STUDIES IN GERMAN LITERATURE

Volume VIII

Title: *Lessing*

and the

Language of Comedy

by

MICHAEL M. METZGER
*State University of New York
at Buffalo*

1966
MOUTON & CO.
THE HAGUE · PARIS

Printed in The Netherlands by Mouton & Co., Printers, The Hague.

For Erika A. Metzger

PREFACE

This study deals with the development of Gotthold Ephraim Lessing's literary style as reflected in the language of his comedies. The transformation of conventional comic character types into autonomous dramatic personalities, Lessing's great poetic contribution to German comedy, can perhaps be best perceived and appreciated through an understanding of the growth of his ability to provide individual and appropriate diction for each of the persons in a dramatic situation. Although this applies equally to Lessing's tragedies, they will be omitted from consideration here, since in Lessing's hands comedy developed a definite unitary form and dialogue style, dramaturgically and functionally isolated from his diverse efforts in tragedy, which the author hopes to treat in a similar study in the future.

The critical interest which Lessing's unique and influential sense for the possibilities of the German language attracted even during his own lifetime and ever since seems to justify specific analysis of his dramatic language, particularly as it first appeared, in comedy. The stylistic affinity between Lessing's conceptually far richer critical writings and his use of language in the drama is one of the verities of Lessing scholarship. The first critic to recognize this relationship was Lessing himself. In the second *Anti-Goeze*, replying to the pastor's objections to his unconventional style, he concedes, "... freylich mag [meinen Stil] das Theater ein wenig verdorben haben". He goes on to make his practice in dramatic dialogue, which imitates the frequently metaphoric nature of speech "in den wirklichen Gesprächen des Umganges", responsible for the "leaps" ("Sprünge") in the exposition of his arguments. He contrasts the logic of the exposition of philosophical questions with that of dramatic dialogue; "Jene [Fragen] erfodern einen gesetzten, immer gleichen Schritt; dieser [Dialog] verlangt mit unter Sprünge: und selten ist ein hoher Springer, ein guter ebner Tänzer."[1] Critics who have since discussed various aspects of Lessing's language, notably August Lehmann,[2] Erich Schmidt,[3] Willi Metzger,[4] August Langen,[5] and, most recently, Eric A. Blackall,[6] have unanimously recognized the strongly dialectical and dramatic qualities in Lessing's prose style. These qualities are present through the conscious employment of various stylistic elements, which Langen enumerates as follows; writing in the first person, frequent direct address of the partner or opponent, apparent interruptions of the train of thought, frequent digressions, many interrogative or exclamatory phrases, and frequent rhetorical repetitions.[7] All of these stylistic traits, which give to Lessing's prose its peculiar pithiness and immediacy, are characteristics of the spontaneously spoken word and also of the language of the stage, particularly as it was evolving in Lessing's own time. In spite of the general recognition of

[1] Gotthold Ephraim Lessing, *Sämtliche Schriften*, ed. by Karl Lachmann, 3rd edn. by Franz Muncker, 23 vols. (Stuttgart-Leipzig-Berlin, 1886-1924), XIII, p. 150 — hereafter cited as *LM*, I, II, etc. Where appropriate, line numbers follow the page number, set off with a period; e.g., *LM*, XIII, 150.5-34.

[2] August Lehmann, *Forschungen über Lessings Sprache* (Braunschweig, 1875), p. 2.

[3] Erich Schmidt, *Lessing: Geschichte seines Lebens und seiner Schriften*, 4th edn., 2 vols. (Berlin, 1923), II, 488 ff.

[4] Willi Metzger, *Die Entwicklung von Lessings Briefstil: eine Analyse der gestaltbildenden seelischen Verfassungen* (= Giessener Beiträge zur deutschen Philologie, XIX) (Giessen, 1926), pp. 1-32.

[5] August Langen, "Deutsche Sprachgeschichte vom Barock bis zur Gegenwart", in *Deutsche Philologie im Aufriß*, ed. Wolfgang Stammler, 3 vols. (Berlin, 1952), I, p. 1203.

[6] Eric A. Blackall, *The Emergence of German as a Literary Language* (Cambridge, 1959), p. 366.

[7] Langen, *op. cit.*, p. 1203.

this relationship between Lessing's expository prose and his dramatic prose, there has not yet been a comprehensive study of Lessing's dramatic language itself.[8]

Before Lessing was a critic, he was a playwright. Before he wrote tragedies, he wrote comedies. The Saxon regular comedy, based on French models, in whose earliest predecessors, the plays of Plautus and Terence, he immersed himself while at St. Afra in Meissen, was Lessing's school of the theatre and, in many respects, a formative influence on his style of writing throughout his life. The surge of creativity in the field of comedy which Lessing experienced between 1747 and 1750, producing *Der junge Gelehrte, Damon, Die alte Jungfer, Der Misogyne, Die Juden, Der Freygeist,* and *Der Schatz;* his desultory activity between 1750 and 1763, which brought forth

---

[8] The studies of Hans Schuchmann, *Studien zum Dialog im Drama Lessings und Schillers* (Giessen, 1927), and Wilhelm Mohri, *Die Technik des Dialoges in Lessings Dramen* (Elbersfeld, 1929), have previously touched upon Lessing's dramatic language. Both, however, concern themselves chiefly with Lessing's fulfillment of the requirements which they consider essential to successful dialogue, and are thus normative in their approaches. Stylistic questions are considered only as they intersect dramaturgic problems. Neither writer concerns himself with the particular criteria for comedy of Lessing's own time. Schuchmann touches only upon *Minna von Barnhelm* among Lessing's comedies. Mohri does treat some of the minor comedies, making some very good points about Lessing's style, but only on the features which are germane to the structural technique of the dialogue. The article by Siegmund Rindskopf, "Der sprachliche Ausdruck der Affekte in Lessings dramatischen Werken", *Zeitschrift für den deutschen Unterricht,* Vol. XV (1901), pp. 545-584, illustrates many of the stylistic features discussed in the present study, but is restricted to expression of passion in dialogue in Lessing's dramas in general, not treating the language of comedy in its totality as a separate entity. The outline and portions published thus far of Bruno Markwardt, "Studien über den Stil G. E. Lessings im Verhältnis zur Aufklärungsprosa", *Wissenschaftliche Zeitschrift der Universität Greifswald; Gesellschafts- und sprachwissenschaftliche Reihe,* 3 (1953-4), pp. 151-180; 4 (1954-5), pp. 1-34, 177-208; 5 (1955-6), pp. 297-338, promise a study of considerable value in this area. Unfortunately, the section in which Markwardt deals specifically with Lessing's comedies had not appeared at this writing. Mention should also be made of Erich Emigholz's dissertation, *Lessings sprachliche Form im Drama: Untersuchungen zum Problem Vers-Prosa in Lessings Dramen* ... (Münster, 1955), a consideration of Lessing's use of prose and verse in drama compared with that of the German dramatists of the next generation.

numerous fragments and even more outlines of projected comedies; his masterpiece of comedy, *Minna von Barnhelm*, and the experimental fragments, *Der Schlaftrunk* and *Die Matrone von Ephesus*, which follow it; all of these reveal a continuing if often sporadic concern on Lessing's part with the problems of comedy during twenty crucial years of his life, the period between 1747 and 1767. These were the years in which Lessing, beginning as an occasional journalist for Voß in Berlin, developed into a mature playwright and formidable critic, producing *Miß Sara Sampson*, *Laokoon*, the *Litteraturbriefe*, and the *Hamburgische Dramaturgie*, to name only the most significant results of his many-faceted activity during this time.

With the exception of *Minna von Barnhelm*, comedies were and are subordinated within Lessing's total literary achievement, most of the completed comedies falling into the period of his poetic apprenticeship. Nevertheless these plays do constitute an element of considerable size in his total production and are not to be overlooked in evaluating Lessing's literary and stylistic personality. They provide the basis for a close scrutiny of the progress of Lessing's development as a writer, of his mastery, increasing with the years, of dramaturgy and dramatic language within a single literary medium. It is to demonstrate how Lessing's style developed within the self-imposed strictures of the comic genre that this study was undertaken. The investigation proceeds chronologically, considering primarily Lessing's use of stylistic devices in character depiction, since, as shall be demonstrated, the representation of characters in action, rather than of the effects of events on characters was, in Lessing's opinion, the function of the proper comedy. We shall seek to determine and describe the ways in which Lessing fulfilled not only the theoretical and practical criteria for the language of comedy in his time but also the dramaturgic requirements of the individual plays and their characters. Lessing saw the "Komödie", or "Lustspiel", in all of its gradations of type, as a genre in its own right, subject to its own principles of form. These principles chiefly governed the means of character representation, the characters in comedy being required to manifest generally recognizable traits in situations close to everyday life in contrast to the specifically historical or mythological characters and situations of tragedy. It therefore seems best to regard comedy and its style, as Lessing did, in relative isolation from the other types of drama. Thus, while Lessing's language in his comedies, an artistic re-creation of the colloquial German of his own time, did influence his own prose style and, with the most significant results, the language of the middle-class tragedy, these aspects will not be considered to any great major in the present study, nor could they be without greatly exceeding its scope.

This book is a slightly condensed version of my doctoral dissertation of the same title which was written under the supervision of Professor Eric A. Blackall of Cornell University, Ithaca, New York. I wish to take this opportunity to thank Professor Blackall for the constant encouragement and perspicacious criticism he gave me during the preparation of the dissertation and for his book, *The Emergence of German as a Literary Language*, which aided me greatly in the execution of this study. I also wish to thank the State University of New York at Buffalo for making the publication of this study possible, and the Graduate School Committee on the Allocation of Research Funds for aid in the preparation of the manuscript. Thanks are also due to the staffs of the Libraries of Cornell University, the University of Illinois at Urbana, and the State University of New York at Buffalo.

Buffalo, New York   MICHAEL M. METZGER
May 1, 1965

CONTENTS

I. LESSING'S THEORY OF
THE LANGUAGE OF COMEDY

Before turning to the analytical portion of this study, we must investigate briefly Lessing's theoretical conception of comedy and its language. The most exhaustive discussion of his thought in this area is to be found in J. G. Robertson's guide to the *Hamburgische Dramaturgie, Lessing's Dramatic Theory.*[1] The following summary does not pretend to such completeness, intending merely to put forth Lessing's views on the language of comedy as the background for the discussion of his actual practice. The lack of great modifications in Lessing's theory of comedy over the years, his very reluctance to stray as far as did, for example, Johann Elias Schlegel from the traditional theories is entirely consonant with the fact that changes in his practice of the language of comedy lie chiefly in the continual refinement of technique and ever deeper insights into its nature.

When Gotthold Ephraim Lessing arrived in Leipzig in 1747 with the sketches for his first comedy in his baggage, the German, or at least the Saxon, theatre had already come far beyond its inchoate and frequently tasteless state at the beginning of the eighteenth century. Although performances were still sporadic, and an organized regular theatre was still far off, advances had been made. Mainly through the theoretical leadership and active sponsorship of J. C. Gottsched, the theatre, and comedy in particular, had been subjected to a series of attempts at reform whose total effect was to try to create a native German theatre in the classical French

[1] J. G. Robertson, *Lessing's Dramatic Theory* (Cambridge, 1938).

mold, following the rules of plausibility and unity dictated by the French arbiters, chiefly Boileau. German comedies of previous eras, such as those of Gryphius or Christian Weise, were out of favor, being too irregular in their construction and, particularly in the case of Gryphius, not sufficiently normative in their plots. From 1730 on, when his *Versuch einer Critischen Dichtkunst* first appeared, Gottsched attempted to give the comedy both a legitimate *raison d'être* in the rationalistic, eudaimonistic Wolffian scheme of things and a form proper to its function. Through the *Deutsche Schaubühne*, appearing between 1740 and 1745, Gottsched presented the German theatre with concrete examples for the improvement of its comedies, such original plays as his wife's *Das Testament* and Quistorp's *Der Hypochondrist* joining the more numerous translations from the French.

Gottsched's view of comedy was morally and socially pragmatic. For him the function of all poetry was the moral betterment of his fellow men. In the case of comedy this was to occur through the display of a vice or socially injurious attitude which is made to seem foolish in the eyes of men. Thus, in an article in his periodical, *Die vernünftigen Tadlerinnen*, Gottsched had said: "Komödien sind oft bessere Beweggründe vom Bösen abzustehen als die besten Vernunftschlüsse der Sittenlehre. Freilich müssen die Stücke danach geschaffen sein. Die Tugend muß stets als belohnt, das Laster als bestraft vorgestellt werden."[2] For Gottsched, however, comedy is not so much a vehicle for the display of virtue as for the ridicule of vice and therefore, although the exact process is never explored in detail, for the healing of the vices of the audience. Guided by Aristotle, Gottsched, in the *Critische Dichtkunst*, defined comedy as follows:

Die Komödie ist nichts anders, als eine Nachahmung einer lasterhaften Handlung, die durch ihr lächerliches Wesen den Zuschauer belustigen, aber auch zugleich erbauen kann. So hat sie Aristoteles beschrieben, und zugleich erkläret, was er durch das Lächerliche

---

[2] Quoted in Mary Beare, *Die Theorie der Komödie von Gottsched bis Jean Paul* (Bonn, 1927), p. 14.

verstünde. Er sagt aber sehr wohl, daß es was ungestaltes oder ungereimtes sey, das doch demjenigen, der es an sich hat, keinen Schmerz verursachet: ... Es ist also wohl zu merken, daß weder das Lasterhafte, noch das Lächerliche für sich allein, in die Komödie gehöret; sondern beydes zusammen, wenn es in einer Handlung verbunden angetroffen wird.[3]

As Betsy Aikin-Sneath points out, comedy was to act as the vehicle of middle-class morality of Gottsched's time, approving the ostensibly reasonable values of the group, of the society, disapproving as unreasonable and making ridiculous the values and actions which the group rejected. "Drama was to be judged by moral as well as by literary standards."[4]

To achieve its double goal of edification and amusement, comedy, according to Gottsched, had to be an accurate imitation of everyday life to the greatest possible extent. The plot and presentation had to conform to the traditional three unities, supposedly dictated by Aristotle and sternly observed in the classical French theatre. In this respect, Gottsched was a "strict constructionist"; "Die ganze Fabel einer Komödie muß, ihrem Inhalte nach, die Einheit der Zeit und des Ortes, eben so wohl als die Tragödie beobachten" (*CD*, p. 647). The social classes appearing in comedy were to be "ordentliche Bürger, oder doch Leute von mäßigem Stande, dergleichen auch wohl zur Noth Baronen, Marquis, und Grafen sind", and "die Großen", presumably meaning actual royalty and upper nobility, were to be omitted, not that they, as Gottsched was at pains to point out, were entirely incapable of vice or folly, but out of respect for their station. Improbable intrigues, fantastic characters, and all other elements detracting from the plausibility and therefore from the proper didactic effect of the play, and which Gottsched deplored in the *théâtre italien*, were to be avoided. The plots were not to be concerned solely with love, seduction, cuckoldry, and the like, as they were in the contemporary French

---

[3] J. C. Gottsched, *Versuch einer Critischen Dichtkunst*, 4th edn. (Leipzig, 1751), p. 643 — hereafter cited as *CD*.
[4] Betsy Aikin-Sneath, *Comedy in Germany in the First Half of the Eighteenth Century* (Oxford, 1936), p. 18.

comedies, since the moral which could be illustrated thus was too slight. Rather, Gottsched suggested somewhat humorlessly, the "Fabel" should be selected to ridicule such social faults as prejudice, intemperance, and bragging.[5]

The implications for the form and language of comedy arising from Gottsched's requirements are clear. The characters must be represented as their counterparts in the real world appear: "Man muß nämlich die Natur und Art der Menschen zu beobachten wissen, jedem Alter, jedem Stande, jedem Geschlechte, und jedem Volke solche Neigungen und Gemüthsarten geben, als wir von ihnen gewohnt sind" (*CD*, p. 649). If characters contrary to expected types, and therefore to plausibility, such as an old man who was not miserly or a youth who was not wasteful were to be represented, Gottsched insisted, the audience must be told why they are contrary to type. Characters, aside from representing types from real life, must also speak as these types do:

Und dieses führet mich endlich auf die Schreibart der Komödien. Sie besteht aus den Gedanken und Ausdrückungen derselben: Und hierinn ist die Komödie von der Tragödie sehr unterschieden. Das macht, daß dort fast lauter vornehme Leute; hier aber Edelleute, Bürger und geringe Personen, Knechte und Mägde vorkommen: dort die heftigsten Gemüthsbewegungen herrschen, die sich durch einen pathetischen Ausdruck zu verstehen geben; hier aber nur lauter lächerliche und lustige Sachen vorkommen, wovon man in der gemeinen Sprache zu reden gewohnt ist. Es muß also eine Komödie eine ganz natürliche Schreibart haben, und wenn sie gleich in Versen gesetzt wird, doch die gemeinsten Redensarten beybehalten... Diejenigen machen es also nicht gut, die sich in ihren Komödien, nach dem bösen Muster der heutigen Franzosen, einer gekünstelten, und durchgehends sinnreichen Schreibart bedienen. Ein so gedrechselter Ausdruck ist der täglichen Sprache des Umganges gar nicht ähnlich, und stellet also ein Stück aus einer andern Welt vor.   (*CD*, pp. 651-2)

Thus, Gottsched required that the language of comedy, in contrast to that of tragedy, be colloquial, persons speaking according to their stations in life as do their counterparts

---

[5]   Aikin-Sneath, *op. cit.*, pp. 20-21.

in the real world, their speech unornamented with bombast or conceits, in order to meet Gottsched's requirement of plausibility in comedy. Comical situations rather than verbal humor were to provide the element of amusement. Just as Gottsched banned the Harlequin as an extraneous and improbably ridiculous figure, the Harlequin's verbal arsenal of jokes, puns, and bawdry, all elements which might detract from the moral process of the play, was to be omitted. Although, for the sake of realism, prose was to be preferred, verse, preferably in five- or six-footed iambs, was a possible medium: "Nur muß keine poetische Schreibart darinnen herrschen, und außer dem Sylbenmaaße sonst nichts gleißendes, oder gekünsteltes dabey vorkommen" (*CD*, p. 652).

For the sake of the betterment of the manners and morals of the public, Gottsched demanded a formally regular comic theatre which should at once entertain and teach through an imitation of life which was, in theory at least, as realistic as possible so that the audience might make an identification between the world on the stage and their own lives, might laugh at the vices ridiculed and avoid similar actions for fear of becoming ridiculous themselves. This last consideration, the effect of comedy on the beholder, was indicated only vaguely by Gottsched in the *Critische Dichtkunst*. It was this theory, consonant with both the Humanistic tradition and the ideas of the German Enlightenment, which dominated the active regular theatre, such as it was, of the 1740's in Leipzig, however imperfectly the comedies which were written as models for the application of the theory reflected Gottsched's intentions. It was the world of this theatre into which Lessing came in 1747.

In discussing the genesis of Lessing's dramatic theory, J. G. Robertson remarks: "Lessing was not a philosopher or aesthetician in any systematic sense of these words. ... He accepted the philosophy of the 'Aufklärung' as a matter of course... The truth is that Lessing's approach to the problems of the drama – as to that of the delimitation of the arts in his 'Laokoon' – was always an empiric one, neither speculative nor metaphysical. His interest began with his ambition to become himself a dramatist; his theories of drama were the outcome of purely practical considerations of ways and means."[6] Lessing's confrontation with the practical problems of comedy preceded by some years his first concern with the theory of the drama. During the period of his greatest productivity, Lessing's views were surely only empirical and personal, rather than directed towards the formulation of any general theory of comedy. How large a role comedy played in his personal development, as a factor in his education as a young man, may be seen in Lessing's letter to his mother of January 20, 1749, in which he gives an accounting of his life since he left St. Afra at Meissen and went to Leipzig. After describing how he had learned fencing, dancing, and riding, and had generally put aside his provincial manners, Lessing tells his mother:

Mein Körper war ein wenig geschickter worden, und ich suchte Gesellschafft, um nun auch leben zu lernen. Ich legte die ernsthafften Bücher eine zeitlang auf die Seite, um mich in denjenigen umzusehn die weit angenehmer, und vielleicht eben so nützlich sind. Die Comoedien kamen mir zur erst in die Hand. Es mag unglaublich vorkommen, wem es will, mir haben sie sehr große Dienste gethan. Ich lernte daraus eine artige und gezwungne, eine grobe und natürliche Aufführung unterscheiden. Ich lernte wahre und falsche Tugenden daraus kennen, und die Laster eben so sehr wegen ihres lächerlichen als wegen ihrer Schändlichkeit fliehen. Habe ich aber alles dieses nur in eine schwache Ausübung gebracht, so hat es gewiß mehr an andern Umständen als an meinen Willen gefehlt. Doch bald hätte ich den vornehmsten Nutzen, den die Lustspiele bey mir gehabt haben, vergeßen. Ich lernte mich selbst kennen, und seit der Zeit habe ich gewiß über niemanden mehr gelacht und gespottet als über mich selbst.   (*LM*, XVII, 8)

Lessing's description almost seems a testimonial to Gottsched's theory of the proper use of comedy. Even if one takes into consideration the possibility that Lessing was overstating its beneficent effects in order to mollify his parents, who disapproved on principle of his having anything to do with such

---

[6]   Robertson, *op. cit.*, pp. 333-34.

frivolous matters, there can be no doubt that Lessing saw the stage as the vehicle for the betterment of men, either through the medium of powerful emotion, as in the tragedy, on which he was to expound more fully much later, or through the sensation of pleasurably scornful laughter at a ridiculous person or act, calculated to make the laugher avoid the same folly. Thus, from his early adulthood on, comedy was not only a school of the theatre for Lessing, but a school of life.

This thought appears again in a letter which Lessing wrote to Friedrich Nicolai on November 13, 1756. Having discussed the function of tragedy, which is the representation of actions arousing pity and fear, and having concluded: "Der mitleidigste Mensch ist der beste Mensch, zu allen gesellschaftlichen Tugenden, zu allen Arten der Großmuth der aufgelegteste", Lessing goes on to treat comedy, clearly and concisely echoing his subjective reaction on a more universal level:

Auf gleiche Weise verfahre ich mit der Komödie. Sie soll uns zur Fertigkeit verhelfen, alle Arten des Lächerlichen leicht wahrzunehmen. Wer diese Fertigkeit besitzt, wird in seinem Betragen alle Arten des Lächerlichen zu vermeiden suchen, und eben dadurch der wohlgezogenste und gesittetste Mensch werden. Und so ist auch die Nützlichkeit der Komödie gerettet.

Beyder Nutzen, des Trauerspiels sowohl als des Lustspiels, ist von dem Vergnügen unzertrennlich; denn die ganze Hälfte des Mitleids und des Lachens ist Vergnügen, und es ist großer Vortheil für den dramatischen Dichter, daß er weder nützlich, noch angenehm, eines ohne das andere seyn kann.   (*LM*, XVII, 66-7)

In Lessing's emphatic mention of the pleasure of both pity and laughter we may perceive a category of aesthetic thinking about drama lacking in Gottsched's rationalistic conception. The idea that one of the uses of laughter is the pleasure it brings had earlier been brought forth in relation to the theory of comedy in a far more absolute form by Johann Elias Schlegel.[7] Lessing's statement that the utility, the moral purpose, of comedy is inextricably bound up with the pleasure

[7]   Beare, *op. cit.*, pp. 29-30.

of beholding it is a modification and synthesis, it would seem, of Gottsched's and Schlegel's theories.

Lessing's ideas about the uses of comedy remained remarkably uniform throughout the twenty years in which he was concerned with such questions. This stability of attitude is reflected in the type and style of his own comedies. Lessing made his final and definitive statement of the uses of comedy in the *Hamburgische Dramaturgie*. It is the distillation of twenty years' experience of men and the theatre, at once more solidly based in actual experience and less optimistic than Gottsched's conception, and yet, in its essentials, resting on the same basic assumptions about the function of the drama:

Die Komödie will durch Lachen bessern; aber nicht eben durch Verlachen; nicht gerade diejenigen Unarten, über die sie zu lachen macht, noch weniger bloß und allein die, an welchen sich diese lächerliche Unarten finden. Ihr wahrer allgemeiner Nutzen liegt in dem Lachen selbst; in der Uebung unserer Fähigkeit das Lächerliche zu bemerken; es unter allen Bemäntelungen der Leidenschaft und der Mode, es in allen Vermischungen mit noch schlimmern oder mit guten Eigenschaften, sogar in den Runzeln des feyerlichen Ernstes, leicht und geschwind zu bemerken. Zugegeben, daß der Geitzige des Moliere nie einen Geitzigen, der Spieler des Regnard nie einen Spieler gebessert habe; eingeräumet, daß das Lachen diese Thoren gar nicht bessern könne: desto schlimmer für sie, aber nicht für die Komödie. Ihr ist genug, wenn sie keine verzweifelte Krankheiten heilen kann, die Gesunden in ihrer Gesundheit zu befestigen. Auch dem Freygebigen ist der Geitzige lehrreich; auch dem, der gar nicht spielt, ist der Spieler unterrichtend; die Thorheiten, die sie nicht haben, haben andere, mit welchen sie leben müssen; es ist ersprießlich, diejenigen zu kennen, mit welchen man in Collision kommen kann; ersprießlich, sich wider alle Eindrücke des Beyspiels zu verwahren. Ein Preservatif ist auch eine schätzbare Arzeney; und die ganze Moral hat kein kräftigers, wirksamers, als das Lächerliche.

(*LM*, IX, 303-4)

Lessing's conception of the role of comedy in the scheme of things did not differ significantly from that of Gottsched. Along different avenues, strongly conditioned by his own practice in the theatre and by a psychology far more subtle and realistic than Gottsched's, Lessing arrived at the same general conclusions. This fact is, of course, a function of Lessing's broad agreement, in this area at least, with the ideas of the Enlightenment. Although Lessing could, on occasion, as the seventeenth *Litteraturbrief* spectacularly testifies, disagree sharply with Gottsched on questions regarding the form which the theatre should take, they were, as men of the Enlightenment, in agreement on the general principle that poetry should be regarded as having a definite normative function. Lessing's conception of comedy takes into account far more the element of aesthetic pleasure in laughter at a ridiculous object. This laughter is "Lachen" and not "Verlachen". The pleasure arises from a pure perception of the ridiculous and through analogy to the beholder's own world, not through scorn of the characters beheld. Comedy is a school for the perception of the ridiculous and exercises faculties which should be applied in the beholder's dealings with other men. The basic tenet which Lessing and Gottsched had in common concerning comedy, the phenomenology of which Lessing attempted to analyze more thoroughly, is that comedy is a morally useful "Nachahmung einer lasterhaften Handlung".

Already early in his literary career, Lessing had very definite ideas about the form which comedy should take. In the following statement, we find described the comedy which Lessing had been striving for several years to produce, the "wahre Komödie", which he was to perfect in *Minna von Barnhelm*. This passage, written in 1754, is from the conclusion of Lessing's presentation in the *Theatralische Bibliothek* of the opposing views of Chassiron and Gellert on the *comédie larmoyante*:

... Noch einmal also mit einem Worte: das Possenspiel will nur zum Lachen bewegen; das weinerliche Lustspiel will nur rühren; die wahre Komödie will beydes. Man glaube nicht, daß ich dadurch die beyden erstern in eine Klasse setzen will; es ist noch immer der Unterscheid zwischen beyden, der zwischen dem Pöbel und Leuten von Stande ist. Der Pöbel wird ewig der Beschützer der Possenspiele bleiben, und unter Leuten von Stande wird es immer gezwungne Zärtlinge geben, die den Ruhm empfindlicher Seelen auch da zu behaupten suchen, wo andre ehrliche Leute gähnen. Die wahre Komödie allein ist für das Volk, und allein fähig einen allgemeinen Beyfall zu erlangen, und folglich auch einen allgemeinen Nutzen zu stiften.   (*LM*, VI, 52)

Lessing's ideal of the comedy was one which should have broad popular appeal with the "Volk", between the extremes of the "Pöbel" and overly effete "Leute von Stande", and which should both amuse and move audiences, but do neither as extremely as the "Possenspiel" and the "weinerliche Lustspiel".

Whereas Gottsched's distinction between tragedy and comedy was based chiefly on the purpose and matter of each, and on the social classes and types of figures which might appear in each, Lessing took not only these elements into consideration, but founded his differentiation between comedy and tragedy upon a formally more distinctive criterion. For him the main function of comedy was the depiction of character and, aside from the traditional identifying feature of the happy ending, the pre-eminent importance of character depiction in comedy was its most significant formal feature. In the *Hamburgische Dramaturgie*, discussing the affinity between *Le philosophe marié* by Destouches with another comedy, Lessing had occasion to state the distinction between comedy and tragedy:

Die verschiedensten Charaktere können in ähnliche Situationen gerathen; und da in der Komödie die Charaktere das Hauptwerk, die Situationen aber nur die Mittel sind, jene sich äußern zu lassen, und ins Spiel zu setzen: so muß man nicht die Situationen, sondern die Charaktere in Betrachtung ziehen, wenn man bestimmen will, ob ein Stück Original oder Copie genennt zu werden verdiene. Umgekehrt ist es in der Tragödie, wo die Charaktere weniger wesentlich sind, und Schrecken und Mitleid vornehmlich aus den Situationen entspringt. Aehnliche Situationen geben also ähnliche Tragödien, aber nicht ähnliche Komödien. Hingegen geben ähnliche Charaktere ähnliche Komödien, anstatt daß sie in den Tragödien fast gar nicht in Erwägung kommen. (*LM*, IX, 402-3)

This idea is central to an understanding of Lessing's own comic productions in which, indeed, the plots are little more than backdrops stitched together for the presentation of the actions of the various individual characters. As a result, the derivation of the plot made very little difference to Lessing, either in writing his own comedies or in appraising the works of others. His main requirements were that the characters be believably depicted, be consistent in their development within the play, and that each should speak with his own characteristic and realistic style. Lessing was conscious of these criteria quite early in his career as a critic, just as he had observed them still earlier in his first comedies. In his defense of Plautus' *Captivi*, for instance, which he had translated and published in the *Beyträge zur Historie und Aufnahme des Theaters* in 1750, Lessing explains why certain characters in the play violated the strictures of Gottsched by punning. Lessing first concedes that there are various literary forms in which puns are out of place, but then continues:

... Ganz anders aber ist es in der Art von Gedichten, wo der Dichter Personen von verschiedner Gattung redend aufführet; ich meyne in den dramatischen. Hier ist es seine vornehmste Pflicht, die Personen zu schildern, wie sie sind, und sie dasjenige sagen zu lassen, was sie nach ihrem Stande und nach ihrer Gemüthsart sagen können.   (*LM*, IV, 181)

Since audiences expected persons of the lower classes to speak in this way, Lessing argues, it was quite proper that Plautus' slaves and parasites would pun, this adding to the reality of the characterization.

Lessing laid stress on the requirement that the characters must be consistent in their actions,[8] and, as we have just seen, that language must be consistent with the character for

---

[8] In the thirty-fourth article of the *Hamburgische Dramaturgie*, discussing Marmontel's *Soliman*, Lessing says: "Uebereinstimmung: — Nichts muß sich in den Charakteren widersprechen; sie müssen immer einförmig, immer sich selbst ähnlich bleiben; sie dürfen sich itzt stärker, itzt schwächer äußern, nach dem die Umstände auf sie wirken; aber keine von diesen Umständen müssen mächtig genug seyn können, sie von schwarz auf weiß zu ändern." (*LM*, IX, 325).

reasons of plausibility and therefore of dramatic effect. The style must be emphatic and clear, and the playwright must not fear to use common or colloquial expressions, since they can greatly augment the dramatic illusion. This point is made in the fifty-first of the *Litteraturbriefe*, of August 16, 1759. Discussing an article by Klopstock in the *Nordische Aufseher*, in which the proper choice and effective placement of words in poetry was considered, Lessing said:

> Die sorgfältige Wahl der edelsten Wörter ... leidet alsdenn einen grossen Abfall, wenn der Dichter nicht in seiner eignen Person spricht. In dem Drama besonders, wo jede Person, so wie ihre eigene Denkungsart, also auch ihre eigne Art zu sprechen haben muß. Die edelsten Worte sind eben deswegen, weil sie die edelsten sind, fast niemals zugleich diejenigen, die uns in der Geschwindigkeit, und besonders im Affecte, zu erst beyfallen. Sie verrathen die vorhergegangene Ueberlegung, verwandeln die Helden in Declamatores, und stören dadurch die Illusion. Es ist daher sogar ein grosses Kunststück eines tragischen Dichters, wenn er, besonders die erhabensten Gedanken, in die gemeinsten Worte kleidet, und im Affecte nicht das edelste, sondern das nachdrücklichste Wort, wenn es auch schon einen etwas niedrigen Nebenbegriff mit sich führen sollte, ergreiffen läßt.   (*LM*, VIII, 145)

Lessing especially admired Shakespeare for his ability to perform this artistry in his tragedies. It was to the language of German tragedy that Lessing was attempting to bring the quality of spontaneous expressiveness, free from all declamatory effects. Comedy had already long since embodied these qualities of language which Lessing required of all drama, and which he had first encountered in comedy. As an expansion of Lessing's requirement of spontaneity and expressiveness from the language of drama, and therefore of faithfulness to life in its imitation, we find a statement in the *Hamburgische Dramaturgie*. In the fifty-ninth essay, Lessing draws a distinction between the language of the ancient and modern drama, saying that the rhetorical and declamatory language of the drama of antiquity was developed for delivery on an open place, and that the characters alternately spoke with each other or with the chorus. In the modern drama,

however, the characters are usually within four walls and
addressing each other as individuals, and therefore a more
natural, less declamatory mode of speaking is required:

> Umsonst beruft man sich desfalls auf den höhern Rang der
> Personen. Vornehme Leute haben sich besser ausdrücken gelernt,
> als der gemeine Mann: aber sie affectiren nicht unaufhörlich, sich
> besser auszudrücken, als er. Am wenigsten in Leidenschaften; deren
> jeder seine eigene Beredsamkeit hat, mit der allein die Natur
> begeistert, die in keiner Schule gelernt wird, und auf die sich der
> Unerzogenste so gut versteht, als der Polirteste.
> Bey einer gesuchten, kostbaren, schwülstigen Sprache kann
> niemals Empfindung seyn. Sie zeigt von keiner Empfindung, und
> kann keine hervorbringen. Aber wohl verträgt sie sich mit den
> simpelsten, gemeinsten, plattesten Worten und Redensarten...
> Nichts ist züchtiger und anständiger als die simple Natur.
> Grobheit und Wust ist eben so weit von ihr entfernt, als Schwulst
> und Bombast von dem Erhabnen. Das nehmliche Gefühl, welches
> die Grenzscheidung dort wahrnimt, wird sie auch hier bemerken.
> Der schwülstigste Dichter ist daher unfehlbar auch der pöbel-
> hafteste. Beide Fehler sind unzertrennlich; ... (LM, X, 30-32)

Lessing's ideal of dramatic language for both tragedy and
comedy is that style combining simplicity, naturalness, and,
when necessary, the greatest possible forcefulness, expressed
not in pathetic bombast, but in natural spontaneity. As Eric
A. Blackall has pointed out, these requirements for dramatic
language are certainly influenced by Lessing's ideal of prose
style, which also aimed towards the greatest clarity, naturalness, and concision.[9] Such an ideal of comic language does
not deviate essentially from that of Gottsched, who also
demanded a natural, simple style in comedy, even if his reasons
for doing so reflected his pragmatic, rather anti-aesthetic bent.

J. G. Robertson has said, "On the subject of comedy, Lessing, like Aristotle, has little to say, and that little of small importance."[10] As true as this statement may be in relation to
the remaining body of Lessing's dramatic theory and aesthetic
theory in Germany in general, Lessing's ideas on comedy are

[9]   Blackall, *The Emergence of German as a Literary Language*, pp. 362-63.
[10]   Robertson, *op. cit.*, p. 387.

illuminating for his own works. In Lessing's activity within the realm of comedy, there is considerable correlation between theory and practice. This is a correlation, however, which is brought about by practice and experience forming theory, and not, as in the case of Gottsched, by a theory which attempts to form the creative efforts of others. Lessing's contribution to the development of German comedy, its language, and that of German drama in general lies not in his theories concerning German comedy and its language, but rather in the plays which he produced.

II. LESSING'S PRACTICE
IN THE LANGUAGE OF COMEDY:
DER JUNGE GELEHRTE

In 1775, Christian Heinrich Schmid, Professor of Poetics at Giessen, wrote in his *Chronologie des deutschen Theaters*:

> Jetzt [1747] spielte die Neuberinn zu Leipzig das erstemal den jungen Gelehrten, ein Lustspiel von Gott. Ephr. Lessing, einem Manne, der durch seine Verdienste um unser Theater allein unsterblich wäre, wenn er nicht auch so viele andre Ansprüche auf Unsterblichkeit hätte. Mit einer innigen Kenntniß der Menschen, hat er zuerst auf unsrer Bühne den scharfsinnigsten Observationsgeist verbunden. Bey aller ungezwungenen Simplicität seiner Entwürfe, sind seine Situationen so anziehend, daß sie den Leser und den Zuhörer gleich hinreißen. Ihm haben wir die ächte komische Sprache zu danken. Natürlich und dennoch gewählt, familiär und dennoch witzig, körnigt und dennoch geschmeidig, hat sein Dialog alle die vornehmsten Eigenschaften des dramatischen Stils, und erhält außerdem durch die mühsamste Feile eine elegante Nettigkeit. [1]

This last sentence, so nicely balanced in itself, sums up the ideal of the language of comedy in Lessing's time. What is desired is language which is true to life, but not excessively verbose, colloquial without being either broad or flat, concise and emphatic, and yet supple and versatile. The young Lessing, compared to such of his contemporaries as Gellert and Frau Gottsched, already at least equalled anyone else writing for the Leipzig theatre of the day in these qualities. How Lessing achieved in *Der junge Gelehrte* the establishment of

---

[1]   Christian Heinrich Schmid, *Chronologie des deutschen Theaters* (n.p., 1775), ed. Paul Legband (Berlin, 1902), p. 82.

new criteria for dramatic language shall be the subject of this chapter.

In respect to its plot *Der junge Gelehrte* does not deviate much from the manner of the time. Elements and ideas are freely borrowed from Holberg's *Erasmus Montanus* and various plays of Molière and Marivaux.[2] Damis, the pedantic and arrogant "junge Gelehrte", is the son of the humorously pretentious merchant, Chrysander, who wants to marry him off to his ward, Juliane, because she has, suddenly and unbeknownst to herself, been found to be in expectation of a considerable fortune.

Juliane, however, is in love with her wealthy suitor, Valer, a friend of Damis's at the university, who has, much to Damis's disgust, given up scholarship for the world of affairs and practical usefulness to the state. Through a ruse involving a falsified letter, and through the aid of the two comic servants, Anton and Lisette, Chrysander's greedy intentions are exposed and the two lovers betrothed. The humor in the play is chiefly at the expense of Damis and Chrysander, and the young pedant, having failed to win the essay contest of the Prussian academy at Berlin, determines to leave ungrateful Germany for a land which will better appreciate his dubious talents.

So much then for the plot, which serves chiefly as the backdrop for the display and comical dissection of Damis. The language of *Der junge Gelehrte*, influenced as it is by the current ideal of comic language derived from the doctrines of Gottsched, holds far more of interest.

Lessing, following the theatrical usage of the time, set out

---

[2] Concerning the borrowed plot elements in *Der junge Gelehrte*, see Erich Schmidt, *Lessing*, I, pp. 134-39, and the notes to the play in the volume *Anmerkungen zu Teil 1 bis 7* of *Lessings Werke*, 25 vols. with 3 vols. of notes and indexes, ed. Julius Petersen and Waldemar von Olshausen (Berlin-Leipzig-Vienna-Stuttgart, Deutsches Verlagshaus Bong & Co., n.d.) — hereafter cited as *PO*, I, etc. C.E. Borden's article "The Original Model for Lessing's 'Der junge Gelehrte'", in *Univ. of Cal. Pubs. in Mod. Phil.*, Vol. 36, No. 3 (Berkeley, 1952) argues effectively that one model was J.E. Schlegel's *Der geschäftige Müßiggänger*.

to create in *Der junge Gelehrte* a linguistic world closely resembling in its vocabulary and tone the actual conversation of middle-class Leipzigers as they might speak at home in what Adelung[3] calls "vertrauliche Sprache" and "gemeine Sprache". Most of the time, Lessing achieves a remarkably credible re-creation of this tone. He does this partly through his choice of vocabulary, which will be discussed when the individual characterizations are dealt with, and through the skillful use of various stylistic devices.

The most elementary devices which Lessing uses are the contraction and elision of unaccented vowels. Certainly these must be directions to the actors to speak the lines in a manner imitating the normal contractions and elisions of colloquial speech. Some of Lessing's indications of contraction are (*Der junge Gelehrte*, Act I):

Und ich wette, *wenns* hoch kömmt...

Will *ichs* denn wissen?

... vielleicht *ists* ein Gang?

... *wers* nur glauben wollte!

Haben Sie meinen Vetter nicht *gesehn*?

Ich dächte, man sähe *mirs* an.

Die Endung *gibts* gewiß nicht?

... wird *ers* thun?

Although they are less ubiquitous than contractions, elisions are also to be found (*Der junge Gelehrte*, Acts I and II):

Lenk ein, Anton.

Hab ichs doch gedacht...

... *guck* einmal in ein lebendiges!

Bleib er mir ... mit den Possen weg...

[3] Johann Christoph Adelung, *Versuch eines vollständigen grammatisch-kritischen Wörterbuches der Hochdeutschen Mundart...* (Leipzig, 1774-86), *passim*.

Was *hör* ich?

O, *pack* dich!

Lessing also utilized ellipsis, the omission of grammatical elements which are unessential because understood as naturally following within the context of the speech. An interesting example is to be found in the first scene of the play, where a sentence whose subject and verb undergo ellipsis is extended over several speeches. In this interchange, Anton is cajoling his master into letting him go to the tavern for a drink, and is trying to find an excuse to leave the house. The triple intrusion of the prepositional phrases standing for whole sentences reinforces the singlemindedness of Anton's intentions:

ANTON. ... Haben Sie mich sonst noch wohin zu schicken? Ich habe ohnedem auf dem Rathskeller eine kleine Verrichtung; vielleicht ists ein Gang? Nu?
    DAMIS. (erzürnt.) Nein, Schurke!
    ANTON. Da haben wirs! Er hat alles gelesen, nur kein Komplimentirbuch. — Aber besinnen Sie Sich. Etwa in den Buchladen?
    DAMIS. Nein, Schurke!
    ANTON. Ich muß das Schurke so oft hören, daß ich endlich selbst glauben werde, es sey mein Taufname. — Aber zum Buchbinder?
    DAMIS. O so schweig, oder —
    ANTON. Oder zum Buchdrucker?...   (*LM*, I, 281.17-282.4)

Again (*LM*, I, 284.7-32), when Damis is demonstrating his prowess at disputation, and trying to prove to him through a paradox that he cannot speak German, Anton says:

Ich? ich? nicht Deutsch! Es wäre ein verdammter Streich, wenn ich Kalmuckisch redte, und wüßte es nicht.

In the same vein, Damis tries to demonstrate that Anton cannot eat either, Anton, in amazement, says:

Ich? ich nicht essen? Und trinken wohl auch nicht?

Damis is equally surprised when Anton tells him that he knows a language which Damis does not, namely Wendish;

Du, eine Sprache, die ich nicht verstünde?

This is verb ellipsis to imitate the spontaneity and syntactical looseness of colloquial speech. Lessing uses it chiefly in situations where surprise or anger are to be expressed. Lessing is, however, also aware of the uses of ellipsis as a rhetorical device to emphasize Damis's pedantic posturings. It is used, for example, to strengthen the vigorous, rather Faustian attack upon the learned professions which Lessing puts into Damis's mouth in the apostrophe to "Gelehrsamkeit":

Der Theolog glaubt dich bey einer Menge heiliger Sprüche, fürchterlicher Erzehlungen und einiger übel angebrachten Figuren zu besitzen. Der Rechtsgelehrte, bey einer unseligen Geschicklichkeit unbrauchbare Gesetze abgestorbner Staaten, zum Nachtheile der gesunden Vernunft, zu verdrehen, und die fürchterlichsten Urthel in einer noch fürchterlichern Sprache vorzutragen.   (*LM*, I, 283.13-18)

The ellipsis of "glaubt dich zu besitzen" in the second sentence gives polemic forcefulness which is enhanced by the oblique "abgestorbner Staaten" and by the intensification of the superlative "fürchterlichsten" through the following "noch fürchterlichern".

An even more important role is played by Lessing's use of aposiopesis. This is the interruption of a speech either by the speaker himself or another character for the purpose of heightening tension between the partners and thus increasing the comic effect. It is used to best effect in Act I, Sc. 2, in the dialogue between Damis and Chrysander. In having the two interrupt each other, and often enough themselves, Lessing masterfully creates the strained, impatient relationship between father and son. It is comical indeed, but with a ring quite true to life. For example:

DAMIS. Ist es nicht so? Aber in eben der Ode warnet Horaz für die Liebe, und für das Frauenzimmer.
    CHRYSANDER. Horaz, Horaz. War Horaz nicht ein Italiäner? Ja für das italiänische Frauenzimmer warne ich dich auch! das ist gefährlich! Ich habe einen guten Freund, der in seiner Jugend —
Doch still! man muß kein Aergerniß geben.   (*LM*, I, 286.20-27)

On occasion, the youthful playwright's enthusiasm for the possibilities of the device runs away with him, and leads him to overwork it somewhat, thus:

CHRYSANDER. ... Nun aber traue ich dir ... so viel zu, daß du Ergötzlichkeiten nicht zu Beschäftigungen machen wirst. Aus diesem Grunde rathe ich dir also —
DAMIS. Ihre Reden haben einigen Schein der Wahrheit. Allein ich dringe tiefer. Sie werden es gleich sehen. Der Status Controversiä ist —
CHRYSANDER. Ey, der Status Controversiä mag meinetwegen in Barbara oder Celarent seyn. Ich bin nicht hergekommen mit dir zu disputiren, sondern —
DAMIS. Die Kunstwörter des Disputirens zu lernen? Wohl! Sie müssen also wissen, daß weder Barbara noch Celarent den Statum —
CHRYSANDER. Ich möchte toll werden! Bleib Er mir, Herr Informator, mit den Possen weg, oder —
DAMIS. Possen? diese seltsamen Benennungen sind zwar Ueberbleibsel der scholastischen Philosophie, das ist wahr; aber doch solche Ueberbleibsel —
CHRYSANDER. Ueber die ich die Geduld verlieren werde, wann du mich nicht bald anhörst...   (*LM*, I, 287.20-288.5)

Besides illustrating his occasionally overconcentrated use of a stylistic element, the passage above serves to display another significant element of Lessing's language in comedy. This is the fact that the characters not only speak colloquially, but actually seem attuned to each other in a naturally intimate relationship. This very effective illusion is consciously created through various stylistic and dramaturgic means. The first of these is a logical extension of aposiopesis. Characters are made not only to interrupt each other's speeches, but the interrupting partner in the dialogue anticipates what the other was going to say and, rightly or wrongly, completes the speech. In the passage just quoted, for example, Chrysander says, "Ich bin nicht hergekommen mit dir zu disputiren, sondern —", and is interrupted by Damis with, "Die Kunstwörter des Disputirens zu lernen?" Similarly, in the dialogue between Anton and Damis quoted on page 32, above, Damis threatens Anton, "schweig, oder —", which Anton twists to his own ends, "Oder zum Buchdrucker?" This device not only generates comical misunderstandings, but also creates the impression that the characters are themselves involved in what they are saying, are listening to each other, and that their conversation is not merely for the benefit of the audience.

A device more generalized in its use is that of prose anadiplosis. Wilhelm Mohri has termed this, which he classifies as a type of symmetrical alternation, a feature peculiar to Lessing and to be found in all of the dramas, but does not discuss its stylistic function.[4] Anadiplosis, as the term is here used, consists in that one character echoes the speech of the other by repeating in the first lines of his speech words from the last lines of his partner's previous speech. The following dialogue between Anton and the maid, Lisette, serves as an excellent example. In this scene, Lisette is trying to coax Anton to give a forged letter to Chrysander:

ANTON. Kömmst du mir schon wieder mit deinem Briefe? Denkt doch; deinetwegen soll ich meinen Herrn betriegen?
    LISETTE. Es soll aber dein Schade nicht seyn.
    ANTON. So? ist es mein Schade nicht, wann ich das, was mir Chrysander versprochen hat, muß sitzen lassen?
    LISETTE. Dafür aber verspricht dich Valer schadlos zu halten.
    ANTON. Wo verspricht er mir es denn?
    LISETTE. Wunderliche Haut! ich verspreche es dir an seiner Statt.
    ANTON. Und wenn du es auch an seiner Statt halten sollst, so werde ich viel bekommen. Nein, nein; ein Sperling in der Hand ist besser, als eine Taube auf dem Dache.
    LISETTE. Wann du die Taube gewiß fangen kannst, so wird sie doch besser seyn, als der Sperling?
    ANTON. Gewiß fangen! als wenn sich alles fangen ließe? Nicht wahr, wann ich die Taube haschen will, so muß ich den Sperling aus der Hand fliegen lassen?
    LISETTE. So laß ihn fliegen.
    ANTON. Gut! und wann sich nun die Taube auch davon machte? Nein, nein, Jungfer, so dumm ist Anton nicht.

(*LM*, I, 337.27-338.11)

Lessing's technique for linking dialogue through anadiplosis

---

[4]   Wilhelm Mohri, *Die Technik des Dialoges...*, pp. 68-71.

is clearly evident in this passage, which is quite typical for the style of this play. The speeches are linked through a series of echoes. Thus, in line 3, above, Lisette throws out "Schade" in a declarative, and Anton returns it in an interrogative (line 4), and with it a form of "versprechen", which Lisette returns with another variation upon "Schade" (line 6). Anton returns "verspricht" in an interrogative, and Lisette again echoes it in a declarative, coupled this time with "an seiner Statt" (line 8). Anton echoes "an seiner Statt", but combined with "halten", and initiates the image of the bird in hand which dominates the next several speeches, being elaborated and enriched to symbolize the minor dilemma in which Anton finds himself. Through this subtle linking, Lessing makes the characters seem closely related, listening and responding to each other within the world of the play.

Lessing further associates his characters more intimately by having them draw upon common stores of allusions, familiar to them from their fictitious everyday lives, but not as yet to the audience. Exposition in dialogue, although certainly important to Lessing for the sake of the plot, does not completely subordinate characterization. Rather, the two are equally powerful considerations in the construction of the dialogue. Exposition is therefore usually unhurried in its pacing. Characters mention matters which are unknown to the audience for a time and then clarified almost casually. Thus, Chrysander mentions Juliane in Act I, Sc. 2 without immediately stating the nature of her relationship to Damis and himself. This relationship does not become clear until Act I, Sc. 4.

The studied gradualness of exposition makes the relationship between the characters, who, after all, live in the same house and in the same matrix of circumstances, seem far more natural than if they repeated these circumstances to each other at the beginning of the play merely for the information of the audience. This latter kind of exposition occurs at the beginning of C. F. Gellert's comedy, *Das Loos in der Lotterie*, published one year before *Der junge Gelehrte* was played. Here,

Herr Orgon, in one fairly lengthy speech, sums up for his sister-in-law, Frau Damon, and, of course, for the audience his entire relationship with his wife, his constitution, and his attitude towards life:

HERR ORGON. Ja, ja, Sie mag ein gut Gemüthe haben. Wenn ich Herr über mein Vermögen wäre: so wollte ich ihr selber dienen. Allein unser beyden Haushaltungen sind einander gleich entgegengesetzt. Bey Ihnen hat der Mann das Geld allein, und bey mir die Frau.

FRAU DAMON. Aber warum geben Sie denn Ihrer Frau Liebste alles, und benehmen sich die Gelegenheit, gegen Ihre Anverwandte und Freunde gefällig und liebreich zu sein?

HERR ORGON. Ich habe recht viele Ursachen dazu, wenn Sie es nur wissen sollten, Frau Schwägerinn. Erstlich, will es meine Frau haben, daß ich ihr alles Geld geben soll. Und warum sollte ichs nicht thun, da mir nicht viel an dem Gelde liegt? Zum andern, was sollte ich mit dem Gelde anfangen? Die Arten, wodurch man es verthut, sind mir fast alle zu beschwerlich. Ich spiele nicht gern, weil es mühsam ist, und man dabey lange nachsinnen muß. Ich trinke nicht gern, weil ich mich vor dem Kopfweh fürchte und in dem Weinkeller sind auch immer so viele Leute. Diese muß ich entweder grüßen, wenn ich hineinkomme, oder ich muß gar mit ihnen reden, oder doch zuhören. Und alles dieses beunruhigt mich, denn ich bleibe gar zu gern in meiner Gelassenheit, und laße mir alles gefallen, wobey ich mich leidend verhalten kann.[5]

This rapid exposition was imposed upon the dramatists of the time by the conventions of the French theatre, whereby the plot must be rapidly founded at the very beginning of the play through a conversation between a major character and his confidant. Hardly has the curtain risen on *Die Pietisterey im Fisenbein-Rocke*, for example, than the tensions which prevail among the main characters have been outlined:

KATHRINE. Ich weiß wohl, daß sie schon seit zwei Jahren an den Herrn Liebmann versprochen ist, und daß die Vollziehung der Heirat nur auf die Mama ankömmt. Allein, meint sie, daß die Frau Glaubeleichten sie einem Manne geben werde, ehe sie recht

---

[5] Christian Fürchtegott Gellert, "Das Loos in der Lotterie", in *Neue Beyträge zum Vergnügen des Verstandes und Witzes*, III, parts 5-6 (Bremen-Leipzig, 1747), pp. 324-25.

doktormäßig und in der Lehre vom wahren inneren Christentume
des Herzens recht befestigt ist? Nicht so, nicht so![6]

While Gellert and Frau Gottsched adhered to this tradition,
Lessing freed himself of it to a remarkable extent. In comparison with the baldly expository passages above, the following exchange between Anton and Lisette seems almost
cryptic in its allusions to events as yet unknown to the audience
and its apparent leisureliness in unfolding the circumstances
behind these allusions:

ANTON. Nu? was will die! in meines Herrn Studierstube? Jetzt
gieng Valer heraus; vor einer Weile Juliane; und du bist noch da?
Ich glaube gar, ihr habt eure Zusammenkünfte hier. Warte,
Lisette! das will ich meinem Herrn sagen. Ich will mich schon
rächen; noch für das Gestrige; besinnst du dich?
    LISETTE. Ich glaube, du keufst? Was willst du mit deinem
Gestrigen?
    ANTON. Eine Maulschelle vergißt sich wohl bey dem leicht, der
sie giebt, aber der, dem die Zähne davon gewackelt haben, der
gedenkt eine Zeit lang daran. Warte nur! warte!
    LISETTE. Wer heißt dich, mich küssen?
    ANTON. Potz Stern, wie gemein würden die Maulschellen seyn,
wenn alle die welche bekommen sollten, die euch küssen wollen. —
Ich will mich schon dafür durch meinen Herrn an dir reiben.
    LISETTE. Dein Herr? Dein Herr wird mir nicht viel thun.
    ANTON. Nicht? Wie vielmal hat er es nicht gesagt, daß so ein
heiliger Ort, als eine Studierstube ist, von euch, unreinen Ge-
schöpfen, nicht müsse entheiliget werden? ... — Und du denkst,
mein Herr würde es so mit ansehen, daß du ihm den lieben Gott
[der Gelehrsamkeit] von der Stube treibest?
    LISETTE. Ich glaube gar, du Narre denkst, der liebe Gott sey nur
für euch Mannspersonen? Schweig, oder —
    ANTON. Ja, so eine, wie gestern vielleicht?
    LISETTE. Noch eine beßre! der Narre hätte gestern mehr, als
eine verdient. Er kömmt zu mir; es ist finster; er will mich küssen;
ich stoße ihn zurück, er kömmt wieder; ich schlage ihn aufs Maul;
es thut ihm weh; er läßt nach; er schimpft; er geht fort — Ich
möchte dir gleich noch eine geben, wenn ich daran gedenke.

                                        (*LM*, I, 311.25-312.22)

---

[6]   Luise Adelgunde Viktorie Gottschedin, "Die Pietisterey im Fischbein-
Rocke", in *Deutsche Literatur, Reihe Aufklärung*, III, ed. F. Brüggemann
(Leipzig, 1935), pp. 143.4-23.

In this subtle casualness of exposition, where the establishment of the relationship between the characters and the development of their peculiarities take precedence over the exposition for the sake of the plot, Lessing distinguishes himself favorably from Gellert and Frau Gottsched. We shall presently have occasion to observe other ways in which Lessing, while carrying on the tradition established in part by these two most significant of his contemporaries writing for the comic stage, surpassed them in language and dramaturgy even within the framework of the current "classical" tradition of comedy.

In order to further heighten the sense of colloquialism and spontaneity in the dialogue, Lessing makes copious use of interjections and exclamatory phrases. Typical examples of interjections to be found are (*Der junge Gelehrte*, Act I):

Ah! wann du es wüßtest!

Ach, man weiß es ja wohl...

Nu?

Nu, Nu, bey allen trift das wohl nicht ein...

Ha! ha! ha!

Hi! hi! hi!

St!

Pfuy doch, Herr!

... au weh, Lisette!

O Herr Vater...

Especially when the character is supposed to be excited or under some degree of stress, these elements give an emphatic emotional force to the language,[7] as do the following exclamatory phrases (*Der junge Gelehrte*, Act. I):

---

[7] In this connection, see also Siegmund Rindskopf, "Der sprachliche Ausdruck der Affekte...", pp. 550-61.

Nun ja doch;

Nein, Schurke!

Potz Stern, was das für Zeug ist!

Sachte!

Ach ob, ob!

Daß ich nicht gar ein Jude wäre!

Ich und Homer? Homer und ich?

Je nun, auch das! wie du willst!

Leider!

To the same ends, oaths, pejorative names, and particularly
the adjective "verdammt" are features favored by Lessing,
especially in enriching the language of such earthy characters
as Anton and Chrysander. The following oaths and pejoratives,
for example, may be found in the nineteen pages of Act I:

Schurke...

Schlingel...

Potz Stern...

Der alte Idiote...

Es wäre ein verdammter Streich...

Ich vergesse über dem verdammten Plaudern...

Immer über den verdammten Büchern!

Du und dein Homer, ihr seyd ein Paar Narren!

Schock tausend!

... nun nennt er mir ein halb Dutzend Menscher!

Himmel, Menscher!

Nu, was für ein Narr muß mich jetzo stören?

Himmel! ich höre meinen Vater wiederkommen.

Der verzweifelte Valer! ... Muß ihn denn der Henker eben heute von Berlin zurückführen?

Mit dem verdammten Schurek!

Die verdammte Post!

Sag mir nur, willst du denn Zeit lebens ein Esel bleiben?

Bist du nun vollends ein Schalk...

Je verflucht!

Ja, darüber hat er schon Teufelsgrillen im Kopfe gehabt.

Aber Gott sei dem Bösewichte gnädig...

Die verdammte Ehre!

This extensive use of interjections, exclamatory phrases, and oaths, the seasoning of colloquial speech, considerably enhances the spectator's sense that he is eavesdropping on actual and impassioned conversation. The use of language of the "niedere Sprechart" in general to achieve this effect was common among the dramatists of the time. Even the staid Gellert, whose dramatic language is generally less vivid than that of Frau Gottsched or Lessing, spices his otherwise bland dialogue with an occasional oath and sometimes does not even stop short of rather questionable allusions:

FRAU ORGON. Sagen Sie mir nur, warum Sie mich nicht fragen, wie ich mich befinde? Sehen Sie denn nicht, daß mir immer schlimmer wird? Die verwünschten Ohrgehenke! Ach die verfluchte Zitternadel! Gab mirs nicht einen Stich ans Herze?
HERR ORGON. Wenn du es für nöthig befindest: so schicke nach dem Doctor. Vielleicht ist deine Unpäßlichkeit eine Frucht unserer ehelichen Liebe.
FRAU ORGON. Schweigen Sie ja mit solchen Reden still. Ihre gemächliche Bequemlichkeit und meine Schwangerschaft, dieß läßt sich ohne Wunder nicht denken. Zehn Jahre habe ich den Himmel um einen Sohn gebeten. Meine Mutter hat dreyzehn Kinder gehabt. An mir kann die Schuld nicht liegen, wenn wir ohne Erben sterben. Essen, trinken und schlafen, das können Sie sehr gut. Mag doch unser Vermögen an lachende Erben kommen. Wenn man die Ursache von allen Dingen wissen könnte, würde

man in den Ausschweifungen der Jugend — Ich mag nichts mehr sagen.[8]

Shortly afterward, the same gracious lady says:

... Ich habe das heillose Thier, meine Magd, nach dem Caffee hierher bestellt... Sehen Sie wohl, daß sie noch nicht da ist? Sollte man ein solches Muster nicht in den Karren sperren lassen?
FRAU DAMON. Liebe Frau Schwägerinn, ärgern Sie Sich nicht von neuem. Ich will gleich nach Ihrer Magd schicken.
FRAU ORGON. Nein! das thun Sie ja nicht. Ich will Wunders wegen sehen, wie lange das verhurte Mensch aussen bleibt. Sie hat ganz gewiß einen Kerl auf der Seite. Wenn Sie nur zu Falle käme, ich wollte es ihr gönnen. Sie hat dieses Unglück tausendmal an mir verdient.[9]

This abrupt coarseness put into the mouth of a lady supposedly belonging to the educated middle classes is in jarring contrast with the generally genteel tone of the play. It is almost as if Hans Wurst, whom Gellert, even more than his fellow playwrights, had banned from his comedies, even to the extent of systematically excluding servants from his plays,[10] had disguised himself as a woman and put in an appearance after all. If this is an attempt by Gellert to bring colloquial flavor and wit into his dialogue, it is merely a clumsy gesture which falls far short of the mark. Many years later, in his preparatory notes to the *Hamburgische Dramaturgie*, Lessing revealed how much this sort of thing irritated him, since its acceptance by the public indicated a sort of double standard:

Man hat über das Wort Hure in meiner Minna geschrieen. Der Schauspieler hat es sich nicht einmal unterstehen wollen zu sagen. Immerhin; ich werde es nicht ausstreichen, und werde es überall wieder brauchen, wo ich glaube, daß es hingehört.
    Aber über Gellerten seine Zweydeutigkeiten, über das verschobne Halstuch und dergleichen, im Loos in der Lotterie, hat sich niemand aufgehalten. Man lächelt mit dem Verfaßer darüber.[11]

[8]   Gellert, "Das Loos in der Lotterie", pp. 347-48.
[9]   *Ibid.*, pp. 364-65.
[10] Woldemar Haynel, *Gellerts Lustspiele* (Emden-Borkum, 1896), p. 82.
[11] *LM*, XV, pp. 61.29-62.6.

In *Die Pietisterey im Fischbein-Rocke,* Frau Gottsched is far more consistent in her use of oaths and interjections, and shows a greater sense of suitability and propriety. As befits an old soldier, for example, Herr Wackermann is equipped with a formidable verbal arsenal bristling with "Zum Henker", "Mein Gott!" and "Potztausend!".[12] Kathrine, the servant, is also permitted a "Zum Henker!" in moments of stress,[13] but if Jungfer Luischen, the daughter of the house, ventures anything of the sort, the rebuke is swift and sure:

JUNGFER LUISCHEN. Zum Henker! wozu soll ich's denn wissen?
KATHRINE. Wie? und sie will heiraten? Pfui, Jungfer Luischen![14]

Frau Gottsched, instead of arbitrarily inserting oaths for the sake of momentary impact, creates on her stage a world of definite socio-linguistic rules reflecting those of the world beyond the stage. The sense of this world definitely is weaker in Gellert's *Loos in der Lotterie.*

Like Frau Gottsched, Lessing observed the decorum of the educated, middle-class world whose language he was bringing to the stage. Oaths, pejorative names, and the more extravagant interjections ("au weh!", etc.) are reserved for the comic characters, chiefly Anton and Chrysander, and are certainly never used by one of the female characters. In this respect, Lessing's early dramatic language surely justifies C. H. Schmid's statement that it is "natürlich und dennoch gewählt".

As strong as the effect of the use of elisions, contractions, ellipsis, aposiopesis, anadiplosis, interjections, and oaths is in making the dialogue emulate colloquial speech, none of these elements contributes as much to its naturalness as Lessing's ear for and re-creation of a colloquial tone. The general shortness of the periods, the frequent occurrence of features like emphatic verb inversion, and the effective use of particles, force

[12] Frau Gottsched, "Die Pietisterey...", pp. 150.7, 152.36, and 153.8, respectively.
[13] *Ibid.,* p. 156.36.
[14] *Ibid.,* p. 143.31-32.

upon the actor the cadence of colloquial, rather than declamatory tone. This may be best illustrated by a comparison
between the opening scenes of Gellert's *Das Loos in der Lotterie*, Lessing's *Der junge Gelehrte*, and Frau Gottsched's *Die
Pietisterey im Fischbein-Rocke*.

At the opening of *Das Loos in der Lotterie*, Herr Orgon and
Frau Damon are conversing:

FRAU DAMON. Bringen Sie mir etwan eine gute Nachricht wegen
der Berlinischen Lotterie? Haben Sie die Liste noch nicht erhalten?
    HERR ORGON. Nein, zur Zeit noch nicht, meine liebe Frau
Schwägerinn. Aber ich bekomme sie entweder mit der heutigen
Post, oder doch mit der morgenden gewiß. Und ich will Ihnen im
voraus von Herzen wünschen, daß Ihr Loos den größten Gewinnst
mag erhalten haben.
    FRAU DAMON. Sie wünschen mir mehr, als ich verlange. Ich
habe nicht in die Lotterie gelegt, um reich zu werden, sondern um
andern gutes zu tun, wenn ich etwas gewönne. Sie wissen wohl,
daß mein lieber Mann mit meiner Freygibigkeit nicht wohl zufrieden ist, und mich durch seine gar zu große Sparsamkeit ausser
den Stand setzet, iemanden Gefälligkeiten zu erzeigen. Wenn ich
nun zum Exempel hundert Thaler gewönne: so wollte ich ihm die
eine Hälfte davon geben, damit er mir erlaubte, die andre
meiner Schwester Tochter Carolinchen zu schenken, welche
sich einige gute Bücher und musikalische Sachen dafür kaufen
würde. Es ist ein recht artiges und geschicktes Mädchen, die von
den meisten Fehlern unsers Geschlechts frey ist.[15]

This style is lucid and functional, giving much important
information in the first few lines of the play. The syntactic
elements of the sentences are logically linked, with no aposiopesis and only the most cautious use of ellipsis (line 5). The
periods tend to be long, dragging behind them trains of subordinate clauses (e.g.; lines 10-13), or rather ponderous verb
constructions, such as Orgon's "mag erhalten haben" (lines
5-7). Grammatical particles appear only rarely and not in
emphatic positions. Interjections and oaths, although they
do occur in slight concentration elsewhere in the play, do not
appear here at all. Certainly this is an approximation to the
way educated people of the better classes wrote or even spoke,

---

[15]   Gellert, "Das Loos in der Lotterie", pp. 323-24.

but just as certainly it is too controlled, too pallid, to seem very natural on the stage. This is, then, a style for the eye rather than for the ear, almost epistolary rather than dramatic.

As the curtain rises on the first act of *Der junge Gelehrte*, Damis and his servant, Anton, have concerns similar to those of Frau Damon and Herr Orgon:

DAMIS. Die Post also ist noch nicht da?
ANTON. Nein.
DAMIS. Noch nicht? Hast du auch nach der rechten gefragt? Die Post von Berlin —
ANTON. Nun ja doch; die Post von Berlin; sie ist noch nicht da! Wann sie aber nicht bald kömmt, so habe ich mir die Beine abgelaufen. Thuen Sie doch, als ob sie Ihnen, wer weiß was, mitbringen würde! Und ich wette, wenns hoch kömmt, so ist es eine neue Schartecke, oder eine Zeitung, oder sonst ein Wisch. —
DAMIS. Nein, mein guter Anton; dasmal möchte es etwas mehr seyn. Ah! wann du es wüßtest —
ANTON. Will ichs denn wissen? Es würde mir weiter doch nichts helfen, als daß ich einmal wieder über Sie lachen könnte. Das ist mir gewiß etwas seltnes? — Haben Sie mich sonst noch wohin zu schicken? Ich habe ohnedem auf dem Rathskeller eine kleine Verrichtung; vielleicht ists ein Gang? Nu?   (*LM*, I, 281.4-19)

This language is not as communicative, as tightly knit as Gellert's, but far more colloquial in its tone. It is rich in repetitions, such as the recurrence of "die Post von Berlin" to bring out the impatience of Damis with the mails and of Anton with Damis. The generous use of particles, beginning with the "also" interposed between subject and verb in the first speech and going on to Anton's fairly spluttering "Nun ja doch!" also enhances the naturalness of the style, as does verb inversion in declarative sentences, such as the "Thuen Sie doch..." on line 7 and the substitution of the phrase "wer weiß was" for a less individually expressive noun or pronoun. The periods are short, and many are interrogative or exclamatory, making for a rapid and seemingly spontaneous interchange of question and answer. The characteristics here illustrated, together with those previously mentioned, make the dramatic language of the young Lessing very much more a language of the living stage than of the writing desk.

The stylistic tradition borrowed from English and French models which Lessing followed most closely in his dramatic apprenticeship is clearly displayed in the following excerpt from the first scene of Frau Gottsched's *Die Pietisterey im Fischbein-Rocke:*

JUNGFER LUISCHEN. Kathrine!

KATHRINE. Jungfer Luischen!

JUNGFER LUISCHEN. Was ist das wieder vor ein Pack Bücher, was du da versteckst?

KATHRINE. Ach! frage sie nur nicht; sie wird's schon zeitig genug erfahren.

JUNGFER LUISCHEN. Wie? ist's schon wieder eine solche verzweifelte Scarteque, die die Mama mir immer zu lesen gibt?

KATHRINE. Ja, ja! das wäre mir eine rechte Scarteque! Nein, meine liebe Jungfer Luischen! es ist ein schönes großes Werk in Oktav, wenn sie es wissen will. Und danke sie noch dem Autor, daß er, wie es scheint, des Lügens müde geworden ist, sonst wäre wahrhaftig ein guter Foliant daraus geworden. Lese sie nur den Titul. Fußstapfen der Wunder Gottes im Hällischen Waisenhause. Ist das nicht lustig?

JUNGFER LUISCHEN. Ach, Kathrine! ich ärgere mich fast zu Tode.

KATHRINE. Ja, ja! ich glaube es wohl, da sie lieber einen Romain oder eine Komödie läse; aber ihre Mama versteht das Ding besser: Hübsche Herzens-Katechismi; ein Heiliger oder ein Vieh; Hoburgs unbekannter Christus; Freylingshausens Grundlegung; das, das gehört zur Erziehung eines Mädgens, welches in der Welt sein Glücke machen soll.

JUNGFER LUISCHEN. Schweige doch nur! [16]

In this passage, written a decade before *Der junge Gelehrte,* may be observed many of the stylistic features which Lessing employed, such as contractions (lines 5 and 7) and numerous exclamatory phrases. The periods are short, and are again frequently interrogatives or imperatives. Frau Gottsched also used aposiopesis, although by no means with the consistency and concentration to be found in Lessing's comedies. Oaths are also frequently in evidence. In her striving for humor

---

[16] Frau Gottsched, "Die Pietisterey...", p. 143.4-25.

generated by linguistic realism and parochialism, Frau Gottsched goes one better than Lessing by introducing a figure
who speaks in dialect, as humorously distinct from the "Hoch-
deutsch" which all of the other characters speak. In the following scene Frau Ehrlichen, who is described among the
"Spielende Personen" as "eine gemeine Bürgersfrau", scolds
Herrn Magister Scheinfromm:

FRAU EHRLICHEN. Ha! ha! Herr Magister! fing eck em hier? He
es en schöner Herr! Eck bedank my vör den schöenn Onderricht,
den he myner Dochter gegewen hefft.
    HERR SCHEINFROMM. Was wollt Ihr denn von mir haben?
    FRAU EHRLICHEN. I! du Schelm! Wat ick von dy heben wöll?
Eck frag dy, wat du von myner Dochter heben wöllst! du ver-
flookter Hund!
    HERR SCHEINFROMM. Meine liebe Frau, was redet Ihr? Habe
ich Eure Tochter nicht gut und gründlich unterrichtet?
    FRAU EHRLICHEN. Gründlich? Ja, freilich! mehr, als 't my löv
es! du Schelm! Eck scheck dy myn Kind, dat du 't in der Gott-
seligkeit onderrechten sollst; on nich en der Gottlosigkeit! Wat
Düvel wöllst du von dem Meeken hebben? Wöllstu Hooren
hebben; so seek dy welcke; op der Lestadie loopen genoog her-
ümmer; aber vertobb my nich myn Kind.[17]

This use of "Plattdeutsch" to equip a comic figure and simultaneously to strengthen, if only briefly, the linguistic realism
of the dialogue, is not to be found in Lessing's early comedies.
The only parallel instance for this use of language in Lessing's
works is the speech of Riccaut de la Marlinière in *Minna von
Barnhelm*, part of whose comic appeal is founded on his
comically imperfect German. Frau Gottsched followed almost to the letter the dictates concerning the language of
comedy laid down by her husband, whose ideas of the proper
comedy were strongly influenced by the French successors of
Molière. In many respects, as did Gellert in his own way,
the young Lessing followed Frau Gottsched.
    One element of the language of *Der junge Gelehrte* betrays
the young and not yet totally controlled craftsman at work.
Frequently there is an unevenness of tone and style, a splitting

[17]   Frau Gottsched, "Die Pietisterey...". p. 190.1-16.

of the language of at least two of the major characters into two discrete levels of function, one being that of characterization, the other of communication.

The language of characterization is predominant in this play so very much concerned with the investigation and dissection of a character humorous in his alienation from the realities of life. One of the most striking stylistic features of *Der junge Gelehrte* is the use of language to give to each of the comic "character" roles its own definite identity. Chrysander, Damis's father, is characterized as the type of the blustering and earthy merchant with philistine pretenses at being as learned as his son. To maintain this pretense, he lards his speech with Latin tags of dubious correctness and punctuates them with the phrase, "Wie wir Lateiner reden..." The trouble with this device of identifying a given character with a certain expression is that it is very easily overworked. This is a difficulty which Lessing himself must have seen, for although he has Chrysander say "wie wir Lateiner reden..." or its equivalent five times within the four pages of Act I, Sc. 2, he does not let him say it more than four times throughout the rest of the play. Chrysander is also characterized by his use of oaths, such as "Schocktausend" or "Potz Element", of such pejoratives as "Bösewicht" and the very low "Menscher", a term reserved, according to Adelung, only for "eine geringe Person weiblichen Geschlechtes im verächtlichen Verstand".[18] Just as often as Chrysander may be found blustering or swearing, however, he may be found speaking quite reasonably with his son, occasionally injecting some mercantile jargon, but in general speaking quite coherently, much in contrast to the style previously illustrated. In Act I, Sc. 5, for example, he says:

Nun das erfreut mich. Kaum hätte ich mir eine so grosse Folgsamkeit von dir versprochen. Glaube mir, Juliane ist ein recht gutes Kind. Ihr Vater war ein rechtschafner Mann, und es war gewiß seine Schuld nicht, daß er nicht noch rechtschafner war. Allein

---

[18]   Adelung, *op. cit.*, III, p. 473.

es fehlte ihm das beste. Das leidige Geld! — Wie ist mir denn?
Hast du ihn nicht gekannt?...
   [after an evasive answer by Damis, leading to an interruption
in the train of thought, Chrysander continues:]
   ... Du hast ihn also nicht gekannt? Ich besinne mich; es ist
auch nicht wohl möglich. Als er starb, war Juliane noch sehr jung.
Ich nahm sie gleich nach seinem Tode in mein Haus, und Gott
sey Dank! sie hat viel Wohlthaten hier genossen. Sie ist schön, sie
ist tugendhaft; wem sollte ich sie also lieber gönnen, als dir? Was
meynst du? —[19]

Here are present virtually none of the elements found in such
high concentration in the characterizing style. This straightforward, neutral style, almost stripped of self-interruptions,
interjections, and other "seasoning", is most efficient for
the communication of facts to the audience, even if not to
Damis, which the style otherwise generally associated with
Chrysander is not. Thus, if the play is to move forward at all,
a splitting of stylistic levels is necessary between the language
of characterization and that of communication. In this play
the young Lessing has not yet mastered the technique of combining these two aspects of dramatic language into an organic
whole.

One of Lessing's best characterizations in *Der junge Gelehrte*,
although showing similar failings as that of Chrysander, is
that of Anton, Damis's servant. Anton's speech is appropriate
to his social level, and features the frequent use of oaths and
words which Adelung considers provincial or low, such as
"Knicker",[20] "Krakelfüße",[21] "Rabenaas",[22] and such verbs

---

[19]   *LM*, I, p. 294, note 2, and p. 295.25-30.
[20]   *Ibid.*, p. 297.3. "Eine Person welche knickt ... im gemeinen Leben und
im verächtlichen Verstande; Er ist ein Knicker; er sucht aus Kargheit
überall etwas abzubrechen oder abzuzwacken." Adelung, *op. cit.*, II, p.
1664.
[21]   *LM*, I, p. 282.11. J. and W. Grimm, *Deutsches Wörterbuch* (Leipzig,
1854, ff.) lists this word as a Saxon dialect form and quotes this passage
from *Der junge Gelehrte*.
[22]   *LM*, I, p. 321.15. "... ein nur in den niedrigen Sprecharten übliches
Schimpfwort, einer höchst strafbaren oder lasterhaften Person". Adelung,
op. cit., III, p. 1219.

as "vexiren"[23] and the regular preterite form "rufte" of the verb "rufen".[24]

As the surrogate Hans Wurst in *Der junge Gelehrte*, Anton is distinguished from the other characters by an even more striking characteristic. In this play, which is otherwise almost totally barren of any images or metaphors, or even of any concretely descriptive adjectives, Anton's dialogue fairly bursts with images and metaphors. His range of images embraces the very folkish and concrete, on one hand, and the rather sophisticated and literary, on the other. Thus, Anton can say, "Zu diesen dreyen, Gott sey Dank, weiß ich mich, wie das Färbepferd um die Rolle",[25] which is as colloquial as one could desire; but also, speaking of Damis, "Die Bücher und die Exempel, die er liest, sind die Winde nach welchen sich der Wetterhahn seiner Gedanken richtet" (*LM*, I, 297), an epigrammatic metaphor of a far more literary cast. These metaphors, however, are still credible within the range of Anton's characterization, for within the economy of the play he wears two masks, that of the stupid servant to Damis and that of the sly confidant of Chrysander. In his pleasure in images, Anton will wittily twist a familiar simile, as when he says to Lisette, "Der Gott der Gelehrsamkeit ... könne kein Weibsbild leiden... Er fliehe davor, wie der Stößer vor den Tauben" (*LM*, I, 312). Or he will self-consciously regret that he cannot think of a suitable image; "Bald aber ward die Grille von einer andern verjagt, so wie etwann, so wie etwann – Schade, daß ich kein Gleichniß dazu finden kann!" (*LM*, I, 300). Anton and Lisette will occasionally develop an image be-

---

[23]   *LM*, I, p. 355.5. "Unnöthige Mühe, Beschwerde, oder Unlust verursachen, nur im gemeinen Leben üblich". Adelung, *op. cit.*, IV, p. 1582.

[24]   *LM*, I, p. 296.19. "Einige oberdeutsche Schriftsteller werfen den Meissnern vor, dass sie dieses Zeitwort wider das Beispiel des grössten Teiles Deutschlands regulär abwandeln. Den Meissnern geschiehet damit zuviel, wohl aber findet man es bei den schlesischen Dichtern häufig in der regulären Form." Adelung, *op. cit.*, III, p. 1518.

[25]   *LM*, I, p. 282.4-5. J. and W. Grimm, *op. cit.*, gives the explanation, "das bei den Färbern die Rolle dreht", and quotes this passage.

tween them, as on page 38, above, and later in the same scene:

ANTON. Ja, ja, mein Aeffchen, ich merk es schon; du willst die Kastanien aus der Asche haben, und brauchst Katzenpfoten dazu.
LISETTE. Je nun, mein liebes Katerchen, thu es immer!
ANTON. Wie sie es einem ans Herze legen kann! Liebes Katerchen! Weis nur her, den Brief; weis her!   (*LM*, I, 338.33-339.3)

Again, however, as with all of the features mentioned thus far, these images are concentrated on the characterizing level of the language. When Anton has to say something of importance to the play, they are almost completely absent, as in the conversation between him and Chrysander in Act I, Scene 6.

The style of the language of the lesser characters in the play, Valer and Juliane, who are present as more or less mechanical accessories to the "serious" element of the plot, is far closer to that of Gellert, as may be seen from the following excerpt from the beginning of Act II, Scene 1:

LISETTE. Nur hier herein; Herr Damis ist ausgegangen. Sie können hier schon ein Wörtchen miteinander im Vertrauen reden.
JULIANE. Ja, ja: mein Entschluß ist gefaßt. Ich bin ihm zu viel schuldig; er hat durch seine Wohlthaten das größte Recht über mich erhalten. Es koste mir was es wolle; ich muß die Heyrath eingehen, weil es Chrysander verlangt. Oder soll ich etwa die Dankbarkeit der Liebe aufopfern? Sie sind selbst tugendhaft, Valer, und Ihr Umgang hat mich edler denken gelehrt. Mich Ihrer werth zu zeigen, muß ich meine Pflicht, auch mit dem Verluste meines Glückes, erfüllen.
LISETTE. Eine wunderbare Moral! wahrhaftig!
VALER. Aber wo bleiben Versprechung, Schwur, Treue? Ist es erlaubt, um eine eingebildete Pflicht zu erfüllen, eine andre, die uns wirklich verbindet, zu vernichten?   (*LM*, I, 306.11-24)

The speech of these characters has not the variety and pungency of that of Chrysander and Anton, or, as shall be seen, of Damis. Indeed, their speech comes closer to what Adelung would call "edle Sprechart". It is noble in sentiment, tight in its syntax, but relatively pallid in comparison with the general style of the play, and falls short of the pithiness and naturalness which are achieved elsewhere. This is because the young lovers are less interesting as characters in themselves than as fixtures in the necessary structure of the plot and move on a different level of feeling and discourse than the other characters.

The most felicitous fusion of the language of characterization with the language of plot function is achieved in the speech of Damis. As we have already seen, he is characterized by stuffy, pedantic manners of speech. His talk swarms with references to Biblical commentators, Greek poetesses, Homer, Horace, and other trappings of scholastic learning. Like his father, Damis frequently uses Latin tags, though less self-consciously. Often Damis will break out in the language of disputation, as when he is trying to demonstrate to Anton by a paradox that he cannot speak German:

> ... Du kannst Deutsch, das ist: du kannst deine Gedanken mit Tönen ausdrücken, die einem Deutschen verständlich sind; das ist, die eben die Gedanken in ihm erwecken, die du bey dir hast. Du kannst aber nicht Deutsch, das ist: du weißt nicht, was in dieser Sprache schlecht oder wohl verbunden, rauh oder annehmlich, undeutlich oder verständlich, alt oder gebräuchlich ist; kurz, du weißt ihre Regeln nicht; du hast keine gelehrte Kenntniß von ihr. (*LM*, I, 284.9-15)

With his father, Damis is pompously rhetorical:

> O Herr Vater, das Studieren ist mir Vergnügens genug. Wer neben den Wissenschaften noch andere Ergötzungen sucht, muß die wahre Süßigkeit derselben noch nicht geschmeckt haben. (*LM*, I, 286. 1-3)

Damis can, however, drop his pose of scholarliness without falling out of character to call Anton "Schurke", or to complain of "die verdammte Post". This rounds out the portrayal of a young man occasionally betraying the childishly petulant personality beneath the learned mask.

Damis is also used by Lessing as a vehicle for his own gratuitous satirical thrusts at the learned professions as in the aforementioned apostrophe to "Gelehrsamkeit", and at women, as when Damis bursts forth with unaccustomed vigor:

Jedes Frauenzimmer ist eitel, hoffärtig, geschwätzig, zänkisch und Zeitlebens kindisch, es mag so alt werden, als es will. Jedes Frauenzimmer weiß kaum, daß es eine Seele hat, um die es unendlich mehr besorgt seyn sollte, als um den Körper. Sich ankleiden, auskleiden, und wieder anders ankleiden; vor dem Spiegel sitzen, seinen eignen Reiz darinne bewundern, auf ausgekünstelte Minen sinnen; mit neugierigen Augen müßig an dem Fenster liegen: unsinnige Romane lesen, und aufs höchste zum Zeitvertreibe die Nadel zur Hand nehmen: das sind seine Beschäftigungen; das ist sein Leben. (*LM*, I, 289.28-290.5)

That this sort of speech is unusual for Damis, and is a gratuitous touch, added to amuse the audience, among the male members of which, at any rate, this sort of gentle misogyny was apparently popular, may be seen in a brief quotation from the parodistic *Versuch eines deutschen Wörterbuches* in the *Bremer Beyträge*, under the article "Verstand":

Das Mädchen hat Verstand, sagt ein Liebhaber, der nur aufs Geld sieht, wenn gleich sein Mädchen weiter nichts thut, als daß es Caffee trinkt, l'Omber spielt, Knötchen macht, zum Fenster heraus sieht, und, wenn es hoch kömmt, über das Nachtzeug der Nachbarinn spottet. In Gesellschaften, wo sie keines von diesen allen thun kann, ist sie nicht im Stande, etwas weiter zu sagen, als ein trocknes Ja und Nein; und spielte sie nicht mit ihrem Fächer; so würde man sie für eine schöne Statue ansehen.[26]

This rhetorical style in the speech of Damis just quoted, with its accumulation of predicative adjectives, with its suspenseful chaining of infinitive phrases rising to the climactic "das sind seine Beschäftigungen; das ist sein Leben" is a distinct deviation from the style otherwise assigned to Damis. So is the apostrophe to "Gelehrsamkeit", with its long periods, its rhetorical exclamations, and its elliptic constructions. But these deviations are still consonant with the image of Damis which has been given, that of a bookish and precociously pompous young pedant, who very easily might spout quotations from books he has only half-digested. Perhaps, too, Damis's language is so much of a piece, with no apparent conflict

[26] *Neue Beyträge zum Vergnügen des Verstandes und Witzes, edn. cit.*, III, Pt. 1, p. 38.

between characterization and communication, for the very reason that he appears chiefly as a humorous character and not so much as an integral part of the actual plot of the play. Damis is rather acted around by the other characters than active himself.

In identifying the level of realism achieved by Lessing in *Der junge Gelehrte*, it might be best to recall once more the adjectives applied to his dramatic language by Christian Heimrich Schmid: "Natürlich und dennoch gewählt". Largely, the language of *Der junge Gelehrte* is an approximation, according to the theatrical usage of the time, to the colloquial speech of the well-to-do, well-bred middle classes, presumably of Leipzig. While using the stylistic and dramaturgic elements described above to re-create the tone and syntax of this language, to achieve a natural effect, Lessing selectively avoids the extremes of realism reached by Frau Gottsched. Dialect is not used, nor is slang. Comparison of the vocabulary of *Der junge Gelehrte* with Adelung's dictionary reveals practically no strictly provincial words in the play. On the other hand, the natural tone of the dialogue, the everyday matter and vocabulary, and especially its striking paucity of images and metaphors, give a matter-of-fact flatness which places it well outside the range of poetic or lyrical language.

Just as the comic dramatic form was concerned with people of the middle estate, between high and low, the language of this first of Lessing's full-length comedies is also generally in the range of colloquial speech, between dialect and slang on one hand, and elevated, poetic speech on the other. Although clearly derivative from the conventions of the time, the young Lessing's dramatic language shows a dexterity of technique and, despite occasional lapses, a sense of total organization and integration which truly distinguish him even at this early date. At its best it is a language that is clear and yet lively, that is realistic and yet terse and theatrical. It is a language showing great promise of things to come.

III. FROM *DAMON* TO *DER FREYGEIST*

The promise so clearly evident in the supple technique and language of *Der junge Gelehrte* was slow in its fulfillment. Lessing's eventual mastery of comic form was gained only at the expense of much experimentation, in the course of which many of his attempts ended in disappointment, as the numerous dramatic fragments indicate. Besides *Der junge Gelehrte*, the products of Lessing's earliest and most prolific preoccupation with comedy are *Damon, oder die wahre Freundschaft, Die alte Jungfer, Der Misogyne, Die Juden*, and *Der Freygeist*, all written between 1747 and 1750. Structurally and thematically there is little about the earliest of these plays which would indicate the possibility of the work in which the two decades of Lessing's interest in comedy are to find their culmination, namely *Minna von Barnhelm*. In these plays, however, developments in Lessing's use of language are to be seen which anticipate this finest of his comedies.

In all of the comedies of the early period, the main features found in *Der junge Gelehrte* are present to some degree, but never again are they used with the same self-confident virtuosity, with the same joy in excess which mark that first triumph. Over the years, Lessing's comic language clearly developed towards a closing of the gap which was apparent in *Der junge Gelehrte* between the diction of humorous characterization and the expression of serious feelings.

Gradually characterization through language becomes more subtle in technique, and the possibilities of making more elevated colloquial language as expressive of character and feeling as the "intimate" and often grossly colloquial variety which dominated *Der junge Gelehrte* are discovered and exploited. If, in *Der junge Gelehrte*, Lessing's language could be described as a mean between the colloquial humor of Frau Gottsched and the genteel sentiment of Gellert, its further development was definitely in the direction of the latter, and beyond to a conception of comedy and its language which transcended previous theories and forms.

In part this may be attributed to increasing maturity on Lessing's part, to a keener sense of proportion and balance. Far more significant, however, is the consideration of genre. Even at the beginning of his career, in such elements as the Valer-Juliane scenes in *Der junge Gelehrte*, Lessing showed an inclination towards the French "comédie larmoyante", a term which he was later to translate as "weinerliches Lustspiel". When this name was used as a pejorative by others, Lessing changed the appellation to "rührendes Lustspiel", which was less literally accurate, but more neutral; indeed, even more so than the French term.[1] Lessing borrowed heavily from the plots of Marivaux and de la Chaussée at this time, as well as from Molière and Holberg. Increasingly the serious characters, the "moving" plot come to dominate the humorous element, until the latter becomes only a comic relief supplementing an essentially earnest action. *Der junge*

---

[1] In the issue of the *Berlinische privilegirte Staats- und gelehrte Zeitung* for May 24, 1753, reviewing Frau Gottsched's translation of Mme. de Graffigny's *Cénie*, Lessing wrote, "Cenie ist ein Meisterstück in dem Geschmacke der weinerlichen Lustspiele" (*LM*, V, p. 168). The following year, in his *Theatralische Bibliothek*, in the introduction to *Abhandlungen von dem weinerlichen oder rührenden Lustspiele*, in which the opinions of the Frenchman, Chassiron, and the German, Gellert, were opposed, Lessing described the genesis of the "comédie larmoyante" in France, saying: "Die erste Veränderung brachte dasjenige hervor, was seine Anhänger das rührende Lustspiel, und seine Widersacher das weinerliche nennen." Continuing, Lessing took credit for having introduced the term "weinerliches Lustspiel" in the passage on *Cénie* quoted above, but suggested it be renamed "rührendes Lustspiel", so that the scornful connotation which the term had taken on might be lost: "Ein rührendes Lustspiel läßt uns an ein sehr schönes Werk denken, da ein weinerliches, ich weis nicht was für ein kleines Ungeheuer zu versprechen scheinet" (*LM*, VI, pp. 6-7).

Gelehrte was the only truly humorous comedy of character which Lessing wrote, and even it had its weak love plot. His remaining comedies show an ever stronger movement towards the dramatic and morally normative rather than the humorous, and eventually, by virtue of their earnestness of content and language, they surpass the conventional bounds of comedy.

Lessing achieved mastery of dramatic language and its techniques long before he completely mastered the dramatic form. In these early plays, the dialogue is often the best thing about an otherwise lifeless and mechanical comedy. Lessing requires many plays and many years of work to evolve the most felicitous relationship between form and content. At first, the content is either too trivial for artistic success or too ruthlessly subordinated to the requirements of the comic form. It is only where language has a truly significant framework of plot and character on which to display itself that true mastery of both form and content is attained.

DAMON, ODER DIE WAHRE FREUNDSCHAFT

It is doubtful whether Lessing ever intended his one-act comedy, *Damon, oder die wahre Freundschaft*, for production on the stage. It was published in the seventh issue of the Hamburg weekly, *Die Ermunterungen zum Vergnügen des Gemüths*, in 1747, and no indication can be found that it was ever performed.[2] In effect Lessing himself later repudiated this comic effort by excluding it from all editions of his works to appear during his lifetime and by his indignation at its unauthorized second publication in C. H. Schmid's *Anthologie der Deutschen* in 1770.[3] In view of the quality of this play, which Erich Schmidt

---

[2]   *LM*, III, p. 178, note 1.
[3]   Schmidt, *Lessing*, I, p. 130. For an opposed view of the significance of *Damon*, see the analysis by Herbert H. J. Peisel, "Damon und Leander", *German Quarterly*, XXXIV, No. 4 (November, 1961), pp. 385-408.

terms, "eine schwächliche Primanerarbeit, ohne Welt- und Theaterkenntnis", this anger is understandable.

The plot of *Damon*, derived from plays of Holberg, Destouches, and Molière,[4] involves two passionate friends, Damon and Leander, who have both staked their entire fortunes upon the safe and profitable return of two merchant ships, and are courting a rich young widow. Disturbed because her two suitors, out of excess of friendship, continually yield each to the other in seeking her hand, neither showing her the proper amount of ardor, the widow resorts to a ruse to settle the matter finally. She reluctantly follows the suggestion of her maid, Lisette, that she say that her choice between Damon and Leander will fall upon the one who is most fortunate in his "affairs". The worthy Damon determines to foil the apparently mercenary widow by offering to share profit and loss from the merchant venture equally with Leander. Leander, who has had erroneous news that his ship has gone down, treacherously agrees, without revealing his supposed mishap, thinking that he will win the fortune and the widow. Next, Damon's blustering cousin Oronte enters and tells Damon that in truth his ship and not Leander's has gone down. Damon believes that he is ruined and resigns himself to the loss of his inheritance and of his beloved. The widow, however, chooses Damon as her husband because he has been the most "fortunate" in having had an opportunity to show his generous spirit and to see his supposed friend in a new light. Damon forgives Leander his shameful lapse, and the friends are reconciled for a happy ending. Certainly Schmidt's condemnation of this rather sentimental piece, with its stiff and overly idealized characters, as "Primanerarbeit" is most valid, despite the touching testimonial to friendship which the play constitutes.

The language of *Damon* shows many of the virtues and failings of the language of *Der junge Gelehrte*. The humorous figures, Lisette and Oronte, are vivid in their speech, whereas the serious characters tend to be stiff and long-winded. Lisette's

---

[4] *PO*, "Anmerkungen zu Teil I bis 7", p. 82.

style at its best may be observed in the following passage. She
has just informed Damon of the widow's supposed intentions:

DAMON. Himmel! wie unglücklich bin ich, wenn Ihr die Wahrheit
redet! Hätte ich mir auch jemals einbilden können, daß der
Reichthum so viel Reizungen für sie haben sollte? Soll der nun
unsere Person erst beliebt machen? Findet sie an mir und an
Leandern nichts, welches dieser verblendenden Kleinigkeit die
Waage halten könnte? Bald sollte es mich gereuen, eine Person zu
lieben, die so niederträchtig —
LISETTE. Nun, nun! Fein sachte, fein sachte! Nur nicht gleich
geschimpft. Zum Geyer, haben Sie es denn besser haben wollen?
Der Reichthum an und für sich selber ist eben dasjenige nicht,
was sie an Ihnen sucht. Die Neigungen meiner Frau gegen Sie und
gegen den Herrn Leander liegen itzo im Gleichgewichte, und dieser
soll also nur ein kleiner Zuwurf seyn, welcher der oder jener
Schale den Ausschlag giebt. O! geizig sind wir eben nicht. Das
sagen Sie uns nur nicht nach. Ob es uns auch gleich keine Schande
seyn würde, wenn wir es wären. Sie zeigen ja dadurch, daß Sie
ihr eine Zeit lang nichts mehr von Ihrer Liebe vorgesagt haben,
ganz deutlich, daß es Ihnen gleichviel seyn würde, ob sie sich für
Sie selbst oder für Ihren Freund erklärte; und Leander desgleichen.
Wie hätte sie es also wohl klüger können anfangen?
DAMON. Ach daß ich so verliebt, ach, daß ich so gewissenhaft in
der Freundschaft bin!
LISETTE. Würde es Ihnen vielleicht lieber gewesen seyn, wenn
meine Frau Sie beyde hätte würfeln lassen, damit die meisten
oder die wenigsten Augen sie dem einen, oder dem andern zur
Frau gegeben hätten? Es ist dieses sonst eine ganz löbliche Sol-
datenmode, wenn von zwey Galgenschwengeln einem das Leben
soll geschenkt werden, und es einer doch eben so wenig verdient,
als der andre. Ja, ja. Nicht wahr, sie hätte der Mode wohl auch
hier folgen können? (*LM*, III, 184.16-185.6)

Within this compass may be seen once again the main elements
of Lessing's humorous colloquial language. Lisette shows
many of the stylistic attributes of Damis's Anton. Her
speech is filled with interjections and exclamatory phrases,
("Nun, nun! Fein sachte, fein sachte!", line 8, above), oaths
("Zum Geyer", line 9, above), and images (the image of the
scales, lines 12-14, above). The tone is lively, the sentences
being short and frequently interrogative or exclamatory.

Lisette's vocabulary is also suited to her station in life, as her familiarity with dicing (lines 23-26, above), and her use of "Galgenschwengel" (line 27) indicate.

Damon's cousin Oronte, and Chrysander in *Der junge Gelehrte* are the ancestors, the most naively constructed prototypes of rich, crotchety older men who are always represented as a type in Lessing's comedies. Like Lisette and the comic man-servant, who is a slightly disguised Hans Wurst, these old men are standard fixtures in European comedy of the time. They are always the butts of humor because of one particular characteristic, be it a linguistic quirk, as in the case of the two just mentioned, or a more deeply rooted trait of character, such as Wumshäter's misogyny in *Der Misogyne* or Lisidor's naive pretensions to philosophizing in *Der Freygeist*. The archetypes for these figures may be sought already in the comedies of Aristophanes (e.g.; *The Birds, The Clouds*) and Plautus (e.g.; *Aulularia, Trinummus*). In this way, too, the French theatre followed the Graeco-Roman, and the humorous old man is rarely missing from any comedy of Molière, Harpagon in *L'Avare* and Orgon in *Tartuffe* being perhaps the most illustrious instances. Their mannerisms are to be found transfigured in the early old men of Lessing's creation, who display that frequently mechanical rigidity of conduct and mannerism, that inability or slowness to adapt their conduct to a new situation which Henry Bergson designates as an essential comic attribute.[5] Orgon and Chrysander share with Harpagon the trait of repeating a single phrase, such as Harpagon's "Sans dot!" (*L'Avare*, I, 5.) the comic effect of which Bergson likens to that of a jack-in-the-box, jumping up again and again, doing the same thing no matter what is done to it. Thus, Oronte, for example, exhibits the extreme of Lessing's use of a single characterizing speech feature:

ORONTE. Ach! Schade um das Geld! Das sind gescheute Reden. Versteh Er mich. Damon, Damon, ein Mensch, der so denken

[5]   Henri Bergson, "Laughter", in *Comedy*, ed. Wylie Sypher (Garden City, 1956), p. 108.

kann, ist nicht werth, daß er mein Vetter sey. Versteh Er mich.
Ach! schade ums Geld! Nein, Gott sey Dank, versteh Er mich, so
albern und gottesvergessen bin ich in meiner Jugend nicht gewesen.
Denkt Er, versteh Er mich, daß Ihn die junge Wittwe nun hey-
rathen wird? versteh Er mich. Sie müste eine Närrinn seyn.
Versteh Er mich.   (*LM*, III, 194.28-34)

Oronte uses this phrase, or its polite variant "Verstehn Sie
mich", a staggering 84 times in the 113 lines allotted to him.
But whereas Harpagon's "Sans dot!" reveals what is closest to
his heart and illuminates an aspect of his character, Oronte's
and Chrysander's repetitions are merely identifying tags
making use of the comic force of repetition, but not telling the
audience much about the essence of their characters. The
transformation which the figure of the humorous old man
undergoes in these early comedies and particularly the changes
in his style of speaking are clear indications of Lessing's general
progress. Oronte, standing as he does at the very beginning
of Lessing's career, still shows all of the earmarks of the old
man arbitrarily introduced just for comic effect. The characterization begins and ends merely with the habit of speech.
As Lessing's art develops, however, the characterizations will
become more subtle and varied, and, as will be the case with
almost all of the characters, penetrate beyond the surface
texture of speech mannerisms.

   Like the styles of speech in *Der junge Gelehrte*, those of *Damon*
fall into two distinct types: the humorous colloquial language
of Oronte and Lisette and the elevated colloquial language
of serious expression, spoken by the characters essential to the
central plot. In *Damon*, however, this second style is far more
in evidence than in *Der junge Gelehrte*, and can be observed and
analyzed more fully. In the following passage, Damon and
Leander, the former sincerely, the latter hypocritically, discuss
the friendship which is supposedly the center of their lives.
Leander has just assured Damon at length that no matter how
great a misdeed Damon might commit against him, he would
never take offense, since his friend is doing it, therefore cannot
be acting out of a low intention, and can thus be forgiven:

DAMON. Ich will wünschen, Leander, daß ich Ihnen mit gleichem Feuer antworten könnte. Ich will mich bemühen, Ihre Freundschaft nie auf eine so harte Probe zu setzen.

LEANDER. Ey, liebster Freund, wie so kaltsinnig? Zweifeln Sie an der Aufrichtigkeit meiner Reden? Zweifeln Sie, ob meine Freundschaft diese Probe aushalten würde? Wollte doch Gott, ja wollte doch Gott, daß Sie mich, je eher je lieber auf eine Art beleidigten, welche bey andern unvergeblich seyn würde! wie vergnügt, wie entzückt wollte ich seyn, die süße Rache einer großmüthigen Verzeihung an Ihnen auszuüben.

DAMON. Und ich will mir dagegen wünschen, daß ich dieser großmüthigen Verzeihung niemals möge nöthig haben.

LEANDER. Ja, Damon, und ich würde, in gleichen Fällen, auch ein gleiches von Ihnen erwarten. O! ich kenne Sie zu wohl. Ihre Seele ist edel und großmüthig. Und diese läßt mich nicht daran zweifeln.

DAMON. Sie trauen mir zu viel zu, werthester Leander. Voll Scham gesteh ich Ihnen, daß ich mich zu schwach dazu befinde. Die Gedanken davon scheinen mir edel und wahr. Die Erfüllung aber unmöglich. Ich zittere schon im voraus, wenn ich mir vorstelle, daß meine Freundschaft einen so harten Versuch vielleicht einmal auszuhalten habe. Doch Ihre Tugend ist mir gut dafür. Und ist ein Freund wohl auch zu einer so allzu großmüthigen Sanftmuth verbunden? Ich weis es, es ist die Pflicht eines Freundes, dem andern zu verzeihen. Doch ist es auch des andern Pflicht, ihm so wenig Gelegenheit dazu zu geben, als ihm nur möglich ist.

(*LM*, III, 189.33-190.22)

Fairly lengthy subordinate clauses and dependent infinitive phrases and the copious use of modals with dependent infinitives combine to make the speeches of Damon and Leander elaborate and somewhat cumbersome. They are enlivened only very slightly by the use of exclamations such as "Ey, liebster Freund..." (line 4, above), or the emphatic repetition of "Wollte doch Gott..." (lines 6-7, above). The vocabulary is generally colorless, the nouns being mostly abstract. Many words are used as part of a ritual of friendship which is being played out between Damon and Leander, through which Leander is trying to prepare Damon for the deception which is to be perpetrated upon him. It is strict in its form, but devoid of real energy of feeling. The way the characters play on words tends to give this dialogue a hollow tone. An example of this is the repeated use of the adjective "großmüthig". In the thirty-odd lines of the passage above, it is used four times, twice as an attributive to "Verzeihung", once as a predicative with "Seele", and finally, again attributively, in a play on words in "großmüthigen Sanftmuth". Lessing apparently was fond of this sort of yoking together of words with the same roots, as may be seen in the speech immediately preceding the passage just quoted, where Leander insists: "Legen Sie doch endlich einmal ... das mir so nachtheilige Vorurtheil ab..." This implies a cerebral playing with the sound of words on Lessing's part, with which Leander's insincere use of the current rhetoric of friendship is nicely satirized.

One of the truly interesting features about the language of *Damon* is the use which Lessing makes of monologues. Like Hédelin, his French preceptor in dramatic theory, Gottsched disapproved of the monologue, since its use in drama violated that all-important principle of "Wahrscheinlichkeit". "Kluge Leute", says Gottsched, "pflegen nicht laut zu reden, wenn sie allein sind; es wäre denn in besondern Affecten, und das zwar mit wenig Worten".[6] Theoretically, then, brief monologues were permissible only for the expression of great agitation. In practice, however, in this as in other respects, the German theatre of Lessing's youth deviated from the canons laid down by its would-be arbiter. Monologues were often very convenient from the dramaturgic viewpoint. They could be used to connect two scenes in order to avoid too improbably rapid a succession on the stage of two characters, each of whom is to speak to a third, who is on stage the whole time. Thus, the third speaker is given a brief reflective or choric monologue to ease the transition. Monologues were also convenient as one way to handle the problem of exposition and to have characters reflect on the actions of others before the audience. The reflective monologue was very much favored by Lessing and is

---

[6] *CD*, p. 648. An excellent treatment of the monologue in Lessing's dramas is: Friederich Düsel, *Der dramatische Monolog in der Poetik des 17. und 18. Jahrhunderts und in den Dramen Lessings* (= *Theatergeschichtliche Forschungen*, XIV) (Hamburg, Leipzig, 1897).

frequently to be found in the early comedies, as shall be seen shortly in the analyses of *Die Juden* and *Der Freygeist*. Damon is given two reflective monologues in the present play. In terms of Gottsched's theory, these are still justifiable, since Damon is evidently in a state of considerable inner agitation. What is of interest here is the expressiveness of these monologues in comparison to the otherwise dry language of the play. This is brought about by the relative brokenness, the almost "stream-of-consciousness" quality of their language, a quality usually associated with the dramatic language of the "Sturm und Drang". In the following monologue, we see Damon just after Oronte has informed him of his financial and therefore his amorous ruin:

— Verdrießliche Nachricht! — Ich verliere mein Vermögen — dieses möchte noch seyn. Wer weis, wenn Leander unglücklich gewesen wäre, ich würde vielleicht nicht großmüthig genug gewesen seyn, ihm zu helfen — Was für eine Schande für mich, wenn ich an ihm untreu geworden wäre! — der Himmel hat mich davor bewahren wollen — ich bin glücklich bey allem meinem Unglücke — aber ich verliere zugleich die liebenswürdige Wittwe — sie wird sich an Leandern nun ohne Schwierigkeit geben — an Leandern — doch Leander ist ja mein Freund — die Liebe — die verdammte Liebe — verdient sie mein Freund nicht eben so wohl, als ich? — was darf ich viel nach einer Frau fragen, deren Herz ich, wenn ich es ja bekommen hätte, bloß meines Geldes wegen bekommen hätte — Aber doch — sie ist liebenswürdig — wie muß ich mit mir selber kämpfen! — Allein Leander — sollte es wahr seyn, daß er diese falsche Nachricht bekommen hätte? — und er sollte es mir verschwiegen haben? — wie hätte er den Vorschlag annehmen können, den ich ihm that — ich falle auf ganz besondre Gedanken — doch weg damit — sie schänden meinen Freund —

(*LM*, III, 196.31-197.14)

The syntax of this monologue is indeed still far too intact, the thoughts too well composed to convey Damon's agitation fully. But the use of a monologue here and an evident attempt to communicate emotion through a character's speech by a partial syntactic disintegration accomplished by the use of aposiopesis and anacoluth shows that the young Lessing already had at his disposal a considerable number of dramaturgic devices which time and experience would teach him to use to fullest effect.

As its subtitle indicates, *Damon* is a play about "die wahre Freundschaft". The action within its twenty-two pages is far more devoted to the unfolding of a sentimental plot than to the dissection of a character, as in *Der junge Gelehrte*. Oronte and Lisette indeed serve to advance the plot, but they are by no means its chief figures, these being the widow, Damon, and Leander. Yet, as the following outline of the play's scenes according to the characters appearing in each makes clear, Oronte and Lisette are carefully woven into the play's structure, their comic presence and speech clearly calculated to lighten the otherwise dry and rhetorical dialogues on Love and Friendship.

Scene	I	The Widow,	Lisette		
„	II		Lisette,	Damon	
„	III		Lisette		
„	IV		Lisette,		Leander
„	V			Damon,	Leander
„	VI			Damon	
„	VII			Damon,	Oronte
„	VIII			Damon	
„	IX		Lisette,	Damon	
„	X	The Widow,	Lisette,	Damon, Leander, Oronte	

Through this structure, Oronte and Lisette speak nearly half of the lines in the play, appearing more or less dominantly in six of its ten scenes. This brings the sentimental and humorous tones closer to achieving quantitative equity than in *Der junge Gelehrte*. In this balance, Lessing achieves a necessary criterion for the "wahre Komödie"; that it contain both sentimental and humorous elements. But the construction of the play as reflected in its two styles of language is still very much the assembly of dissociated elements into a proportioned whole rather than their blending together into an organic unity.

DIE ALTE JUNGFER

The next comedy by Lessing to reach the stage after *Der junge Gelehrte* was the three-act play, *Die alte Jungfer*, written in 1748 and shortly thereafter performed by Koch's troupe.[7] This play must have enjoyed some degree of popularity at the time. It was first published in Berlin in 1749 as a book by itself and not, as was more usual, as part of an anthology or literary journal.[8] With *Damon*, however, *Die alte Jungfer* shares the fate of having been excluded from all editions of his works which Lessing himself edited, and was thus rejected by him as an example of his youthful follies, some of which, as he wrote in 1754, had unfortunately seen the light of day here and there already.[9]

There is certainly less justification to be found for this disavowal than in the case of *Damon*. *Die alte Jungfer* is a well-ordered and integrated farce, betraying, as Erich Schmidt concedes, far more knowledge of the theatre than *Damon*, if no more knowledge of life.[10] Indeed the characters of *Die alte Jungfer* have much less immediacy and reality than do those of *Der junge Gelehrte*, and are for the most part drawn from the standard cast of the contemporary comic theatre.

As C.C.D. Vail points out, *Die alte Jungfer* and *Der Misogyne*, written at about the same time, are Lessing's two "pure comedies of manners".[11] "The English source [for *Die alte Jungfer*] is unquestionably Congreve's *The Way of the World*" for Vail. Although the plot is not nearly as complicated as Congreve's, and other elements are to be found in it, *Die alte Jungfer* does show some essential resemblances to the English work. The rich old maid, given the Anglo-German comic name Ohldin, is, if we accept Vail's premise, Lessing's counterpart to Lady Wishfort.

[7]   C. H. Schmid, *Chronologie...*, p. 90.
[8]   *LM*, III, p. 201, note 1.
[9]   *LM*, V, p. 271.
[10]   Schmidt, *Lessing*, I, p. 131.
[11]   Curtis C. D. Vail, *Lessing's Relation to the English Language and Literature* (New York, 1936), p. 106.

At the play's outset Ohldin agrees to a marriage arranged by Herr Oronte, the humorous old man of the piece, who claims to be happily married, but constantly quarrels with his wife. Jungfer Ohldin's prospective bridegroom is Kapitän von Schlag, a debt-ridden, fortune-hunting army officer, cashiered because of his unfitness for service, who possesses none of the ethical compunctions of his far better fellow officer, Tellheim. Ohldin's young cousin Lelio, an indolent ne'er-do-well, who had expected to inherit her fortune upon her death, together with Lisette, the maid, ponders upon a way to prevent the marriage. In the play's only plot element truly parallel to *The Way of the World*, they engage Peter, a sweets-hawker, to dupe Ohldin by disguising himself with a beard and wooden leg and trying to foist himself upon the old maid as the captain, repelling her the while with his boorish behavior. This is similar to Mirabell's device of disguising the servant, Waitwell, as his uncle, Sir Rowland, and having him court Lady Wishfort in order to blackmail her for permission to marry Millamant. Peter behaves abominably, and just as the old maid is about to reconsider her engagement, the real captain arrives and saves the situation for himself, winning the hand of the self-deluding Jungfer Ohldin. When Lelio threatens to protest the marriage, the captain privately promises him that his financial interests will be protected if he makes no trouble. The play ends with a procession of all of the characters to dinner, Lisette taking the captain's arm, which is, as Herr Oronte remarks in the curtain line, "Ein böses Omen".

The tone of this farce, strongly dependent indeed upon the English comedy of manners, is an entirely new one in Lessing's works up to this time. The urbanity and cynicism of a Congreve are lacking, it is true, but so are the sentimentality and moralizing of a Gellert, which latter elements were evident in *Der junge Gelehrte* and even more so in *Damon*, and will become significant again in later works. Here, however, the element of feeling is entirely lacking. No distinction is to be made between humorous and serious characters, between caricatures and idealized figures of noble sentiment. All of the characters are possessed of flaws, either of stupidity, cupidity, or both. This is cold comedy, of a kind intended to make the audience laugh at the foibles of the characters and the world in which they live, rather than to move it by any of their actions, as in the "rührendes Lustspiel" or even in Lessing's ideal of "wahre Komödie". It is comedy of a kind which Lessing is never to write again, possibly because it moves only to cruel laughter and achieves no improvement in the beholder as the comedy must to be justified in the thinking of the Enlightenment. *Die alte Jungfer* stands alone in this respect among Lessing's comedies, and this may well be the reason why Lessing never included it in editions of his works.

Mainly because of the uniformity of characterization and tone, the language of *Die alte Jungfer* shows an evenness of handling not previously to be observed in Lessing's comedies. It is colloquial, sometimes even vulgar, throughout, showing none of the internal variations between ordinary and elevated speech of the earlier plays. Such discrepancies will still be found in later plays, though to a significantly modulated degree. All of the devices used to impart the illusion of common colloquial reality to comedy are in this play, but here are shared by all of the characters.

There is, however, an important quantitative and qualitative difference between the comic colloquial language of *Die alte Jungfer* and that of the plays written earlier. The stylistic elements first favored by Lessing are used with greater moderation, resulting in a more subdued and natural tone of dialogue. The following scene, between Lelio and Lisette, is quite typical of the general tone of *Die alte Jungfer*. Here, Lisette wants to give Lelio the news of the impending engagement of his cousin:

LISETTE. O! allerliebste Post für ihren Vetter! Ob er denn in seiner Stube ist? Herr Lelio! Herr Lelio! Die Männersucht ist doch eine recht wesentliche Krankheit des Frauenzimmers. Es mag so jung, oder so alt seyn als es will. Ach — ich befinde mich in der That auch nicht gesund. Herr Lelio!

LELIO. Was giebts? Ey, Mademoiselle Lisette! Ich dächte, mein Närrchen, du hättest dich können zu mir in meine Stube bemühen.

LISETTE. Ergebene Dienerin! Das hiesse sich zu weit in des Feindes Länder wagen. Der Platz hier ist neutral. Hier kan ich Ihren Anfällen trotzen.

LELIO. Ach! Wer nur den Angriff wagen will, gewinnt dich aller Orten.

LISETTE. Schade, daß es niemand hört. Sonst würde ich Ihnen für gütige Recommendation danken. Doch zur Sache! Ich habe Ihnen eine recht besondre neue Neuigkeit zu sagen.

LELIO. Gut! daß du auf das Capitel von Neuigkeiten kömmst. Ich habe dir auch etwas sehr drolligtes daraus mitzutheilen.

LISETTE. Meines ist doch wohl noch drollichter.

LELIO. Unmöglich! Was wetten wir?

LISETTE. Schade auf das Wetten! ich bekomme doch nichts von Ihnen.

LELIO. Ey. Du bist närrisch. Warte nur, bis meine Muhme stirbt. Denn —

LISETTE. O, die hat noch viel vor ihrem Tode in willens.

LELIO. Du redst, als wenn du schon wüßtest, was ich dir sagen wollte.

LISETTE. Nu? Nur heraus! was ist es denn?

LELIO. Laß nur erst deine Neuigkeit hören.

LISETTE. Nu so hören Sie. Ihre Muhme —

LELIO. Meine Muhme —

LISETTE. Will heyrathen.

LELIO. Will heyrathen. Das wollte ich dir auch sagen. Wo, Henker, has du es schon her?   (*LM*, III, 207.6-208.2)

Comparing the language of this scene with that of the exchange between Anton and Lisette on page 38, above, it may be seen that the alternation of speeches in this dialogue is not as agitated through ellipsis and aposiopesis, not as strongly punctuated by oaths and exclamations, although the moods of the scenes are quite similar. A very lively tone is achieved, however, through the use of the device of linking speeches through anadiplosis, which was described earlier. The device of anadiplosis is again supported by a linkage of images. When Lelio suggests that Lisette could have come into his room, she answers by initiating a military image, saying that that would be venturing too far into enemy territory, and that she can defy his attacks on the neutral ground of the

"Saal". Lelio replies that whoever will dare the attack can conquer her anywhere, thus rounding off the image from strategy. Lisette then gets to the point of her visit by telling Lelio, with a comical adjectival reinforcement, of the "recht besondre neue Neuigkeit" she has for him. Lelio picks up the word "Neuigkeiten", and introduces the word "drolligt", which Lisette tosses back in the comparative. Lelio offers to bet that his news is droller, and Lisette parries this by alluding to his impecunity, with a repetition of "Wetten". This prompts Lelio to state his hopes upon the eventual death of his cousin, Jungfer Ohldin, which brings Lisette back to her original mission, which she announces again by taking up Lelio's allusion to dying and saying that her mistress still intends to do much before her death. This brings the conversation back to the word "Neuigkeit", and from there on, Lelio's and Lisette's speeches are virtually a series of parallel repetitions until the end of the passage quoted. Here again, Lessing has keyed the characters to one another by making the speeches of their dialogue interconnect through links established by word repetitions, words modulated in repetition, and the play of words around a single concept. Through this linking of the speeches, together with the copious use of interjections and exclamatory phrases, and the crisp brevity of the individual lines, a brisk, lively pace is achieved and maintained throughout the play, without the occasional slackening to be observed in *Der junge Gelehrte*.

The characters in *Die alte Jungfer* are, as noted above, drawn from standard figures upon the European comic stage of the time, and are definitely to be seen as types rather than as individualized personalities. This was also the case in the comedies examined previously. Particularly in *Der junge Gelehrte*, each humorous role was given an appropriate diction, with the serious roles having elevated colloquial diction practically undifferentiated as to character. Since *Die alte Jungfer* is a comedy of manners, depending largely on the humor of the situation for its effect, rather than on the humor of the feeling generated by differences in character, there are no

such serious roles in the play and no idealized characters.
Therefore the characters are not very much to be distinguished
from each other through their language. All are on the same
common colloquial level and all share the same speech features.
A good demonstration of the more moderate use of characterizing features in this play is a comparison of the styles of
Jungfer Ohldin and Lisette in the following passage. Herr
Oronte has just left with Ohldin's consent to marry Kapitän
von Schlag:

LISETTE. Was war denn das wieder für ein Besuch? Nicht wahr,
Herr Oronte wollte Geld borgen?
  OHLDIN. Die Närrin denkt, bey mir sey sonst nichts, als nur das
leidige Geld zu suchen.
  LISETTE. Nu, einen Freyer hat er Ihnen doch wohl nicht gebracht? Obgleich jeziger Zeit die Freyer auch zu einer Art von
Geldborgern geworden sind. Ueber dergleichen Sachen sind Sie
weg. Es ist auch wahr, der Ehestand ist eine rechte Hölle —
  OHLDIN. Gott behüte uns! Lisette bedenkst du auch, was du
sagst?
  LISETTE. Nichts, als was Sie unzähligmal gesagt haben. Ach,
daß mich doch niemand will in die Hölle hohlen! So lange hätte
ich nimmermehr Gedult, als Sie. Und wenn Sie nicht bald darzu
thun, so wirds zu spät.
  OHLDIN. Zu spät — unvernünftiges Mensch! Wie alt bin ich
denn?
  LISETTE. Für mich ist das keine Rechnung. Ich kan nicht bis
funfzig zählen.   (*LM*, III, 206.6-21)

Even considering what is expected of her type by the audience,
Lisette is unusually candid to Ohldin in comparison with
other Lisettes to be found in Lessing's comedies. Ohldin, however, puts herself on one social and stylistic level with her
servant, using such unladylike terms as "unvernünftiges
Mensch" and even discussing her age with her. In respect to
vocabulary and syntax, there is little difference between their
manners of speech, which further adds to the uniformity of the
general tone of the play. Since all of the characters are reduced to the same level of ridicule, the differences in speech
arising from supposed differences in social class have all but

disappeared. The full impact of the evenness of this style, newly developed here by Lessing, may best be felt by comparing the passage just quoted with a similar passage from *Damon* in which, again, a Lisette is talking to her mistress:

LISETTE. Das sind sie noch? So? Damon ist also des Leanders Nebenbuhler, und Leander des Damons. Und gleichwohl sind Leander und Damon die besten Freunde? Das wäre eine neue Mode. Wider die streite ich mit Händen und Füssen. Was? Nebenbuhler, die sich nicht unter einander zanken, verleumden, schimpfen, betrügen, herausfordern, schlagen, das wären mir artige Creaturen. Nein. Es muß bey dem Alten bleiben. Unter Nebenbuhlern muß Feindschaft seyn, oder sie sind keine Nebenbuhler.

DIE WITTWE. Es ist wahr, ich habe mich über ihr Bezeigen einigermaßen selbst gewundert. Ehe beyde noch wußten, daß sie einerley Zweck hätten, bezeigte sich niemand gegen mich verliebter, als eben sie. Niemand war zärtlicher, niemand bestrebte sich um meine Gegengunst mehr, als sie. So bald sie gewahr wurden, daß einer des andern Nebenbuhler wäre, so bald wurden beyde, in ihrem Bestreben, mir zu gefallen, nachlässiger. Einer redete bey mir dem andern das Wort, Damon dem Leander, und Leander dem Damon. Beyde schwiegen von ihren eigenen Angelegenheiten.   (*LM*, III, 179. 20-34)

The widow's language is decorous and elaborate compared to Lisette's. The servant's speech is enlivened by exclamations, interrogatory clauses, and one of the rare instances of asyndeton to be found in Lessing's comedies (lines 5-6, above). In marked contrast, the widow uses no such figures. Rather, the flow of her language is slowed down by such periphrastic constructions as "gewahr wurden" and "einer redete ... dem andern das Wort".

The genteelness of the widow's style is reinforced by her use of abstract euphemisms in speaking of matters of the heart. The use of nouns colorless in their meaning, such as "Bezeigen" and "Angelegenheiten", and of "Gegengunst" sap the force of the more concrete adjectives in the comparatives "zärtlicher" and "verliebter". Thus, in *Damon*, there is a marked difference between the language of the servant and that of the mistress, a difference which corresponds to the two disparate stylistic levels observed in *Damon* in general, and which is here reinforced by disparity of social class. *Die alte Jungfer* shows a considerable contrast to *Damon* in the matter of levels of language. *Die alte Jungfer* is unique in its uniformity of tone among Lessing's comedies, a quality attributable less to any progress on Lessing's part than to the nature of the plot of the play, and possibly also to the tone of Lessing's English source, where differences of stylistic level are often less acute than in the French plays which Lessing usually used as models at this time.

That the language of *Die alte Jungfer* is more unified in its tone by no means implies that none of the characters are distinguished from others in their language. At least three of the characters have distinctive manners of speech, but the technique for characterizing language has changed considerably. Simple and monotonous tags are no longer used. The characterizing features are more subtly contrived and woven into the speech of the character involved. Lessing's refinement in technique is best seen in the figure of Clitander, a friend of Lelio's and a definitely tertiary character, added merely for comic effect. Here, he is teasing Jungfer Ohldin about her impending marriage:

CLITANDER. Mademoiselle, Jungfer Braut, Madam — Wie Teufel soll man Sie nennen? Ist es wahr, oder ist es nicht wahr, daß Sie heyrathen wollen?

OHLDIN. Ja. Es ist allerdings wahr. Wer kann wider sein Schicksal? Ich versichre Sie, Herr Clitander, es ist eine ganz besondre Vorsehung dabey gewesen. Ich hatte an nichts weniger, als an einen Mann, gedacht, und plötzlich —

CLITANDER. Und plötzlich ist Ihnen der Appetit angekommen?

OHLDIN. Sie können gewiß glauben, daß es mein Betrieb gar nicht gewesen ist. Die Heyrathen werden im Himmel gestiftet, und wer wollte so gottlos seyn, sich hier zu widersetzen?

CLITANDER. Da haben Sie recht. Die ganze Stadt lacht zwar über Sie; aber das ist das Schicksal der Frommen. Kehren Sie sich nicht daran. Ein Mann ist doch ein ganz nützlicher Hausrath.

OHLDIN. Ich weis nicht, worüber die Stadt lachen sollte. Ist denn eine Heyrath so was lächerliches? die gottlose böse Stadt!

CLITANDER. Sie thun der Stadt unrecht. Sie lacht nicht darüber, daß Sie heyrathen, sondern, daß Sie nicht schon vor 30 Jahren geheyrathet haben.

OHLDIN. Ist das nicht närrisch. Vor dreyßig Jahren! Vor dreyßig Jahren war ich noch ein Kind.   (*LM*, III, 214.15-215.2)

Clitander is characterized through his singular bluntness in relation to the other characters in the play. It is seen here, of course, in its most extreme form. His use of oaths, such as "Wie Teufel..." and "Zum Henker!" in the presence of a lady sets him off from all of the other characters except Peter, the sweets-hawker, who can be expected to use such language. These oaths, however, are the only specifically characterizing mannerisms which can be found in Clitander's language. Otherwise, he is defined by *what* he says, his insulting frankness, his preoccupation with pleasure, gossip, and gallantry. Clitander is an ironist of sorts, breaking off every gallant gesture with an almost brutal twist. He begins by addressing Ohldin, "Mademoiselle, Jungfer Braut, Madam", and insultingly sets off the extravagance of this with "wie Teufel soll man Sie nennen?", and then the categorical question of whether or not it is true that she intends to marry. It is his irony which defines Clitander when he responds to Ohldin's simpering concerning the unexpectedness of her marriage by interrupting with, "Und plötzlich ist Ihnen der Appetit angekommen?". The use of the down-to-earth "Appetit" strips the conventional innocence from Ohldin's situation and reveals her in a truer light. Again, this represents a considerable change from the decorous tone of the widow and her suitors in *Damon*. In short, Lessing's creation of the character of Clitander reveals an increasing ability on his part to penetrate below the surface mannerisms of a character's speech, and to portray not only these, but the nature unterlying them. Increasingly, Lessing's characterizations will depend on utterances arising from this inner nature, mannerisms of speech serving only to support and underline the characterization of a personality rather than constituting it. One of the first steps in this direction has been taken with the creation of such a minor character as Clitander.

Die alte Jungfer, despite its neglect by Lessing himself and subsequent critics, shows significant developments in Lessing's stylistic technique in the comedies. First of all, the general tone of the dialogue, while still lively in its pacing, is more subdued, less extravagantly larded with stylistic tricks, and therefore more uniformly sustained. In part, this evenness of style comes about through the fact that *Die alte Jungfer* is unique among Lessing's comedies in having only one level – humorous colloquial speech – in contrast to the two levels of humorous and elevated colloquial speech to be found in the earlier comedies, eliminating completely the discrepancy in tones caused by contrasting manners of speech. Also, possibly most significantly for the development of Lessing as a dramatic writer, the first signs are to be found in this comedy of a more penetrating and valid variety of stylistic characterization.

DER MISOGYNE

The other comedy which Lessing wrote in 1748 had quite a different history in his affections than did *Die alte Jungfer.* *Der Misogyne* was not only included in the first collection of Lessing's *Schriften* (1753-55), but the one-act play was also expanded to three acts for the edition of the *Lustspiele* which appeared in 1767. For the present, however, the one-act version, "verfertiget im Jahre 1748", shall be considered exclusively.[12]

In his *Formgeschichte der deutschen Dichtung*, Paul Böckmann regards *Der Misogyne* as entirely typical of the comedies of Lessing's Leipzig and Berlin periods and his involvement with the formative principle of wit. Böckmann says: "Das Lustspiel

---

[12] The text of *Der Misogyn* presented in *LM*, II is based on the second edition of Lessing's *Lustspiele* of 1770. The text of the one-act play, *Der Misogyne*, published in the sixth part of the *Schriften* in 1755, is presented in variorum form. In this study, all quotations are from the 1755 edition, as are, in order to have the earliest possible texts, those of the plays treated later in this chapter.

wird vom Witz getragen, nicht von Komik oder Humor."[13] Although this is true of Lessing's earlier comedies only with reservations, it is fully the case in *Der Misogyne*. That is to say, it is the use which the characters make of their rational faculties to overcome the antisocial irrationality of the old man which is intended to delight the audience, rather than any directly comic devices or characters. The misogynist is a figure to be ridiculed, a comic character not because of a surface trait of manner or speech, but because of an impairment of his rational function through an obsession which does not permit him to see the world as other men see it and thus removes him from the society of rational men. A structural indication of this dependence on wit rather than on humor is the use made of the element of disguise. In *Die alte Jungfer*, Peter was disguised in order that, through his humorously shocking behavior, he would dissuade the old maid from marrying Kapitän von Schlag, whom he was impersonating. There the disguise motif was used in a strictly comic manner. In *Der Misogyne* it is used to approach the old man by way of his intellect, his "Witz".

Wumshäter, the misogynist of the title, is firmly resolved to let neither his son Valer nor his daughter Laura marry. Valer is to be spared the bitter experiences which Wumshäter has garnered in his own three ventures into matrimony, and Laura, being a woman, cannot be given to any man whom Wumshäter respects, and a marriage to any other man would be damaging to Wumshäter's reputation. Valer and his beloved Hilaria hit upon a witty ruse to wrest the father's consent from him. Hilaria disguises herself as her own fictitious brother, Lelio, and through "his" intelligent agreement with Wumshäter's views on women gains the old man's affection. Hilaria herself then appears, and much is made of her resemblance to her "brother". Wumshäter denies that there is any resemblance at all between the "brother" and sister, claiming that Hilaria is both shorter and stouter than "Lelio", and demands

[13]   Paul Böckmann, *Formgeschichte der deutschen Dichtung*, vol. I (Hamburg, 1949), p. 583.

to see them both together. In the final scene, confronted by Hilaria in half-male, half-female costume, Wumshäter is shamed because he has failed to see that Lelio and Hilaria are one and the same. Because he has let his prejudices blind and shame him to such an extent, Wumshäter is forced to give his consent to Valer's marriage, warning that before the year is out, his son will regret his rashness. Wumshäter's misogyny has not been overcome, and his character has not developed; he merely has been duped, and is thus an object for laughter. Laura's suitor, Leander, also wins her hand by outwitting her father. His lawyer, Herr Solbit, tells Wumshäter that Leander will concede a lawsuit to him if Laura is given him in marriage. Delighted that his legal adversary will have what is to him a double punishment, a lost lawsuit and a wife, Wumshäter gleefully consents. It is the witty intrigue, then, rather than humor or the force of feeling, which impels this play. Sentiment, though frequently expressed, is unfailingly superficial and the only character infused with any seeming passion at all is Wumshäter. The young lovers, Valer and Hilaria, Leander and Laura, in no way transcend pale stereotypes. Their characters are in no way individualized.

In many respects, the language of *Der Misogyne* shows a continuation of the trends of development observed in *Die alte Jungfer*. Largely because of the plot elements involved, however, the tone of the play is quite different from that of its predecessor. It is only rarely sprightly and mocking, as was *Die alte Jungfer* most of the time. Such lively dialogues as that between Wumshäter and Lisette in Scene 1 are few, and not typical. Elevated colloquial language, the language of serious expression, completely lacking in the previous play, here penetrates into the diction of nearly all of the characters with fairly uniform effect. It is not restricted only to a few figures, as in *Damon* and *Der junge Gelehrte*. Thus, while the general tone remains colloquial, it is considerably modified by the relative dryness and elaborateness of the elevated colloquial diction which Lessing used at this time to depict the expression of serious sentiment. Such stylistic devices as aposiopesis, ellipsis, the use of expressive particles, oaths, and exclamatory phrases associated with the strictly humorous colloquial language are far less in evidence.

The relative scarcity of these stylistic devices is most striking in Lessing's handling of the character whose language might be expected to contain them in the greatest abundance, namely Wumshäter. His is clearly the humorous role in the play, and his the comic aberration around whose deception and defeat it revolves. Wumshäter is the latest in Lessing's succession of garrulous, cantankerous fathers to stand in the way of young love's progress. His character is rapidly established through his relish in telling of his misery at the hands of his three wives, now safely buried, and through his abusive references to womankind in general as "die verdammten Weiber", "Weibsstück", "Weibsvolk", and "Weibsbild". Hilaria is termed, "ein Geschöpf, ... das desto giftiger wird, jemehr es sein Gift verbergen kann". His misogyny has something of the nature of a cosmic *idée fixe*, as when he says to Lisette, "... so bald du und deines gleichen sich unter die Menschen rechnen, so bald bekomme ich Lust, mich mit dem Himmel zu zanken, daß er mich zu einem gemacht hat." His extravagant misogyny is comical because of the heights of rhetoric to which it can bring him, as the following passage bears ample witness:

Und wenn die Treue selbst vom Himmel käme, die Erde nochmals zu beglücken, so dürfte sie nur einen weiblichen Körper, uns sichtbar zu werden, annehmen; ich bin versichert, die Wohnung würde bald den Geist verderben, und in kurzen würde sie und die Untreue nur dem Namen nach unterschieden seyn...

(*LM*, II, 7.14)

Wumshäter is not defined, as were his earlier counterparts, merely by an external trait of language. His language, rather, is made the medium of expression of his particular humor, that of misogyny, which dominates his character. Because of this, Wumshäter's style is not so much that of a caricature in relation to the other characters as was that of Chrysander. This is well illustrated by the following scene between Wumshäter and Valer.

WUMSHÄTER. Welch Geschöpf! — Ich will auch heute noch alles Weibsvolk aus meinem Hause schaffen; auch meine Tochter. Sie mag sehen, wo sie bleibt — Gut, gut, mein Sohn, daß du kömmst; ich habe eben nach dir gefragt.
VALER. Wie glücklich wär ich, wenn ich glauben dürfte, daß Sie meinen Bitten hätten wollen zuvor kommen. Darf ich mir schmeicheln, die so oft gesuchte Einwilligung endlich von Ihnen zu erhalten?
WUMSHÄTER. O! du fängst wieder von der verdrüßlichen Sache an. Kränke doch deinen alten Vater nicht so, der dich bis jetzt für den einzigen Trost seines Alters gehalten hat. Es ist ja noch Zeit.
VALER. Nein, es ist nicht länger Zeit, liebster Vater. Ich habe heute Briefe bekommen, welche mich nöthigen, auf das eheste wieder zurück zu reisen.
WUMSHÄTER. Je nun, so reise in Gottes Namen; nur folge mir darinn; heyrathe nicht. Ich habe dich zu lieb, als daß ich zu deinem Unglücke Ja sagen sollte.
VALER. Zu meinem Unglücke? Wie schlecht müssen Sie oder ich dieses kennen? Ich werde es für mein Unglück halten, wenn ich eine Person länger entbehren muß, die mir das Schätzbarste in der Welt ist. Und Sie —
WUMSHÄTER. Und ich werde es für dein äußerstes Unglück halten, wenn ich dich deiner blinden Neigung folgen sehe. Ein Weibsbild für das Schätzbarste auf der Welt zu halten? Ein Weibsbild! Doch der Mangel der Erfahrung entschuldiget dich —

(*LM*, II, 4.32-5.22)

Linking of the speeches through anadiplosis is done again in a very effective way. Wumshäter and Valer counter each other's arguments using each other's words. When the father responds to the son's pleas for his consent to the marriage by saying, "Es ist ja noch *Zeit*", Valer responds, insisting emphatically, "Nein, es ist nicht länger *Zeit*", adding that he has letters which urge him, "auf das eheste wieder zurück zu *reisen*". Wumshäter inflects this infinitive in giving his permission; "... so *reise* in Gottes Namen", but implores him not to marry, since he loves him too much, "als daß ich zu deinem *Unglücke* Ja sagen sollte". This begins a play around the word "Unglück" and the opposed ideas of father and son about what

constitutes misfortune, which ends with Wumshäter's intensification; "Und ich werde es für dein äußerstes *Unglück*
halten..." He then repeats Valer's last utterance, twisting it
about: "ein Weibsbild für das Schätzbarste auf der Welt zu
halten?", and, being brought back to his favorite theme
through the compound with "Weibs-", Wumshäter rants on,
immune to any further imprecations. Again, this sort of intricate linkage gives the dispute, even on the printed page, added
intensity through the illusion that each of the characters is
acutely aware of what the other is saying.

In Valer's speeches, the elevated colloquial features associated with the language of expression used by the serious
characters found in the earlier plays are to be found again.
Yet his style, though polite, is not as elaborate, not as stiff as
that of Damon, for example. The individual speeches are
shorter, the tendency to hypotaxis more controlled than was
the case earlier. Still, the use of reinforcing superlatives, such
as "liebster Vater", "auf das eheste", and "das Schätzbarste"
serves to give Valer's language a decorousness not apparent
in Wumshäter's. Like other characters of his cast, Valer
speaks in a way most reminiscent of the complimentary style
adopted in very formal address or letter-writing at the time.
This effect is further heightened by the relatively large number
of elaborate verb constructions in his speech. Even in the
brief passage just quoted, there may be found; periphrasis,
"daß Sie meinen Bitten hätten wollen zuvor kommen";
dependent infinitive phrases, "die Einwilligung endlich zu
erhalten?", "auf das eheste wieder zurück zu reisen"; and a
surfeit of modal constructions with dependent infinitives,
"wenn ich glauben dürfte", "daß Sie hätten wollen zuvor
kommen", "Darf ich mir schmeicheln...", "Wie schlecht
müssen Sie oder ich dieses kennen!", "... wenn ich eine Person
länger entbehren muß, ...". These features, while not
restricted to the language of Valer and the other "serious"
characters, strongly determine the tone of their language
through the density in which they occur. Valer's style of
speaking and that of the other characters of his age and

station in the play, Hilaria, Laura, and Leander, are indistinguishable from each other as to tone and level of diction. This tone is still more decorous and sententious than that of the humorous roles of Wumshäter and his lawyer, Herr Solbit. Although he does not rant in the same way earlier characters of his type did, Wumshäter's tone is earthier and more colloquial than Valer's. As noted before, Wumshäter's unreasoning misogyny moves him frequently to rhetoric, which is then often strongly tinged with pathos. An example of this is his request to Valer on lines 10-11, above: "Kränke doch deinen alten Vater nicht so, der dich bis jetzt für den einzigen Trost seines Alters gehalten hat." The double loading of this sentence with allusion to old age, "alten … Alters", coupled with the idea of the son being his father's *sole* consolation, and juxtaposed to the idea of irritation, give this sentence an undeniable quality of overpathetic self-pity, which is frequently present elsewhere in the play, and which sounds strange coming from a man who has just resolved to send his daughter out of the house to fend for herself. Pathos and coarseness are parallel and contradictory in Wumshäter's style, as the contrast between the speech just quoted and his use of such terms as "Weibsvolk" and "Weibsbild" already indicate. Wumshäter's flights of misogynistic rhetoric are often dragged down to earth by extremely concrete phrases. While his style is generally less decorous, less observant of polite forms than that of Valer, an internal contradiction of styles exists in his speech, just as a contradiction of feelings which is incompatible with reasonable humanity exists in him, namely, love for his son and hatred for all womankind, including his own daughter and his son's beloved. Wumshäter's stylistic contradictions may be seen in the following passage, in which he is telling Valer of his misfortunes with his first wife. Valer's interruptions, since they are not germane to the present discussion, are omitted.

… Ich war in deinen Jahren eben so feurig, eben so unbedachtsam. Ich sah ein Mädchen mit rothen Backen, ich sah es; und beschloß meine Frau daraus zu machen. Sie war arm —

... Sie war arm, und ich besaß auch nicht viel. Nun stelle dir
einmal vor, was ein angehender Handelsmann, wie ich dazumal
war, für Kummer, Sorge und Plage hat, wenn er mit leeren
Händen anfängt.
... Zu meinen Anverwandten durfte ich bey meinen mühseligen
Umständen keine Zuflucht nehmen. Warum? sie hätten mir vorgeschlagen, eine alte reiche Wittwe zu heyrathen, wodurch mir in
meiner Handlung auf einmal wäre geholfen gewesen. Ich stieß sie
also vor den Kopf, da ich mich in ein schön Gesicht vergaffte, und
lieber glücklich lieben, als glücklich leben wollte.
... Was dabey das Schlimmste war, so liebte ich sie so blind, daß
ich allen möglichen Aufwand ihrentwegen machte. Ihr über-
mäßiger Staat brachte mich in unzähligen Schulden —
... Glaubst du, daß ich mich aus den vielen Schulden hätte
herausreißen können, wenn der Himmel nicht so gütig gewesen
wäre, mir, nach Jahres Frist, die Ursache meines Verderbens zu
nehmen? Sie starb, und sie hatte kaum die Augen zugethan, als
mir die meinigen aufgiengen. Wo ich hinsah, war ich schuldig.
Und bedenke, in was für eine Raserey ich gerieth, da ich nach
ihrem Tode ihre verfluchte Untreue erfuhr. Meine Schulden
fiengen an, mich zweymal heftiger zu drücken, als ich sah, daß ich
sie einer Nichtswürdigen zu Liebe, einer verdammten Heuchlerin
zu gefallen, gemacht hatte...   (*LM*, II, 6.5-7.3)

To support his arguments and increase the pathos of this
favorite discourse, Wumshäter employs various stylistic
devices of rhetoric. First of all, there are pleonastic constructions, such as the triplet "Kummer, Sorge und Plage", and
the final phrase, "einer Nichtswürdigen zu Liebe, einer verdammten Heuchlerin zu gefallen". The most important feature of Wumshäter's style, however, is his penchant for antithesis, in which this passage abounds. Several more or less
complex antithetical constructions are to be found here.
When Wumshäter says, "da ich ... lieber glücklich lieben,
als glücklich leben wollte", the antithesis is between the
infinitives modified by the same adverbs. Then he reports,
"... sie hatte kaum die Augen zugethan, als mir die meinigen
aufgiengen", the antithesis here depending on the opposition
of "die Augen zugethan" and "die meinigen aufgiengen".
The effectiveness of this construction stems from the yoking
together of the literal and figurative meanings of closing and

opening the eyes. Finally, in a combination of pleonastic and antithetical style, Wumshäter concludes that he had incurred his debts, "einer Nichtswürdigen zu Liebe, einer verdammten Heuchlerin zu gefallen". Both phrases say the same thing, yet are pleonastically linked for emphasis. "Heuchlerin" and "Nichtswürdigen" are in an antithetical relationship to "zu Liebe" and "zu gefallen".

This high-flown manner is accompanied, however, by very down-to-earth words and phrases which directly contradict the rhetorical elevation and, by contrast, produce a humorous effect. Thus, to the elaborate, almost elegant periphrasis of the sentence "... sie hätten mir vorgeschlagen eine alte reiche Wittwe zu heyrathen, wodurch mir in meiner Handlung auf einmal wäre geholfen gewesen", he juxtaposes, "Ich stieß sie also vor den Kopf, da ich mich in ein schön Gesicht vergaffte." The idiomatic straightforwardness of the verb forms "stieß ... vor den Kopf" and "vergaffte" almost obliterates the impression of the decorous tone of the previous sentence. The most dramatic example of this sort of juxtaposition occurs in lines 17-20, above. Here Wumshäter, again in a sort of pleonastic sequence, tells how he was relieved of his intolerable burden. First he relates it in a pathetic rhetorical tone: "Glaubst du, daß ich mich aus den vielen Schulden hätte herausreißen können, wenn der Himmel nicht so gütig gewesen wäre, mir, nach Jahres Frist, die Ursache meines Verderbens zu nehmen?" The second member of the construction is much shorter: "Sie starb", and completely deflates the pompous rhetoric of the first part. Wumshäter, through this stylistic contradiction, is made to be unconsciously ironic in constantly revealing the bare truth which lurks behind the contrived façade of his rhetoric. Thus, while Valer's speech and that of most of the remaining characters is decorous and polite, even in the expression of passion, Wumshäter's is a mixture, occasionally humorous in its contradictory nature, of long-winded rhetorical elements set off by very earthy, often commonly colloquial words and phrases.

The inclusion of the figure of Herr Solbit, the comical

lawyer, while necessary to the plot, allows Lessing to make fun of the legal profession and parody its language. Thus, when Solbit arrives and asks to see Wumshäter in privacy, Lelio/ Hilaria exclaims: "Sie dürfen nur im Stylo Curiä mit ihm reden; es wird so gut seyn, als ob wir nicht da wären." Even the characters of the play are conscious of the discrepancy between the rhetoric of law and their own colloquial speech. "Stylo Curiä" is just the style which Solbit uses to present his proposition to Wumshäter:

Hochedelgebohrner, insbesonders hochzuehrender Herr und Gönner! Als Gott den Adam erschaffen, und in das schöne Paradies gesetzt hatte — Beyläufig will ich erinnern, daß man bis jetzo noch nicht weiß, wo eigentlich das Paradies gewesen ist. Die Gelehrten streiten sehr heftig darüber. Doch es sey gewesen, wo es wolle. — Als nun Gott den Adam in dieses uns unbewußte Paradies gesetzt hatte — ...
   Verzweifelt, daß ich die Rede vergessen habe. Sie hätten ein recht ciceronianisches Meisterstück hören sollen. Nun hören Sie nur, ich will Ihnen die *Contenta* kurz sagen. *Pro primo* hatte ich in dieser Rede ein richtiges Verzeichniß aller bösen Weiber, von der Eva an bis auf die Ihrigen drey, mit vieler mühsamen Belesenheit gemacht. *Pro secundo* hatte ich gründlich erwiesen, daß eine Frau das größte Unglück auf der Welt sey, und daraus unwidersprechlich hergeleitet, daß das Heyrathen eine sehr unsinnige Sache seyn müsse, welches ich dann noch weitläufig mit *Testimoniis*, besonders mit den Ihrigen, bestärkt hatte. *Pro tertio tandem et ultimo*, kam ich darauf, daß Herr Leander eben diese Unsinnigkeit begehen wollte, und zwar mit der Ehr und Tugendsamen belobten Jungfer, Jungfer Laura, eheleiblichen einzigen Tochter des Hochedelgebohrnen Herren, Herren Zacharias Maria Wumshäter —   (*LM*, II, 28. 15-30)

The elaborate complimentary forms, laden with honorific adjectives, to be found at the beginning and end of this passage, the use of Latin terms and scholastic asides, such as the small disquisition on the Garden of Eden; these are elements comprising the parodistic legal speech with which Lessing has equipped Herr Solbit. Solbit has quite another tone when not in his professional capacity. In the following speech, he is telling Lisette about his activities as an inciter to lawsuits and marriages in a tone rather more frank than usual:

— Aber das ist wahr; eine Lust ist es, wenn ich des Vormittags meinen Klienten Gehör gebe. Alles hat seine Zuflucht zu mir. Will der Bauer mit seinem Herrn proceßiren; so kömmt er zu mir. Will ein altes Mütterchen einen gesunden frischen Mann haben; so kömmt sie zu mir. Will ein Hundsvott den andern Injuriarum belangen; so kömmt er zu mir. Will eine junge Frau ihren alten Ehekriepel los seyn; so kömmt sie zu mir...   (*LM*, II, 33.19-25)

When Solbit is out of court, so to speak, his sentence structure becomes simpler and more straightforward, and his vocabulary more common. His speech, it is true, still abounds in legalisms such as "Klienten", "Gehör", "proceßiren", "Injuriarum belangen". Yet, extralegal concepts also enter gradually into Solbit's vocabulary as he speaks with Lisette. His descriptions grow ever more drastic and vulgar, from the little old lady who wants to find a healthy young husband, to the "Hundsvott" going to law, and finally to the young wife who wants to be rid of her "Ehekriepel". Thus, Lessing is not only making fun of lawyers, a favorite target of satire since satire's birth, but, through the figure of Herr Solbit, of their pompous and empty style, behind which can lurk the crudest baseness.

The style of speaking of the character roles in *Der Misogyne* has come well beyond the simple repetition of a comic tag for the sake of a running humorous effect. The language of Wumshäter subtly reflects, in its contradictory aspects of rhetoric and plain speech, of pathos and coarseness, the inner nature of the old man. Because of its language, the characterization of Wumshäter is not merely a linear depiction of the type of the misogynist, but he is given some of those contradictory traits in addition to misogyny which initiate the transition from character as two-dimensional type to that of character as more rounded personality. Both Wumshäter and Solbit, for all of their oddities and fixed ideas, are still part of the world of the other, the "earnest" characters. Reflecting this fact, neither of them departs as radically from the norm of polite, elevated colloquial language established by Valer and Lelio/Hilaria as does, for example, Chrysander in *Der junge Gelehrte* from that of Juliane and Valer.

The two levels of serious and characterizing language, of elevated and more common colloquial speech, are still present in *Der Misogyne*, but are much less sharply distinguished from each other than they were before. In this play, one level of language affects the other, the elevated colloquial language moderating the common colloquial in its earthiness, and the common colloquial style, on the other hand, making the elevated style less complex, freer, and more straightforward in its expression.

DIE JUDEN

In the introduction to the third and fourth parts of his *Schriften*, published in 1754, which, with the exceptions already noted, contained his completed dramatic works up to that time, Lessing wrote:

Das zweyte Lustspiel, welches man in dem vierten Theile finden wird, heißt die Juden. Es war das Resultat einer sehr ernsthaften Betrachtung über die schimpfliche Unterdrückung, in welcher ein Volk seufzen muß, das ein Christ, sollte ich meinen, nicht ohne eine Art von Ehrerbietung betrachten kann. Aus ihm, dachte ich, sind ehedem so viel Helden und Propheten aufgestanden, und jetzo zweifelt man, ob ein ehrlicher Mann unter ihm anzutreffen sey? Meine Lust zum Theater war damals so groß, daß sich alles, was mir in den Kopf kam, in eine Komödie verwandelte. Ich bekam also gar bald den Einfall, zu versuchen, was es für eine Wirkung auf der Bühne haben werde, wenn man dem Volke die Tugend da zeigte, wo es sie ganz und gar nicht vermuthet. Ich bin begierig mein Urtheil zu hören.   (*LM*, V, 270.24-36)

Die Juden, written in 1749, is the celebrated first instance in which a Jew is sympathetically depicted upon the German stage, without the slightest trace of caricature, as an educated and cultured man. As the above quotation shows, Lessing's intention in writing this one-act comedy had a most serious origin; the desire to vindicate a downtrodden and wrongly maligned people, and through this vindication to elevate his audiences morally by catching unawares and disappointing their prejudices.

This was to be done by a surprise tantamount to the various intrigues and surprise motifs found in the earlier comedies. Rather than being offered a dramatic exploration of the relationship between the Jew and society, the audience was to be forced to associate a Jew with virtue by a dramatic trick, to its own surprise and betterment. The virtuous Jew in this play, named only "Der Reisende", was not to identify himself until the very end. This "medicine" to cure the audience of its prejudices was to be made more palatable by "sweetening" with comedy plot techniques of the conventional type. The didactic revelation, the *raison d'être* of the entire play, had to be properly introduced, and Lessing borrowed from various French and English sources[14] to provide a comic guise for his earnest purpose. Possibly the very incongruity of intention and form was intended to make the surprise of the audience even greater and thus the moral lesson even more effective. Because the fact that the hero is a Jew has to be saved until the very end of the play, however, its plot is excessively padded, which disperses the force of Lessing's intent in the execution. Such trappings, for example, are to be found as disproportionately long comic scenes between servants, and the introduction of a snuffbox, which changes hands four times in the course of the play. These elements, while serving to further the plot to some degree, are, by intention, retardant in their overall effect, and take up most of the play. With such devices against which to contend, the main characters of the serious plot are often more or less forced into the background.

The servants are again the most humorous characters in the play. This effect is heightened in *Die Juden* because the play lacks a central comic figure possessed of a humorous

---

[14] Concerning the sources of *Die Juden*, see Paul Albrecht, *Leszings Plagiate*, 6 vols. (Hamburg-Leipzig, 1891), II, pp. 864-93, and Paul P. Kies, "The Sources of Lessing's 'Die Juden'", *Philological Quarterly*, VI (1927), pp. 406ff.

excess around which such plays as *Der junge Gelehrte* and *Der Misogyne* turn, and who acts as a foil and counterweight for his witty servants. The characters of the serious plot are in surface respects devoid of conventional characterizing features, which is emphasized by their having names which simply describe their functions or stations: "Der Reisende", "Der Baron", "Das Fräulein". They do not correspond to any simple types, but rather, for the first time, are given very individualized characterizations.

On the night previous to the beginning of the play, the Baron has been rescued by the Traveler and his servant from would-be robbers, actually the Baron's own "Vogt" and "Schulze". Since the highwaymen had beards, they are assumed to have been Jews, and many disparaging remarks about Jews in general are made by the "Vogt" and the Baron. The Traveler's only reaction is to disparage these overgeneralizations mildly. The Baron tries to win the Traveler's friendship, feeling much obligated and drawn to him through his noble nature and bearing as an educated man of the world who seems to share many of the Baron's own ideas. The Baron is puzzled by the stranger's reticence about his name and station and, misled by this reticence and the lies of the Traveler's servant, assumes that he is a nobleman. When the true culprits of the previous night are apprehended by the Traveler when the false beards fall out of the "Vogt's" pocket, the Baron's enthusiasm knows no bounds. He offers to his benefactor his daughter's hand in marriage and the inheritance of his entire fortune. His generosity is in vain, the Traveler tells him, for Fate prevents him from accepting the Baron's daughter, for he is not a nobleman, but a Jew. After the shock has worn off slightly, the Baron observes that there are times when Heaven itself prevents one from fully showing gratitude. The Baron offers the Traveler a generous reward. But the Traveler declines, saying that the God of his fathers has provided well for him. All are impressed by his virtue and generosity, and leave the stage to a final comic love scene between the two servants, Christoph and Lisette.

In the last two plays examined, *Die alte Jungfer* and *Der Misogyne*, a clear trend was noted of coalescence of the discrete levels of language found earlier to a generally colloquial and familiar tone in the former play and a more elevated tone in the latter. *Die Juden* represents a reversal of this trend of coalescence. More than in any other comedy written by Lessing before, the characters in this play are distinguished in their language by their reflection of their individual stations in life and functions within the economy of the piece. Social stratification plays a greater role here than in the previous plays, where the divisions made between masters and servants were not always reflected in the ways in which either group spoke. This is not to say that there is a return here to the type of division to be found in *Damon*, for in *Die Juden*, each group's style seems quite natural to it, and there is far less artificiality in the ways the characters differ in their styles of speaking.

In *Die Juden*, the language which each character speaks corresponds with remarkable precision to his station in life. Three levels of language are discernible, as are three social estates; the rough-hewn language of the bucolics, Stich and Krumm, which is heavy with images, oaths, and specifically dialectal characteristics; the witty, sprightly, and more sophisticated language shared by Christoph and Lisette; and the elevated language of the educated wealthy, shared by the Baron, his daughter, and the Traveler. This last group must in turn be divided according to age and sex, considerations which are more important here than in the first two groups. Each character remains consistently on his own level of language in *Die Juden*, in contrast to the situation in *Der junge Gelehrte*, where the language of comic characterization was abandoned any time one of the characters had to say clearly something which was of importance to the plot.

Since a division of the varieties of language in *Die Juden* along social lines suggests itself, it will perhaps be best to start an analysis of this language on the lowest rung of the social ladder. Michael Stich and Martin Krumm, the mayor and steward, respectively, of the Baron's domains, who have tried to rob and possibly kill him, are rare examples of rural figures to appear on the German comic stage at this time. Usually the scene of a comedy was a town house, and all of the characters urban, either belonging to the upper middle class or its servants. That Stich and Krumm are the villains of the piece corresponds to a prevalent prejudice of the time, which had been handed down from the previous century, that farmers were the lowest variety of mankind, and were both stupid and morally corrupt. In *Die Juden*, Lessing might thus be said to have been combating one kind of prejudice with another. Since Stich only appears briefly in the first scene of the play, it is Krumm's language which will be most closely examined.

As the play begins, Stich and Krumm are discussing the events of the previous night:

KRUMM. Du dummer Michel Stich!

STICH. Du dummer Martin Krumm!

KRUMM. Nu, nu, wir wollens nur gestehen, wir sind beyde erz-dumm gewesen. Es wäre ja auf einen nicht angekommen, den wir mehr todt geschlagen hätten!

STICH. Du bist närrisch. Wie hätten wir es können klüger an-fangen? Waren wir nicht gut vermummt? war nicht der Kutscher auf unsrer Seite? konnten wir was dafür, daß uns das Glück so einen Querstrich machte? Hab ichs doch viel hundertmal gesagt: das verdammte Glücke! ohne das kann man nicht einmal ein guter Spitzbube seyn.

KRUMM. Je nu, wenn ichs beym Lichte besehe, so sind wir kaum dadurch auf ein Paar Tage länger dem Stricke entgangen.

STICH. Ah, es hat sich was mit dem Stricke! Wenn alle Diebe gehangen würden, die Galgen müßten dichter stehn. Man sieht ja kaum aller zwey Meilen einen; und wo noch einer ist, sieht man doch nichts daran. Ich glaube, die Herren Richter werden, aus Höflichkeit, die Dinger gar eingehen lassen. Zu was sind sie auch nütze? Zu nichts, als aufs höchste, daß unser einer, wenn er vorbey geht, die Augen zublinzt.

KRUMM. O! das thu ich nicht einmal. Mein Vater und mein Großvater sind daran gestorben, was will ichs viel besser ver-langen? Ich schäme mich meiner Eltern nicht.

STICH. Aber die ehrlichen Leute werden sich deiner schämen. Du hast noch lange nicht so viel gethan, daß man dich für ihren rechten und ächten Sohn halten kann.

KRUMM. O! denkst du denn, daß es deswegen unserm Herrn soll geschenkt seyn? Und an dem verzweifelten Fremden, der uns so einen fetten Bissen aus dem Munde gerissen hat, will ich mich gewiß auch rächen. Seine Uhr soll er so richtig müssen da lassen, als — ha! ha! sieh, da kömmt er gleich. Hurtig geh fort! ich will mein Meisterstück machen.

STICH. Aber halbpart! halbpart!   (*LM*, I, 375.3-376.9)

The Traveler describes the language spoken by Stich and Krumm as "die ordentliche hiesige Bauernsprache", although the particular locality intended is not mentioned. In its phonology, syntax, and content, this is surely not a realistic rendering of any "Bauernsprache". It is merely the common colloquial language associated with the lower social levels in Lessing's plays with a few dialect forms added. One of the chief ways in which Lessing conveys the idea that these are men of a lower class of society is through the use of vocabulary items considered below the standard of polite language of the time. Aside from the unsavory content of the conversation, such expressions as "Spitzbube", and the verb "zublinzen", both described by Adelung as being used "nur im gemeinen Leben", are certainly intended by Lessing to place these characters in this sphere. Dialect words are also used, such as "halbpart", which is a specifically Lower Saxon form indicating a claim to half of the article in question.[15] Krumm uses other specifically dialectal forms elsewhere in the play, and they are clearly there to make this language sub-standard and somewhat humorous. Which dialect is intended, however, is unclear, since some items are, like "halbpart", northern forms, while others, like "Mädel"[16] and "Schubsack"[17] are, according to Adelung, "oberdeutsch". Thus, Lessing was aiming not to imitate any particular dialect or "Bauernsprache", but merely to give an impression that the language of these characters is provincial and below the accepted standard. Of course, the use of oaths, such as "Zum

---

[15] Karl Müller-Fraureuth, *Wörterbuch der obersächsischen und erzgebirgischen Mundarten*, I: A-J (Dresden, 1911), p. 465.
[16] *LM*, I, p. 401.12; Adelung, *op. cit.*, III, p. 303.
[17] *LM*, I, p. 401.25; Adelung, *op. cit.*, IV, p. 285.

Teufel"[18] and the adjective "verdammt" also strengthen this impression.

As is Anton in *Der junge Gelehrte*, Krumm and Stich are distinguished peculiarly by the vividness with which they express themselves. There are more images and metaphors in the short scene between them just quoted than in the entire rest of the play. Such expressions as "daß uns das Glück so einen Querstrich machte" and the graphic metaphor for their escaped prey, "... so einen fetten Bissen..." are unique to Stich and Krumm, and are obviously intended again to produce the effect of colloquial spontaneity and color.

Krumm's language is particularly distinctive when he attempts to converse with his social betters. His archaic pomposity in the following exchange with the Traveler, combined with his coarseness and bad manners, put Krumm into the worst possible light, further effectively defining his character and bringing out the generosity and gentility of the Traveler in this first scene in which he appears:

KRUMM. ... — Ganz dienstwilliger Diener, mein Herr, — ich werde Martin Krumm heissen, und werde, auf diesem Gute hier, wohlbestallter Vogt seyn.

DER REISENDE. Es kann seyn, mein Freund. Aber habt Ihr nicht meinen Bedienten gesehen?

KRUMM. Ihnen zu dienen, nein; aber ich habe wohl von Dero preißwürdigen Person sehr viel gutes zu hören, die Ehre gehabt. Und es erfreut mich also, daß ich die Ehre habe, die Ehre Ihrer Bekanntschaft zu geniessen. Man sagt, daß Sie unsern Herrn gestern Abends, auf der Reise, aus einer sehr gefährlichen Gefahr sollen gerissen haben. Wie ich nun nicht anders kann, als mich des Glücks meines Herrn zu erfreuen, so erfreu ich mich —

DER REISENDE. Ich errathe es, was Ihr wollt; Ihr wollt Euch bey mir bedanken, daß ich Eurem Herrn beygestanden habe —

KRUMM. Ja, ganz recht; eben das!

DER REISENDE. Ihr seyd ein ehrlicher Mann —

KRUMM. Das bin ich! Und mit der Ehrlichkeit kömmt man immer auch am weitesten.

DER REISENDE. Es ist mir kein geringes Vergnügen, daß ich mir, durch eine so kleine Gefälligkeit, so viel rechtschaffne Leute ver-

---

[18]   *LM*, I, p. 393.23.

bindlich gemacht habe ... Kann ich Euch sonst worinn dienen, mein Freund?

KRUMM. O! mit dem Dienen, mein Herr, will ich Sie nicht beschweren. Ich habe meinen Knecht, der mich bedienen muß, wanns nöthig ist...   (*LM*, I, 376.12-377.11)

Krumm's baseness is clearly brought out here through his abuse of polite phrases, such as the meaningless and tiresome coupling of "Ehre" and "erfreuen" in his longwinded and empty speech. What Krumm does not succeed in saying, the Traveler is able to reduce to a single line. Krumm's coarseness is emphasized by his complete misunderstanding of the Traveler's polite phrase, "Kann ich Euch sonst worinn dienen?", which he answers with a crude boast.

The language of Stich and Krumm, while by no means a realistic rendering of dialect or even slang, represents the socially and stylistically lowest level of colloquial language in *Die Juden*. As rural figures unique in Lessing's comedies, they occupy the level in the hierarchy of comic language usually reserved for servants. The effect of this is to raise the level of the servants' language to a tone much closer to that of polite conversation.

Christoph and Lisette, the two servants in this play, provide a comical, weakly romantic sub-plot. They are more urbane and witty in their conversations than the servants encountered thus far in Lessing's comedies. They show the direct French influence on Lessing, and one scene between them, in its outlines and the movement of its dialogue, is clearly borrowed from Marivaux's *La seconde Surprise de l'Amour*, as Albrecht demonstrates. Christoph and Lisette address each other in the formal third person plural, rather than in the more usual familiar second person singular, raising the general tone of their language and making them, too, unique among representatives of their class in Lessing's comedies.

According to Hermann Paul,[19] the third person plural in second person address was the standard form of polite address in German in the eighteenth century. Lessing was well aware,

[19]   Hermann Paul, *Deutsche Grammatik*, III (Halle a.S., 1919), p. 123.

however, of the nuances that could be achieved with the various levels of second person address, as he was to demonstrate in *Minna von Barnhelm*. This awareness is to be sensed in *Die Juden* too, for on occasion, especially when she is annoyed with him, Lisette addresses Christoph in the third person singular, which, in the eighteenth century, was used by persons of low estate to address respectfully persons of their station with whom they were not intimate. In the final scene of the play, when she knows of the deception which Christoph has practiced upon her in telling her that his master was a Dutch nobleman, Lisette addresses him as follows, with Christoph taking his cue from her:

LISETTE. Also, mein Freund, hat Er mich vorhin belogen?
CHRISTOPH. Ja, und das aus zweyerley Ursachen. Erstlich, weil ich die Wahrheit nicht wußte; und anderns, weil man für eine Dose, die man wiedergeben muß, nicht viel Wahrheit sagen kann.
LISETTE. Und wanns dazu kömmt, ist Er wohl gar auch ein Jude, so sehr Er Sich verstellt?
CHRISTOPH. Das ist zu neugierig für eine Jungfer gefragt! Komm Sie nur!   (*LM*, I, 411.19-26)

This tone, in which the servants jocularly condescend to each other, using a less respectful, but still distant address form, is very different from their usual tone. This is an early example of how Lessing skillfully uses conventional features of style, second person address in this case, to display the state and degree of closeness of a relationship.

Despite an admixture of polite repartee and formal terms in their language, there is still a considerable amount of earthy coarseness in the dialogues of Christoph and Lisette, as the following scene between them will demonstrate. Christoph and Lisette are sitting on the Traveler's saddlebags, and Christoph should be unsaddling the horses when Lisette attempts to coax from him information concerning his master:

CHRISTOPH. Wo blieben wir denn? — Ja, — bey der Liebe — Ich liebe Sie also, Mamsell. Je vous aime, würde ich sagen, wenn Sie eine französische Marquisinn wären.
LISETTE. Der Geyer! Sie sind wohl gar ein Franzose?

CHRISTOPH. Nein, ich muß meine Schande gestehn: ich bin nur ein Deutscher. — Aber ich habe das Glück gehabt, mit verschiedenen Franzosen umgehen zu können, und da habe ich denn so ziemlich gelernt, was zu einem rechtschaffnen Kerl gehört. Ich glaube, man sieht mir es auch gleich an.

LISETTE. Sie kommen also vielleicht mit Ihrem Herrn aus Frankreich?

CHRISTOPH. Ach nein! —

LISETTE. Wo sonst her? freylich wohl! —

CHRISTOPH. Es liegt noch einige Meilen hinter Frankreich, wo wir herkommen.

LISETTE. Aus Italien doch wohl nicht?

CHRISTOPH. Nicht weit davon.

LISETTE. Aus England also?

CHRISTOPH. Beynahe; England ist eine Provinz davon. Wir sind über funfzig Meilen von hier zu Hause — Aber, daß Gott! — meine Pferde, — die armen Thiere stehen noch gesattelt. Verzeihen Sie, Mamsell! — Hurtig! stehen Sie auf! — (er nimmt die Mantelsäcke wieder untern Arm.) — Trotz meiner innbrünstigen Liebe, muß ich doch gehn und erst das nöthigste verrichten — Wir haben noch den ganzen Tag, und, was das meiste ist, noch die ganze Nacht vor uns. Wir wollen schon noch eins werden...

(*LM*, I, 392.17-393.5)

In comparison to the bucolic crudeness shown by Stich and Krumm, these servants have a wide range of awareness. Lessing puts into their mouths satirical comments on the literature of the day, as when Christoph says of his master's traveling-library; "Sie besteht aus Lustspielen, die zum Weinen, und aus Trauerspielen, die zum Lachen bewegen; aus zärtlichen Heldengedichten, aus tiefsinnigen Trinkliedern, und was dergleichen neue Siebensachen mehr sind" (*LM*, I, 392.1-4). In addition, Christoph is supplied with a smattering of French, and Lisette with at least the vague awareness that there are such places as France, Italy, and England. Thus, in addition to making them address each other more formally, Lessing has made the servants almost cosmopolitan in order to distinguish them from Krumm and Stich. In marked contrast to the relative sophistication of the content of the servants' dialogue, however, is the occasional crudeness of their style. They use oaths, such as "Zum Geyer", and "daß Gott".

Furthermore, the coarse *double entendre* playing on the literal and idiomatic meanings of the expression "eins werden", shows the thinness of the veneer of Christoph's clumsy gallantries towards Lisette.

At the top of the social scale in *Die Juden* stand the Traveler, the Baron, and his daughter, "das Fräulein". While they all have the elevated colloquial speech seen in Lessing's earlier comedies, there is noticeable here a greater flexibility than was apparent in *Der Misogyne*. In that play, although the stiffness formerly associated with this style in Lessing's previous plays was alleviated, the tone of the characters whose speech belonged exclusively in the elevated colloquial sphere was uniform; men and women spoke exactly like each other, with no sort of variation according to character. This is no longer the case in *Die Juden*. Within the realm of elevated colloquial speech, Lessing has found ways to give to each character speaking it an individualized diction, just as he did in *Der junge Gelehrte* on the level of characterizing common colloquial speech. Despite the fact that these characters are given neither comic nor regular proper names, and yet correspond to prevalent theatrical types, they still have more individuality as characters than do the earlier Valers or Orontes.

"Das Fräulein" is characterized in a few simple stylistic strokes. She is supposed to be quite young, perhaps two years short of marriageable age, although she has an eagerness much in advance of her tender years. The Traveler calls her "eine so angenehme und muntre Tochter", and goes on to say: "Sie bezaubert durch ihre unverstellten Reden, in welchen eine liebenswürdige Unschuld, und der aller natürlichste Witz herrschet." The Baron explains, "Sie ist wenig unter Leuten ihres gleichen gewesen, und besitzt die Kunst zu gefallen, die man schwerlich auf dem Lande erlernen kann, und die doch oft mehr, als die Schönheit selbst vermag, in einem sehr geringen Grade" (*LM*, I, 384.1-7). It is questionable whether Lessing really succeeded in creating such a character in the short time in which he lets the girl appear. Perhaps these things must be said about her because he has not succeeded. Her speech in the following scene indicates, at least, that she is naive and outspoken:

FRÄULEIN. Warum verlassen Sie uns, mein Herr? Warum sind Sie hier so allein? Ist Ihnen unser Umgang schon die wenigen Stunden, die Sie bey uns sind, zuwider geworden? Es sollte mir leid thun. Ich suche aller Welt zu gefallen; und Ihnen möchte ich, vor allen andern, gerne nicht mißfallen.

DER REISENDE. Verzeihen Sie mir, Fräulein. Ich habe nur meinem Bedienten befehlen wollen, alles zur Abreise fertig zu halten.

FRÄULEIN. Von was reden Sie? Von der Abreise? Wenn Sie etwa schon ein Jahr bey uns wären, so könnte man es Ihnen noch verzeihen, wenn Sie eine melancholische Stunde auf diesen Einfall gebracht hätte. Aber wie, nicht einmal einen völligen Tag aushalten wollen? das ist zu arg. Ich sage es Ihnen, ich werde böse, wenn Sie noch einmal daran gedenken.

DER REISENDE. Sie könnten mir nichts empfindlichers drohen.

FRÄULEIN. Nein? im Ernst? ist es wahr, würden Sie empfindlich seyn, wenn ich böse auf Sie würde?

DER REISENDE. Wie sollte uns der Zorn eines liebenswürdigen Frauenzimmers gleichgültig seyn können?

FRÄULEIN. Was Sie sagen, klingt zwar beynahe, als wenn Sie spotten wollten: doch ich will es für Ernst aufnehmen; gesetzt, ich irre mich auch. Also, mein Herr, — ich bin ein wenig liebenswürdig, wie man mir gesagt hat, und ich sage Ihnen noch einmal, ich werde entsetzlich, entsetzlich zornig werden, wenn Sie, binnen hier und dem neuen Jahre, wieder an Ihre Abreise gedenken.

(*LM*, I, 382.23-383.16)

Here may be seen how Lessing has refined his technique of linking a character with a definite feature of speech. In crafting the young lady's diction, he relies heavily on one stylistic feature; the use of many interrogatives. This gives a naive but teasing effect, the impression of constantly questioning youth, but also of coquetry. Lessing does not overdo his use of this device here, as he might have only two years earlier, and varies the interrogatives with several short declarative clauses. The general tone is light and colloquial, and complex sentences are avoided. The girl begins the dialogue coyly, seeking out the Traveler after he has briefly left her and her father, and, in polite periphrasis, expresses her intense desire to please him: "Ich suche aller Welt zu gefallen, und Ihnen möchte ich, vor allen andern, gerne nicht mißfallen." When the Traveler answers that he has made arrangements for his departure, she coquettishly threatens to become angry if he even thinks of leaving so soon again. The Traveler responds politely with a pallid euphemism, that she could threaten him with nothing worse. She seems, however, to take this polite gesture seriously, and pursues the subject, apparently excited that her anger could be noticed by such a man, and twists the word "empfindlich" into something other than the Traveler meant. The Traveler answers her question with another coolly polite phrase, coupling the conventional "liebenswürdiges Frauenzimmer" with the neutral adjective "gleichgültig", and using the collective pronoun "uns" rather than "mir" to further increase the formality and indirectness of the question, and reducing it merely to a polite gesture. This gesture, however, is again taken at face value by the girl, and she accuses him of teasing, but then resolves that she will take him seriously after all, because she wants to. She repeats her threat, and the reality of her feeling breaks through in the redoubling of the adverb in her intention of becoming "entsetzlich, entsetzlich zornig". Thus, through the use of relatively sparse stylistic means, namely interrogatives and the device of having the girl misunderstand the Traveler's euphemistic phrases, which is to be expected in a girl not experienced in the verbal game of polite society, Lessing achieves a definite and skillful characterization, beyond the bare requirements of the plot, in a relatively small scope.

The Baron and the Traveler are distinguished from each other by age and station. By his own account, the Baron is fifty years old and has seen military service, but has been rather isolated from the world of men. As he says, "Bekannte habe ich gehabt, aber noch keinen Freund." Although his intentions are good, the Baron is given to overgeneralizations and haste in forming judgments. In Lessing's delineation of his character, there is an echo to be detected of the testiness of

such earlier purely humorous characters as Chrysander and
Wumshäter. Though in a very much modified form, the
Baron's language has elements in common with theirs, and he
is the heir to the technique of Lessing's depiction of older men
upon the comic stage. The Traveler, aside from the courage
and generosity displayed in his actions, is not distinguished
in characterization by any more individual traits, presumably
also to counteract earlier overdrawn caricatures and to make
the final surprise more striking. Accordingly, his language,
except for the lofty quality of his sentiment, is most similar
to the rather bland elevated colloquial language found in
earlier comedies, although it, too, is less dense, less hypotactic
in its quality. Good examples of the language of both the
Baron and the Traveler are to be found in the following scene,
in which the Baron is unsuccessfully suing for the Traveler's
friendship:

BARON. ... Und niemals ist mir die Freundschaft so reizend vor-
gekommen, als seit den wenigen Stunden, da ich nach der Ihrigen
strebe. Wodurch kann ich sie verdienen?
DER REISENDE. Meine Freundschaft bedeutet so wenig, daß das
bloße Verlangen darnach ein genugsames Verdienst ist, sie zu
erhalten. Ihre Bitte ist weit mehr werth, als das, was Sie bitten.
BARON. O, mein Herr, die Freundschaft eines Wohlthäters —
DER REISENDE. Erlauben Sie, — ist keine Freundschaft. Wenn
Sie mich unter dieser falschen Gestalt betrachten, so kann ich Ihr
Freund nicht seyn. Gesetzt einen Augenblick, ich wäre Ihr Wohl-
thäter: würde ich nicht zu befürchten haben, daß Ihre Freund-
schaft nichts, als eine wirksame Dankbarkeit wäre?
BARON. Sollte sich beydes nicht verbinden lassen?
DER REISENDE. Sehr schwer! Diese hält ein edles Gemüth für
seine Pflicht; jene erfordert lauter willkührliche Bewegungen der
Seele.
BARON. Aber wie sollte ich — Ihr allzuzärtlicher Geschmack
macht mich ganz verwirrt. —
DER REISENDE. Schätzen Sie mich nur nicht höher, als ich es
verdiene. Aufs höchste bin ich ein Mensch, der seine Schuldigkeit
mit Vergnügen gethan hat. Die Schuldigkeit an sich selbst ist
keiner Dankbarkeit werth. Daß ich sie aber mit Vergnügen gethan
habe, dafür bin ich genugsam durch Ihre Freundschaft belohnt.

BARON. Diese Großmuth verwirrt mich nur noch mehr. — Aber ich bin vielleicht zu verwegen. — Ich habe mich noch nicht unterstehen wollen, nach Ihrem Namen, nach Ihrem Stande zu fragen. — Vielleicht biete ich meine Freundschaft einem an, der — der sie zu verachten —

DER REISENDE. Verzeihen Sie, — Sie — Sie machen Sich — Sie haben allzugroße Gedanken von mir.

BARON. (bey Seite.) Soll ich ihn wohl fragen? Er kann meine Neugierigkeit übel nehmen.

DER REISENDE. (bey Seite.) Wenn er mich fragt, was werde ich ihm antworten?

BARON. (bey Seite.) Frage ich ihn nicht? Er kann es als eine Grobheit auslegen.

DER REISENDE. (bey Seite.) Soll ich ihm die Wahrheit sagen?

BARON. (bey Seite.) Doch ich will den sichersten Weg gehen. Ich will erst seinen Bedienten ausfragen lassen.

DER REISENDE. (bey Seite.) Könnte ich doch dieser Verwirrung überhoben seyn! —

BARON. Warum so nachdenkend?

DER REISENDE. Ich war gleich bereit, diese Frage an Sie zu thun, mein Herr —

BARON. Ich weiß es, man vergißt sich dann und wann. Lassen Sie uns von etwas andern reden — Sehen Sie, daß es wirkliche Juden gewesen sind, die mich angefallen haben? Nur jetzo hat mir mein Schulze gesagt, daß er seit einigen Tagen dreye auf der Landstraße angetroffen. Wie er mir sie beschreibt, haben sie Spitzbuben ähnlicher, als ehrlichen Leuten, gesehen. Und warum sollte ich auch daran zweifeln? Ein Volk, das auf den Gewinnst so erpicht ist, fragt wenig darnach, ob es ihn mit Recht oder Unrecht, mit List oder Gewaltsamkeit erhält — Es scheinet auch zur Handelschaft, oder deutsch zu reden, zur Betrügerey gemacht zu seyn. Höflich, frey, unternehmend, verschwiegen, sind Eigenschaften die es schätzbar machen würden, wenn es sie nicht allzusehr zu unserm Unglück anwendete. — (er hält etwas inne.) — Die Juden haben mir sonst schon nicht wenig Schaden und Verdruß gemacht. Als ich noch in Kriegsdiensten war, ließ ich mich bereden, einen Wechsel für einen meiner Bekannten mit zu unterschreiben; und der Jude, an den er ausgestellet war, brachte mich nicht allein dahin, daß ich ihn bezahlen, sondern, daß ich ihn sogar zweymal bezahlen mußte — O! es sind die allerboshaftesten und niederträchtigsten Leute — Was sagen Sie dazu? Sie scheinen ganz niedergeschlagen.   (*LM*, I, 384.19-386.16)

The conversation starts out in the language of polite sentiment.

The Baron quite openly asks for the Traveler's friendship. The Traveler, unwilling to reveal his identity, politely parries this suit by deprecating the value of his friendship in relation to that of the Baron's request. Here, the two men are dealing in the euphemistic platitudes of the conventions of friendship current at the time. The Baron's exclamation concerning the friendship of a benefactor is politely interrupted and damped by the Traveler's hypothesis and demonstration, delivered almost in the tone of a logical theorem, of the incompatibility of gratitude and friendship. When the Baron still persists, the Traveler becomes even more distant in his style, demonstrating in an antithetical statement the difference between gratitude and friendship, and goes on to make the sententious theoretical statement that gratitude is not due one who merely does his duty, but that he accepts, as a reward for having done it with pleasure, the Baron's friendship. Here again, the Traveler's style is characterized by abstractness and objectivity. This is achieved by his talking chiefly in generalities with the Baron, dealing with the abstract concepts of friendship and gratitude, and avoiding a direct personal statement. In this respect, his speech on lines 19-23, above, is to be noted. He begins by speaking of himself, asking that the Baron not estimate him more highly than he deserves. In the very next sentence, from one clause to the next, the Traveler turns his statement about himself into a general axiom, beginning the sentence in the first person, and finishing it in the third. "Aufs höchste bin ich ein Mensch, der seine Schuldigkeit mit Vergnügen gethan hat." This is followed by a further platitude: "Die Schuldigkeit an sich selbst ist keiner Dankbarkeit werth", which completely lifts the conversation into the abstract sphere, whence it is only partly retrieved by the frostily conciliatory gesture of the Traveler's last sentence in the speech. In the same distantly intellectual way in which he has fended off the "Fräulein's" offers of love, the Traveler has fended off the Baron's suit for friendship. Throughout this conversation, the Traveler has been speaking from his intellect, from his "Witz". His style is entirely controlled and cool, at least up to line 29, above, while he is conversing with the Baron.

In contrast to the Traveler, the Baron speaks from the heart, eschewing the polite abstractness of tone taken by the Traveler. Indeed, the Baron begins by speaking in the reserved style of polite sentiment, but as he is rebuffed and puzzled by the Traveler's apparent coolness, his style gradually unravels. He protests the Traveler's first rebuff with an exclamatory, "O, mein Herr...", and after the Traveler's analysis of the difference between gratitude and friendship, is virtually reduced to stammering, interrupting himself and beginning anew. The Traveler's style is also disjointed through aposiopesis, although he retains the polite phrases in his speech.

Finally, through mutual embarrassment, which Lessing expresses by having each of the two men talk to himself although the other is still on the stage, both the Baron and the Traveler drop their masks of polite convention while each asks himself, in straightforward interrogatives, what he is to do next. In the case of the Traveler, especially, there is a striking difference in the style of the monologues compared to that of the dialogues. In the monologue, the euphemisms and periphrases of polite convention are gone, and the immediate situation is confronted in a more direct style.

The Baron takes up the thread of the dialogue again, and presently launches into a diatribe against the Jews which, in its style, not to mention its reasoning, is strongly reminiscent of one of Wumshäter's attacks upon women. Particularly in this speech, the typological affinity between the Baron and the older men in Lessing's early comedies is very apparent. Little by little, as he warms to his subject, the Baron drops the phrases of polite conversation, reverting more and more to common colloquial speech, and culminating in a splenetic outburst. He begins by wanting to dispel the embarrassment created by his touching upon the question of the Traveler's identity and station and talks about the incidents of the previous night, thinking that here he is on neutral ground. His use of the term "Spitzbube" and the adjective "erpicht", both of which are described by Adelung as belonging to common colloquial usage, betrays the Baron's lapse in style when entering upon a subject which causes him some inner agitation, despite the presence of an honored and respected guest. As he mentions the deceitfulness of the Jews, the Baron consciously exchanges his vocabulary of polite euphemism for more drastically direct description: "[Das Volk] scheinet auch zu Handelschaft, oder deutsch zu reden, zur Betrügerey gemacht zu seyn." From this point onward, the Baron "speaks German" more and more, and the language of polite periphrasis less and less. Significantly, the Baron is made to pause, apparently deciding whether he should drop his last reserve on the subject, and then storms on, revealing the details of his personal unfortunate encounter with a Jew. Although his language is perfectly contained and controlled, still within the realm of elevated colloquial usage, the Baron ends his diatribe with a hyperbolic exclamatory outburst: "O! es sind die allerboshaftesten und niederträchtigsten Leute –."

In contrast to the occasionally splenetic Baron, the Traveler, who for practical dramaturgic reasons must conceal more than he reveals, remains generally cool and dignified in his language as in his bearing. When he comments on the central matter of the play at all, he does so in the form of a brief moralizing monologue. Thus, after Krumm had delivered himself of some abusive remarks against the Jews and has left the stage, the Traveler, not revealing himself to the audience, but seemingly commenting chiefly on Krumm and apparently only by coincidence on the place of the Jew in the world, says:

Vielleicht ist dieser Kerl, so dumm er ist, oder sich stellt, ein größrer Betrieger, als nie einer unter den Juden gewesen ist. Wenn diese hintergehen so überlegt man nicht, daß sie die Christen darzu gezwungen haben. Ich zweifle ob sich einer von ihnen rühmen kann, mit einem Juden aufrichtig verfahren zu seyn. Dieser thut aufs höchste nichts, als daß er ihnen gleiches mit gleichem zu vergelten sucht. Wenn zwey Nationen redlich mit einander umgehen sollen, so müssen beyde das ihre darzu beytragen.
(*LM*, I, 380.9)

This calm on the part of the Traveler has been criticized as lacking verisimilitude and the grandeur of the later *Nathan*. This is true, and is symptomatic of Lessing's preoccupation at the time with turning every subject into a comedy, which he confessed himself in the introduction to *Die Juden* quoted at the beginning of this section, and which extended even to as personally vital a matter as this. On one hand, the Traveler's reticence is necessary to the economy of the comedy, and on the other, he must speak with a clear voice as Lessing's advocate in the theater. The play, whatever its faults in focusing on the central problem may be, still does not fail entirely in putting its message across. In this monologue, where he is at once serving as chief character and choric commentator, the Traveler's style is again less elevated than in the dialogues in which he has been observed. His periods are shorter and less intricate, his vocabulary less euphemistic. He uses words like "Betrieger" and "Kerl", which are in the realm of the commonly colloquial, but would not use "Spitzbube", as does the Baron. Despite the fact that his language is more direct in the monologues, the Traveler still adheres to the conventions of polite speech, for his language must and does remain plain, compact, and lofty in its statements, with all the clarity and straightforwardness of Lessing's own didactic prose.

The feature of the language of *Die Juden* which most represents a progressive change from that of earlier comedies is the new realization of characterization through elevated colloquial language. This level of language is handled more subtly and variously than ever by Lessing, and through this, each role in the serious plot has its individual voice. Indeed, in the writing of the parts of Stich and Krumm and the servants, techniques are to be found which have their roots in in the language of Lessing's earliest efforts, but the opposition which existed in these works between the language of characterization and that of earnest communication no longer exists. Henceforth, expression and characterization will be indissolubly linked.

DER FREYGEIST

Lessing's impulse for the vindication of a misjudged man, group, or ideal was as strong as his instinct for unrelenting attack on shallow or badly reasoned notions. Both urges were vigorous in his early manhood and stayed with him throughout his life, affecting every aspect of his work. In the two plays written in 1749, the polemic element is unmistakable. In *Die Juden*, Lessing was vindicating the Jewish people and attacking those who wrongly condemned the entire nation for the faults of a few of its number. His aim in *Der Freygeist* was a doubly significant one for him; the vindication of himself as a dramatist and of comedy as a morally valid art form before the strongly critical eye of his father, the pastor of Kamenz, who very much disapproved of the theater and of his son's involvement with it when he should have been carrying on his studies.

In answer to one of many critical letters from his father, Lessing wrote in April, 1749:

Wenn man mir mit Recht den Tittel eines deutschen Moliere beylegen könnte, so könnte ich gewiß eines ewigen Nahmens versichert seyn. Die Wahrheit zu gestehen, so habe ich zwar sehr große Lust ihn zu verdienen, aber sein Umfang und meine Ohnmacht sind zwey Stücke die auch die gröste Lust erstücken können. ... Den Beweiß warum ein Comoedienschreiber kein guter Christ seyn könne, kan ich nicht ergründen. Ein Comoedienschreiber ist ein Mensch der die Laster auf ihrer lächerlichen Seite schildert. Darf denn ein Christ über die Laster nicht lachen? Verdienen die Laster so viel Hochachtung? Und wenn ich ihnen nun gar verspräche eine Comoedie zu machen, die nicht nur die H. Theologen lesen sondern auch loben sollen? Halten sie mein Versprechen vor unmöglich? Wie wenn ich eine auf die Freygeister und auf die Verächter ihres Standes machte? Ich weiß gewiß, sie würden vieles von ihrer Schärfe fahren laßen.   (*LM*, XVII, 16)

The play with which Lessing fulfilled his promise to his stern father, whose wrath was not noticeably mollified by it, is a peculiar blending of didactic and sentimental plot elements, each supporting the other. The opposition between the two protagonists, the freethinker Adrast and the pious pastor, Theophan, is, as Paul Böckmann has pointed out, one between the principles of "Witz" and "Herz".[20] Adrast's intellectual skepticism, reinforced by previous unfortunate experience, about the sincerity of declared religious precepts and the honesty of clergymen is finally overcome by Theophan's limitless generosity of heart. In a plot patterned chiefly on de Lisle's *Caprices du cœur et de l'esprit*, Adrast and Theophan are brought together in the house of Lisidor, to whose daughters they are to be married. According to Lisidor's plan of yoking like with like, Theophan is to marry the modest, pious Juliane, and Adrast the sprightly, witty Henriette; "der Fromme sollte die Fromme, und der Lustige die Lustige haben", as Lisidor says. Adrast, however, loves Juliane, and therefore the contempt he feels for Theophan as a pastor is turned to hatred for him as a rival. Theophan, long unaware of the true basis of Adrast's hostility, is determined, despite rude rebuffs, to gain his friendship. When Theophan's cousin, Araspe, who is also Adrast's creditor, arrives to collect his money, Theophan pleads for Araspe's mercy, saying that Adrast can be won over to religion again if he is not hurt by those who profess it. Araspe gives Theophan the promissory notes which Adrast signed, and Theophan tears them up before the freethinker's eyes. Adrast's only reaction is one of scorn for what he regards as merely another part of Theophan's devious plot to gain power over him and destroy his happiness. Finally, however, Theophan's consistent generosity, culminating in his admission that Juliane loves Adrast as Adrast loves her, and more and less consenting to take Henriette as second best, convince Adrast that his skepticism has been exaggerated, and he is ashamed, and exchanges pledges of friendship with Theophan. They exchange brides as well, to the satisfaction of both ladies.

Humorous relief in *Der Freygeist* is provided by the figures of Johann and Martin, the servants of Adrast and Theophan.

---

[20]   Böckmann, *op. cit.*, I, p. 589.

Each is a caricature of the extreme of his master's intellectual position; Johann uses atheism as an excuse for his boisterous and drunken existence, and Martin is meanly smug in his superstitious orthodoxy. Lisette describes them as "ein Paar allerliebste Schlingel! Adrasts Johann, und Theophans Martin: die wahren Bilder ihrer Herren, von der häßlichen Seite! Aus Freygeisterey ist jener ein Spitzbube; und aus Frömmigkeit dieser ein Dummkopf." They appear together in only one humorous scene, in which Johann attempts for his own ends to turn Martin into a freethinker, and is himself duped. Otherwise, Johann is merely used as a messenger and informant as the plot requires. Lisette plays her usual role as witty commentator upon the proceedings of the play and serves to bring together Theophan and Henriette. In general, the servants are much less in evidence than before and never actually dominate the action, which here is far more important to Lessing than considerations of mere entertainment.

This suppression of the servants and thus of the comic element of the play is indicative of Lessing's progress as a dramatist. In *Die Juden*, he had turned a serious theme into comedy, subjecting the formal requirements of that theme to those of comedy. The resulting play was artistically unsuccessful because of the basic incongruity of form and content. In *Der Freygeist*, the serious matter is cast in a far more appropriate form and given the proper attention at the center of the plot. The comic elements, which so disturbed the unity of *Die Juden* are made to serve the purposes of the main plot by underlining its action satirically.

Thus, the mood of *Der Freygeist* is almost uniformly earnest, with little of the bantering tone found in the earlier plays. The major characters, particularly Adrast and Theophan, are almost continually engaged in trying to refute each other's arguments and allegations, sometimes through logic, and sometimes, as they are quick to remind each other, by impromptu sermons. Adrast, Theophan, Juliane, and Araspe occasionally give long polemical speeches, which accentuate further the formal tone of the play and its didactic elements, which such characters as Johann, Martin, and Lisidor, by virtue of their brief and infrequent appearances, do little to counter with humor.

The trend towards characterizing variety within elevated colloquial style noted in *Die Juden* is continued and strengthened in *Der Freygeist*. The language of *Der Freygeist* is almost entirely of this variety. Lisidor, Johann and Martin, all three traditional comic figures, whose language is more vulgar, have very little to say. Of the play's thirty-five scenes, Lisidor appears in only seven, and does not dominate any of them, and Johann, except for his one scene with Martin, is even more firmly restrained, appearing in only five scenes. Lisette, although she is on stage through one-third of the comedy, is still not as much in evidence as maids have been in earlier plays.

The tone of the play, then, is set by the chief characters of the sentimental-didactic plot; Adrast, who is volubly present for all but nine scenes, Theophan, who is on stage about half the time, and Juliane and Henriette. All of these characters speak the language of the educated upper classes. But again, as in *Die Juden*, Lessing has found ways to differentiate the language of individual characters even more effectively than in the previous play. The male characters are set off in their speech from the female characters, and the two main figures in each of these categories from each other.

The characters in *Der Freygeist* comment liberally upon each other. Theophan, the young cleric, is characterized by Henriette: "Theophan ... hat das liebenswürdigste Gesicht von der Welt. Es herrscht eine Freundlichkeit darinn, die sich niemals verleugnet." He is represented as pious, learned, and generous, ever patient and courteous. Adrast, on the other hand, is frequently ill-tempered and almost uncouth, as Henriette's comment on his behavior shows. "Was für ein Stolz, was für eine Verachtung aller andern blickt dem Adrast aus jeder Miene! ... Umsonst sind seine Gesichtszüge noch so regelmäßig: sein Eigensinn, seine Lust zum Spotten hat eine gewisse Falte hineingebracht, die ihm (sic) in meinen Augen

recht häßlich läßt." Adrast is not the creature of the devil
which Theophan's servant, Martin, believes all freethinkers
to be, and, necessarily, he is far more sympathetic as a character than Gellert's Herr Simon in *Das Loos in der Lotterie*, who
is portrayed as a cynical and atheistic fop, preening himself
with French mannerisms. Adrast is a man of high ideals, but,
as Theophan says, his intellectual faculty, "Witz", dominates
his emotional faculty, "Herz", which Adrast mistrusts. The
redressing of the balance between these two faculties is the
business of the play. But through most of its action, Adrast is
haughty, quick-tempered, and immoderate in his judgment
of men's intentions.

The following scene may serve to illustrate the ways in
which the differences in character between Adrast and Theophan are reflected in the language of each. In this passage
from the first scene of the play, Adrast and Theophan are
discussing their opposing views of friendship. In order to give
a broader sampling of his speech in this particular situation,
part of Adrast's monologue in the scene following is also
included.

THEOPHAN. ... Sagen Sie mir, ist die Liebe unter der Freundschaft,
oder die Freundschaft unter der Liebe begriffen? Nothwendig das
letztere. Derjenige also, der die Liebe in ihrem allerweitesten Um-
fange gebietet, gebietet der nicht auch die Freundschaft? Ich
sollte es glauben; und es ist so wenig wahr, daß unser Gesetzgeber
die Freundschaft seines Geboths nicht würdig geschätzt habe, daß
er vielmehr seine Lehre zu einer Freundschaft gegen die ganze
Welt gemacht hat.

ADRAST. Sie bürden ihm Ungereimtheiten auf. Freundschaft
gegen die ganze Welt? Was ist das? Mein Freund muß kein Freund
der ganzen Welt seyn.

THEOPHAN. Und also ist Ihnen wohl nichts Freundschaft, als
jene Uebereinstimmung der Temperamente, jene angeborne Harmonie der Gemüther, jener heimliche Zug gegen einander, jene
unsichtbare Kette, die zwey einerley denkende, einerley wollende
Seelen verknüpfet?

ADRAST. Ja, nur dieses ist mir Freundschaft.

THEOPHAN. Nur dieses? Sie widersprechen Sich also selbst.

ADRAST. O! daß Ihr Leute doch überall Widersprüche findet,
außer nur da nicht, wo sie wirklich sind!

THEOPHAN. Ueberlegen Sie es. Wenn diese, ohne Zweifel nicht willkührliche, Uebereinstimmung der Seelen, diese in uns liegende Harmonie mit einem andern einzeln Wesen allein die wahre Freundschaft ausmacht: wie können Sie verlangen, daß sie der Gegenstand eines Gesetzes sein soll? Wo sie ist, darf sie nicht geboten werden; und wo sie nicht ist, da wird sie umsonst geboten. Und wie können Sie es unserm Lehrer zur Last legen, daß er die Freundschaft in diesem Verstande übergangen ist? Er hat uns eine edlere Freundschaft befohlen, welche jenes blinden Hanges, den auch die unvernünftigen Thiere nicht missen, entbehren kann: eine Freundschaft, die sich nach erkannten Vollkommenheiten mittheilet; welche sich nicht von der Natur lenken läßt, sondern welche die Natur selbst lenket.

ADRAST. O Geschwätze!

THEOPHAN. Ich muß Ihnen dieses sagen, Adrast, ob Sie es gleich eben so wohl wissen könnten, als ich; und auch wissen sollten. Was würden Sie selbst von mir denken, wenn ich den Verdacht nicht mit aller Gewalt von mir abzulenken suchte, als mache mich die Religion zu einem Verächter der Freundschaft, die Sie nur allzugern aus einem wichtigen Grunde verachten möchten? — Sehen Sie mich nicht so geringschätzig an; wenden Sie Sich nicht auf eine so beleidigende Art von mir —

ADRAST. (bey Seite.) Das Pfaffengeschmeisse!

THEOPHAN. Nichts mehr! Ich mag Sie in diesem Tone nicht hören. Ich würde unmöglich darinne antworten können; und ich bleibe keine Antwort gerne schuldig. Ich will Sie verlassen. Ich erfuhr eben jezt, daß einer von meinen Anverwandten mit der Post angelangt sey. Ich gehe ihm entgegen, und werde die Ehre haben Ihnen denselben vorzustellen. [exit Theophan.]

ADRAST. [solo.] — Daß ich ihn nimmermehr wiedersehen dürfte! Welcher von euch Schwarzröcken wäre auch kein Heuchler? — Priestern habe ich mein Unglück zu danken. Sie haben mich gedrückt, verfolgt, so nahe sie auch das Blut mit mir verbunden hatte. Hassen will ich dich, Theophan, und alle deines Ordens! Muß ich denn auch hier in die Verwandtschaft der Geistlichkeit gerathen? — Er, dieser Schleicher, dieser blöde Verleugner seines Verstandes, soll mein Schwager werden? — ...   (*LM*, II, 55.2-56.21)

As befits a pastor, Theophan is logical and not a little rhetorical in his speech, especially when, as here, he is occupied with the attempted conversion of a freethinker. He tries to convince Adrast by the Socratic method, trapping him into contradictions and demonstrating, in the manner of the disputation, the necessary subordination of friendship to love, and why friendship cannot be subject to law as Adrast first demands. His tone is almost always friendly, calm, and factual, a feature which infuriates the more hot-blooded Adrast. This effect is brought about by Theophan's speaking in lengthy but well-organized periods, whose subordinate clauses stand in a clear syntactic relationship to their main clauses. The deliberateness of Theophan's tone is further emphasized by his use of extended adjectival phrases ("... diese, ohne Zweifel nicht willkührliche, Uebereinstimmung der Seelen, diese in uns liegende Harmonie...") and appositional phrases ("... jene Uebereinstimmung der Temperamente, jene angeborene Harmonie der Gemüther, jener heimliche Zug gegen einander, jene unsichtbare Kette, ..."). Appropriately to his calling, too, his vocabulary is uncolored by vivid elements, save conventional, abstract metaphors. Theophan has in common with characters such as "Der Reisende" elevated colloquial language. In *Der Freygeist*, this bland and rather stiff style is credibly linked with Theophan's characterization, and Theophan alone speaks it exclusively.

Adrast, on the other hand, speaks like a man of the world, and is much less in control of his emotions than is the clergyman. Adrast's language imparts much of his impatience and skepticism through his frequent use of interrogatives and exclamations ("Freundschaft gegen die ganze Welt? Was ist das?"; "O! daß Ihr Leute doch überall Widersprüche findet, außer nur da nicht, wo sie wirklich sind!"). This is especially true of the "O Geschwätze!" with which he responds to Theophan's long speech on friendship, and of his contemptuous "Das Pfaffengeschmeisse!" Adrast's passionate nature, and the violence of his dislike for Theophan are also betrayed by his addressing the absent cleric in the familiar second person singular in the monologue: "Hassen will ich dich, Theophan, und alle deines Ordens!" His individual sentences are, as a rule, much shorter than Theophan's and more subject to ellipsis, as the exclamatory examples just cited indicate. His vocabulary especially marks Adrast as having knowledge of a world of which Theophan is not directly aware. In mentioning that the most attractive masks usually hide the ugliest faces, Adrast says that this is "eine Karnevalserfahrung" and certainly such expressions as "Pfaffengeschmeisse" and "Schwarzröcke" must have been popular in the galant circles in which Adrast must be presumed to have squandered his fortune.

In addition, Adrast is also given to more graphic expression than is Theophan, and occasionally uses quite forceful images to reinforce his arguments. Here, he is expounding upon why religion, though not needed by educated men, is necessary for the common people.

Ihm [dem Pöbel] die Religion nehmen, heißt ein wildes Pferd auf der fetten Weide los binden, das, so bald es sich frey fühlt, lieber in unfruchtbaren Wäldern herumschweifen und Mangel leiden, als durch einen gemächlichen Dienst alles, was es braucht, erwerben will.   (*LM*, II, 99.19-22)

Despite his professed atheism and worldly ways, Adrast is still intended to be seen as a basically honorable man, made bitter by bad experiences with the clergy and by temporarily thwarted love. Accordingly, his speech is not permitted to sink below the level of the freer colloquial tone described above. Unlike Damis, the "junge Gelehrte", Adrast does not use oaths, except for one "Himmel", and the strongest pejoratives he uses are "Schurke" and "Dummkopf" in speaking to Johann. Thus, the contrasting characterizations of Theophan and Adrast are clearly expressed in their language as well. This represents a considerable refinement of technique as compared with *Damon*, for example, where both the honest Damon and the deceptive Leander spoke in almost the same way, the contrast in their characters being only very slightly reflected in their speech.

Henriette and Juliane, the prospective brides of Adrast and Theophan, are as opposed to each other in their characters as are their bridegrooms. As their father sees it:

Die Juliane ist eine geborne Priesterfrau; und Henriette — in ganz Deutschland muß kein Mädchen zu finden seyn, das sich für Ihn, Adrast, besser schickte. Hübsch, munter, fix; sie singt, sie tanzt, sie spielt; kurz, sie ist meine leibhafte Tochter. Juliane dargegen ist die liebe, heilige Einfalt.   (*LM*, II, 58.27-31)

To this description, Adrast, barely able to hide his true feelings for Juliane, adds:

Ihre Schönheit blendet nicht; aber sie geht ans Herz. Man läßt sich gern von ihren stillen Reizen fesseln, und man biegt sich mit Bedacht in ihr Joch, das uns andere in einer fröhlichen Unbesonnenheit überwerfen müssen. Sie redet wenig; aber auch ihr geringstes Wort hat Vernunft.   (*LM*, II, 58.33-59.3)

As with Adrast and Theophan, the diametric opposition between Henriette and Juliane is also clearly detectible in their language. The two sisters have just recruited Lisette as the judge to decide an argument which they have been having:

LISETTE. Ohne weitere Umstände; erzählen Sie mir nunmehr Ihre Streitigkeit. — Unterdessen lege ich mein Gesicht in richterliche Falten.

JULIANE. Streitigkeit? Eine wichtige Streitigkeit? Ihr seyd beide Schäkerinnen. — Ich will nichts mehr davon hören.

HENRIETTE. So? Du willst keinen Richter erkennen? Ein klarer Beweis, daß Du Unrecht hast. — Höre nur, Lisette! wir haben über unsre Anbeter gezankt. Ich will die Dinger immer noch so nennen, mag doch zuletzt daraus werden, was da will.

LISETTE. Das dachte ich. Ueber was könnten sich zwey gute Schwestern auch sonst zanken? Es ist freylich verdrießlich, wenn man sein künftiges Haupt verachten hört.

HENRIETTE. Schwude! Mädchen; du willst ganz auf die falsche Seite. Keine hat des andern Anbeter verachtet; sondern unser Zank kam daher, weil eine des andern Anbeter — schon wieder Anbeter! — allzu sehr erhob.

LISETTE. Eine neue Art Zanks! wahrhaftig, eine neue Art!

HENRIETTE. Kannst du es anders sagen, Juliane?

JULIANE. O! verschone mich doch damit.

HENRIETTE. Hoffe auf kein Verschonen, wenn du nicht wiederrufst. — Sage, Lisette, hast du unsre Männerchen schon einmal gegeneinander gehalten? Was dünkt dich? Juliane macht ihren armen Theophan herunter, als wenn er ein kleines Ungeheuer wäre.

JULIANE. Unartige Schwester! Wenn habe ich dieses gethan?

Mußt du aus einer flüchtigen Anmerkung, die du mir gar nicht hättest aufmutzen sollen, solche Folgen ziehen?
HENRIETTE. Ich seh, man muß dich böse machen, wenn du mit der Sprache heraus sollst. — Eine flüchtige Anmerkung nennst du es? Warum strittest du denn über ihre Gründlichkeit?
JULIANE. Du hast noch närrische Ausdrücke! Fiengst du nicht den ganzen Handel selbst an? Ich glaubte, wie sehr ich dir schmeicheln würde, wenn ich deinen Adrast den wohlgemachtesten Mann nennte, den ich jemals gesehen hätte. Du hättest für meine Gesinnungen danken, und nicht widersprechen sollen.

(*LM*, II, 66.1-33)

Henriette's gay, frivolous character is underlined in her speech by her reference to her and her sister's "Anbeter" as "Dinger" and "Männerchen". Her use of "Schwude",[21] a coachman's instruction to his horses to turn left, a specifically Upper Saxon dialect form, in order to bring Lisette upon the right path of thought, also betrays her lack of concern for appearances of gentility. Interrogative clauses are again used to establish a light and somewhat impertinent tone in Henriette's language. Juliane, the more serious and quiet of the two, shares none of these features. Although it is not marked by the same logical deliberateness and tendency to hypotaxis as that of Theophan, Juliane's language is very similar to it in tone. Her vocabulary is limited entirely to words befitting a young lady of her social class. As does Theophan, Juliane on occasion takes on a didactic, almost preaching tone with Adrast, which, however, does not contradict her characterization in the least. In the following speech, for example, Juliane is upbraiding Adrast for his contempt of religion and the women who believe in it:

Halten Sie, Adrast! Sie erweisen meinem Geschlechte eben so wenig Ehre, als der Religion. Jenes setzen Sie mit dem Pöbel in Eine Klasse, so fein auch Ihre Wendung war; und diese machen Sie aufs höchste zu einer Art von Schminke, die das Geräthe auf unsern Nachttischen vermehren kann. Nein, Adrast! die Religion ist eine Zierde für alle Menschen; und muß ihre wesentlichste

[21]   Adelung, *op. cit.*, IV, p. 375.

Zierde seyn. Ach! Sie verkennen sie aus Stolz; aber aus einem falschen Stolze. Was kann unsre Seele mit erhabenern Begriffen füllen, als die Religion? Und worinn kann die Schönheit der Seelen anders bestehen, als in solchen Begriffen? in würdigen Begriffen von Gott, von uns, von unsern Pflichten, von unserer Bestimmung? Was kann unser Herz, diesen Sammelplatz verderbter und unruhiger Leidenschaften, mehr reinigen, mehr beruhigen, als eben diese Religion? Was kann uns im Elende mehr aufrichten, als sie? Was kann uns zu wahrern Menschen, zu bessern Bürgern, zu aufrichtigern Freunden machen, als sie? ...

(*LM*, II, 99.28-100.8)

This speech is a little sermon. Juliane starts off with a double antithesis, contrasting her sex with the "Pöbel" and religion with "Schminke". She then develops the image of "Schminke, die das Geräthe auf unsern Nachttischen vermehren kann" into a denial of Adrast's premise, calling religion not only a cosmetic for women, but an essential ornament for all mankind. Accusing Adrast of misunderstanding religion because of his pride, Juliane goes on, in a series of rhetorical questions, to expand on the beauties of religion. Aiming at Adrast's strong ethical instincts, she demonstrates how religion can make men's lot better on earth, cleanse the soul, and contribute to the felicity of the society. Juliane's chain of reasoning here is strictly empirical and rationalistic. Her vocabulary, however, while not employing the abstract compounds associated with the language of Pietism, at times reveals traits hardly to be associated with the language of rationalistic speech. Such an idea as "unser Herz, dies[er] Schauplatz verderbter und unruhiger Leidenschaften", conveys a hint of the religious imagery of the Baroque. Yet, this element is linked with such terms as "Begriff", and "Klasse" in the sense of a philosophical category, terms which seem rather to belong again to the world of philosophic reasoning. In its logical structure and its mixture of philosophical and religious concepts, Juliane's language, at least in its didactic phase and function, has a great affinity with Theophan's.

The three comic figures, Lisidor, Johann and Martin show the features associated with Lessing's earliest techniques of characterization. Lisidor is described in Lessing's preliminary sketches for *Der Freygeist* as "ein alter reicher Kaufmann: ungewiß und schwankend in seinen Grundsätzen, jezt auf des Adrasts, jezt auf des Theophans Seite; beydes ohne zu wißen warum?"[22] His language is characterized by his misuse and mixing of metaphors, and the generally lower level of his vocabulary. He says to Adrast, for example, "Wenn ihr euch in den Haaren liegt, so fische ich im Trüben. Da fällt manche Brocke ab, die keiner von euch brauchen kann" (*LM*, II, 57.32-58.2). He refers frivolously to the philosophical rivals as "Ihr Herren Grillenfänger", and denies that he is a "Katzenkopf", a slang word synonymous with "Dummkopf".[23] Thus, even more than Wumshäter in *Der Misogyne*, Lisidor still bears many traces in common with characters from Lessing's earliest plays. While he is developing his stylistic techniques in the language of comedy, Lessing does not discard, but merely modifies the devices with which he began. They are no longer much in evidence, but useful on occasion, as the characterization of Lisidor shows.

This is also evident in the language of Johann and Martin, which is distinctly set apart from that of the other characters. Theirs constitutes once again the socially lowest level of language in the play. Here, Johann is scornfully telling Martin of his travels:

JOHANN. ... Du bist zu beklagen, armer Schelm!
MARTIN. Arm? Laß einmal sehen, wer die vergangene Woche das meiste Trinkgeld gekriegt hat. (Er greift in die Tasche.) Du bist ein lüderlicher Teufel, du versäufst alles —
JOHANN. Laß stecken. Ich rede von einer ganz andern Armuth, von der Armuth des Geistes, der sich mit lauter elenden Brocken des Aberglaubens ernähren, und mit lauter armseligen Lumpen der Dummheit kleiden muß. — Aber so geht es euch Leuten, die ihr nicht weiter, als höchstens vier Meilen hinter den Backofen kommt. Wenn du gereiset wärest, wie ich —
MARTIN. Gereist bist du? Laß hören, wo bist du gewesen?
JOHANN. Ich bin gewesen — in Frankreich —

---

[22]   *LM*, III, p. 262.4-6.
[23]   *LM*, II, p. 57.8; Adelung, *op cit.*, II, p. 1520.

MARTIN. In Frankreich? Mit deinem Herrn?

JOHANN. Ja, mein Herr war mit.

MARTIN. Das ist das Land, wo die Franzosen wohnen? — So wie ich einmal einen gesehen habe, — das war eine schnurrige Kröte! In einem Augenblicke konnte er sich siebenmal auf dem Absatze herum drehen, und dazu pfeifen.

JOHANN. Ja, es giebt große Geister unter ihnen! Ich bin da erst recht klug geworden.

MARTIN. Hast du denn auch Frankreichsch gelernt?

JOHANN. Französisch, willst du sagen: - vollkommen.

MARTIN. O! rede einmal!

JOHANN. Das will ich wohl thun, — Quelle heure est-il, maraut? Le pere et la mere une fille des coups de baton. Comment coquin? Diantre diable carogne à vous servir.

MARTIN. Das ist schnakisch! Und das Zeug können die Leute da verstehen? Sag einmal, was hieß das auf Deutsch?

JOHANN. Ja! auf Deutsch! Du guter Narre, das läßt sich auf Deutsch nicht so sagen. Solche feine Gedanken können nur französisch ausgedruckt werden. (*LM*, II, 74.33-75.29)

Compared to the servants in *Die Juden,* Johann and Martin are low comedy figures indeed. Martin's use of such dialect forms as "schnakisch" and "schnurrig"[24] marks his language as belonging to that of the lowest order of society, and his misnomer "Frankreichsch" defines the level of his education, as does his later question about "Engländsch". Johann's French gibberish speaks for itself. His German vocabulary is also that of the vulgar, with such items as "Maul" and "Ohrenbläser". The language of Johann and Martin, then, cleaves very much to the standard established by Lessing earlier, except that, by virtue of the subordination of these figures in the play's structure, it is not very much in evidence.

Of the comedies which Lessing wrote before *Minna von Barnhelm, Der Freygeist* represents his highest achievement. In its dramaturgic organization and subtly differentiated lan-

---

[24] "schnakisch ... welches ... nur in der vertraulichen Sprechart, besonders der Ober und Niedersachsens üblich ist, was Lachen erreget, spaßhaft, lustig." Adelung, *op. cit.*, IV, p. 229. "schnurrig ... welches für poßierlich, lächerlich, schnakisch, drollig, doch nur in der vertraulichen Sprechart, besonders Nieder-Deutschlandes, üblich ist." Adelung, *op. cit.*, IV, p. 229.

guage, it is the logical culmination of the three years of intensive preoccupation and practical experience with the comic
stage which lie between *Damon* and *Der Freygeist*. New possibilities for the comedy as a medium of personal conviction
rather than merely as a popular moral lesson, have been seen
and partially fulfilled by Lessing. The language of the comedies has changed with his use of the medium. It has become
more flexible and individualized. The early differences in
levels of colloquial language in the comedies, although still
present, are not as drastically defined as they were. The role
of vulgar humorous language has been much diminished, and
a new and expressive medium has been discovered in elevated
colloquial language, which is modulated from its formality
and syntactic rigidity and made to display individual traits
of style as the character being created might require. The
experience which Lessing gained in this time, the techniques
which he developed, are present, modified further to a remarkably small degree, throughout his remaining comic productions.

IV. *DER SCHATZ* AND THE COMIC FRAGMENTS
1749-1767

Der Freygeist represents the high-water mark of Lessing's desire to establish himself as "ein deutscher Molière". For fifteen years Lessing was not to produce a comedy to match *Der Freygeist* as a drama of opposed principles and as a subtly shaped portrayal of individualized characters simultaneously representing these principles. If *Der Freygeist* were Lessing's last comedy, its critical reputation might well be more lustrous than at present. Considering the state of the German theatre of the time, it surpasses in quality all contemporary plays and all that were to come for some time. But Lessing's production did not cease, although his immediate interest in the comedy as a creative form seems for some time to have been quiescent. The fragments on which Lessing worked between 1750 and 1767 dramaturgically give little promise of his potential to write *Minna von Barnhelm*, a play bearing many of the traits of its predecessors, but representing simultaneously a new standard towards which German writers might strive, which in most cases was never again achieved. If *Minna von Barnhelm* put Lessing's early plays in a shade, whence they are only rarely called forth, it banished its immediate predecessors, from whose lineage it had most definitely evolved, to an obscurity so complete that today their existence is barely remembered. The present chapter is to be occupied with the plays of this quiescent phase, which show the experimental aspect of Lessing's career as a writer of comedies both before and after the creation of *Minna von Barnhelm*.

During the period in question, bounded by Lessing's departure from Leipzig for his first sojourn in Berlin and the beginning of his engagement in Hamburg by the ill-fated "Nationaltheater", he became too much involved with the more theoretical aspects of the theatre and with other forms of dramatic production, notably the "bürgerliches Trauerspiel", and with the problems of art theory for comedy to retain the central position in his interests which it had assumed earlier. Comedy had to some extent become a medium for Lessing's personal ideas, the vehicle in which he sent them out into the world. But just as Lessing, the writer of satirical poems and fables had made way for the writer of comedies, so the latter had to make way for the tragedian, and finally for the writer in aesthetics, art history, and religion. Undoubtedly the dramatist was alive in Lessing throughout his life, but appeared at each phase motivated by different considerations. Comedy became the object of experimentation and theoretical speculation rather than a meaningful personal medium for Lessing in this period. Consequently, with the exceptions of *Der Schatz* and *Minna von Barnhelm*, all of Lessing's comic efforts between 1749 and 1767 remained in the form of outlines or, at best, fragments. Except for *Palaion*, a consummately mediocre fragment in French, *Vor diesen!*, the German translation of this fragment, and the late *Der Schlaftrunk*, all of the fragments to be discussed are borrowed from single sources, and display little of the eclectic interweaving of various plot elements found in the comedies before 1750. All indicate more interest in form than in content, and in all, excluding *Der Schatz*, increasing attention is paid the individualization of character depiction by stylistic means. *Der Schatz* and *Weiber sind Weiber* are directly derived from plays of Plautus; the extant scenes of *Die glückliche Erbin* are, for the most part, little more than translations or rearrangements of scenes from Goldoni's *L'Erede fortunata*. *Die Matrone von Ephesus* is, of course, based on the famous tale interpolated into the *Satyricon* of Petronius, but recast entirely by Lessing, indicating a possible new direction in his career as a writer of comedies after *Minna von Barnhelm*. In the following sections, it will be necessary to explore the origins and contents of each of the fragments in order to bring into proper perspective the stylistic features of each.

PLAUTINE PLAYS

Die Gefangenen

Lessing's acquaintance with the drama of antiquity and especially with the Roman comedy well antedates his acquaintance with the Franco-German regular comedy he encountered in Leipzig. He had studied the comedies of Terence and Plautus intensively at St. Afra in Meissen, where they had been his whole world, "Schon in Jahren, da ich die Menschen nur aus Büchern kannte – beneidenswürdig ist der, der sie niemals näher kennen lernt!"[1] Plautus in particular exerted a strong indirect influence on Lessing's earliest comedies. Anton in *Der junge Gelehrte*, for example, is far more reminiscent of the sly slaves of the Roman comedy than of the Pasquins or Arlecchinos who were the servants of the *théâtre italien*. It cannot be said with certainty, however, to what extent Lessing was directly influenced by Plautus in his earliest comedies and to what extent seeming affinities result from Plautine influences on the comic theatre of the time in general, for the Roman comedies were known, admired, and copied in all of Europe at the time. It is not surprising then, that Plautus should eventually exert a more direct and definite influence on Lessing. Plautus was the first author to be treated in the *Beyträge zur Historie und Aufnahme des Theaters*, a series which Lessing and his cousin, Christlob Mylius, planned for the improvement and diversification of the German theatrical repertory. In the first part, which appeared in 1750, Lessing presented a vindicating biography of Plautus with an inventory of his works and the editions available at the time. In the second part of the *Beyträge*, Lessing published his trans-

---

[1] *LM*, V, p. 268.

lation of Plautus' *Captivi*, which he called "das vortrefflichste Stück ... welches jemals auf den Schauplatz gekommen ist."[2] Lessing claims this distinction for the play because it comes closest to fulfilling the function of comedy, to educate and improve the spectators, and is amply provided with the necessary artistic attributes, even though it does not adhere absolutely to Gottsched's rigid neoclassical rules.[3] At about the same time Lessing was working on a very free adaptation of Plautus' *Stichus*, which he entitled *Weiber sind Weiber*, and on a re-casting of *Trinummus*, *Der Schatz*.

For purposes of comparison with the language of the adaptations just mentioned, it seems germane to the question of Plautus' influence on Lessing's language to examine briefly Lessing's style in translating the *Captivi* into *Die Gefangenen*. The plot of the play is perhaps most concisely given by Plautus himself, as was his habit, in an anacrostic "argumentum" preceding the play. The translation follows:

One of Hegio's sons has been taken prisoner in a battle with the Eleans; the other was stolen by a runaway slave and sold when he was four years old. The father, in his great anxiety to recover the captured boy, bought up Elean prisoners of war; and among those that he had purchased was the son he had lost many years before. This son, having exchanged clothes and names with his Elean master, secured the latter's release, taking the consequences himself. This master of his returned, bringing Hegio's captive son, and along with him that runaway slave, whose disclosures led to the recognition of the other son.[4]

In his introduction to *Die Gefangenen*, Lessing says of the translation: "Ich habe mich bestrebt [die Übersetzung] so einzurichten, daß sich Plautus darinnen ähnlich bleiben möge. Ich habe getreu übersetzt, wo es möglich gewesen ist; ich bin von dem Originale abgegangen, wo es der natürliche oder komische Ausdruck der Gedanken, oder unübersetzliche Wort-

---

[2]   *LM*, IV, p. 79.
[3]   *LM*, IV, p. 191.
[4]   *Plautus*, with an English translation by Paul Nixon, 5 vols. (London-Cambridge, Mass., 1928), I, p. 461.

spiele nothwendig erfoderten."[5] He went on to say that he had tried to translate the puns with similar German ones or to demonstrate the untranslatable ones in footnotes. Thus, although philological accuracy was an aim, it was not to stand in the way of a lively translation and one understandable and enjoyable for German readers. That this is no simple task in the case of Plautus may be seen from the following juxtaposition of a short scene from the Latin original and the same scene in a consciously artless and literal English translation. In this scene, Hegio, having just given instructions for the care of the prisoners he has bought, is accosted by the parasite, Ergasilus, who is anxious that his favorite patron, Hegio's son, should return safe and sound:

ERG. Tum denique homines nostra intellegimus bona, quem quae in potestate habuimus, ea amisimus, ego, postquam gnatus tuos potitust hostium, expertus quanti fuerit nunc desidero.
HEGIO Alienus cum eius incommodum tam aegre feras, quid me patrem par facerest, cui ille est unicus?
ERG. Alienus ego? alienus illi? aha, Hegio, numquam istuc dixis neque animum induxis tuom; tibi ille unicust, mi etiam unico magis unicus.
HEGIO Laudo, malum cum amici tuom ducis malum. nunc habe bonum animum.
ERG. Eheu, huic illud dolet, quia nunc remissus est edendi exercitus.
HEGIO Nullumne interea nactu's, qui posset tibi remissum quem dixti imperare exercitum?
ERG. Quid credis? fugitant omnes hanc provinciam, quoi optigerat postquam captust Philopolemus tuos.
HEGIO Non pol mirandum est fugitare hanc provinciam. multis et multigeneribus opus est tibi militibus: primumdum opus est Pistorensibus: eorum sunt aliquot genera Pistorensium: opus Paniceis est, opus Placentinis quoque; opus Turdetanis, opust Ficedulensibus; iam maritumi omnes milites opus sunt tibi.
ERG. Ut saepe summa ingenia in occulto latent; hic qualis imperator nunc privatus est.[6]

[5] *LM*, IV, p. 194.25-28; p. 83.24-26.
[6] Plautus, *ed. cit.*, I, pp. 474-76.

ERG. Then at last do we men know our blessings, when we have lost those things which we once had in our power. I, since your son fell into the power of the enemy, knowing by experience of what value he was, now feel his loss.

HEGIO. Since you, who are no relation, bear his misfortune so much amiss, what is it likely that I, a father, should do, whose only son he is?

ERG. I, no relation to him? He, no relation to me? Oh, Hegio! Never do say that, or come to such a belief. To you he is an only child, but to me, he is even more only than an only one.

HEGIO. I commend you, in that you consider the affliction of your friend your own affliction. Now be of good heart.

ERG. Oh, dear! oh, dear! here's (rubbing his stomach) where it hurts: my whole comissary department has been disbanded now, you see.

HEGIO. Meanwhile, have you found no one to command for you the [department] you say is disbanded. [7]

ERG. What do you think? All to whom it used to fall are in the habit of declining that province since your son Philopolemus was taken prisoner.

HEGIO. I' faith, 'tisn't to be wondered at, that they're in the habit of declining that province. You have necessity for numerous troops, and those of numerous kinds. Well, first you have need of the Bakerians. Of these Bakerians, there are several kinds. You have need of Rollmakerians, you have need too of Confectionerians, you have need of Poultererians, you have need of Beccaficorians; besides, all the maritime forces are necessary for you.

ERG. How the greatest geniuses do frequently lie concealed! How great a general now is this private individual! [8]

As Lessing saw and stated, the main problem in translating Plautus, once the impossibility of retaining his metre is accepted, is a retention of the flavor of his style, especially some sense of the frequent doubleness of meaning of his words, his frequent use of puns. In Hegio's last speech, above, a particularly volatile battery of puns presents itself, linking the names of various Italian cities of Plautus' time with those of various

[7]   Plautus, *ed. cit.*, I, p. 475. Used as translation for this speech only, since the Riley translation, preferred here for its greater literalness, did not correspond well to Lessing's translation at this point.

[8]   Plautus, *The Comedies of Plautus*, translated by Henry Thomas Riley, 2 vols. (London, 1889), I, pp. 432-33.

kinds of cooks and bakers.[9] A literal rendering of this speech is impossible without losing the doubleness of meaning. Lessing chooses to sacrifice the aspect of the place-names, and all in all, it is probably the best choice:

ERGASILUS. So gehts. Wir Menschen erkennen unser Glück nicht eher, als bis wir es wiederum verlieren. Seit dem dein Sohn ist gefangen worden, seit dem habe ich erst eingesehen, wie hoch ich ihn zu schätzen habe. Ach wie sehne ich mich nach ihm!

HEGIO. Da einem Fremden sein Unglück so nahe geht, wie soll es mich nicht schmerzen, da er mein einziger Sohn ist?

ERGASILUS. Ich ein Fremder? Dein Sohn mir ein Fremder? O Hegio, sage dieses nicht; glaub es nicht. Er ist dein einziger Sohn, aber mir — mir ist er noch viel einziger.

HEGIO. Ich lobe dich, daß dich deines Freundes Ungemach wie das deine schmerzt. Doch sey nur gutes Muths.

ERGASILUS. Ach!

HEGIO. Der gute Schelm ist ganz betrübt, weil die Schmausereyen nunmehr abgedankt sind. Hast du denn aber niemanden gefunden, der unterdessen diese abgedankten Schmausereyen in seinen Sold nehmen und commandiren will?

ERGASILUS. Du glaubst es wohl; aber nein. Nachdem dein Sohn Philopolemus ist gefangen worden, bedankt sich jedermann für dergleichen Commando.

HEGIO. Es wundert mich auch eben nicht, daß sie sich dafür bedanken. Man hat gar zu viel und gar zu vielerley Soldaten dazu nöthig. Da sind erstlich Beckersoldaten. Und von diesen Beckersoldaten giebts wieder unterschiedne Arten. Man braucht Brodsoldaten; man braucht Kuchensoldaten. Hernach kommen die Ziemersoldaten, die Schnepfensoldaten. Und was hat man nicht endlich für eine Menge Fischsoldaten nöthig?

ERGASILUS. Wie doch manchmal die größten Köpfe im Ver-

---

[9] In explaining this speech, Riley says, "In the word 'Pistorienses' [Plautus] alludes to the bakers and the natives of Pistorium, a town of Etruria; in the 'Panicei', to the bread or roll bakers, and the natives of Pana, a little town of the Samnites, mentioned by Strabo; in the 'Placentini', to the 'confectioners' or 'cake-makers', and the people of Placentia, a region in the north of Italy; in the 'Turdetani', to the 'poulterers' or 'sellers of thrushes', and the people of Turdetania, a district of Spain; and in the 'Ficedulae', to the 'sellers of beccaficos', a delicate bird, and to the inhabitants of Ficedulae, a town near Rome. Of course these appellations, as relating to the trades, are only comical words coined for the occasion." Plautus, Riley edn., I, pp. 432-33.

borgnen bleiben! Was solltest du nicht für ein General seyn, und mußt doch als eine Privatperson leben?   (*LM*, IV, 90.16-91.8)

In his desire to be true to the Roman comedian, Lessing has completely subordinated his own style to that of Plautus. He renders the Latin into lively and readable German, avoiding the pitfalls presented by the puns better than do some later translators. Although, as K. R. Bergethon demonstrates,[10] *Die Gefangenen* belongs to the period in which Lessing favored strict translation, as literal as possible, he was aware that absolutely complete transfer from one language to the other was not feasible if the translation was to be clearly understandable and enjoyable. Aside from limiting the effects of the puns on the food-soldiers, Lessing chose to render "exercitus" in the original version with "Schmausereyen" for the sake of clarity, and to add Hegio's reference to Ergasilus as a "Schelm" in order to make his cry of pain more comprehensible. There are no attempts made, however, to bring the play up to date through local references, as Plautus had done in transferring the play from the Greek original. There are no additions of oaths or interjections or other features of style typical of Lessing to season the dialogue further. The speech is plain and, for all of its joy in double meanings, clear, remaining colloquial, as did the language of the Roman original. Lessing's style, even when he is most strongly obligated to Plautus, is still essentially that of his language in the comedies already examined, although, through his desire to be faithful to the original, many of the techniques which might have been used to enliven the dialogue are missing.

Weiber sind Weiber

How differently Lessing worked when he had a free hand in adapting Plautus may be seen in *Weiber sind Weiber*, an adaptation of *Stichus*. Lessing's outline for the plot of the play

---

[10]   Kaare Roald Bergethon, "Lessing's Theory of Translation". unpublished diss., Ithaca, N.Y. (1940), p. 20.

has been lost, and only a completed first act and the first scene of a second act are extant. According to Reinhardstoettner,[11] there had been no adaptations of *Stichus* before Lessing's time, making it clear that he worked directly from the original. Influences of previous adaptors of Plautine comedies upon the author shall be more of a problem in the discussion of *Der Schatz*.

Plautus's *Stichus* is little more than a farce. What serious content there is centers around the return of two brothers, who, after an absence of three years to recoup in trade their losses in carousing, come back to their wives. The wives, who are sisters, have resisted their father' efforts to make them give up hope for their husbands and remarry. Upon their return, the brothers, now wealthy, refuse to associate with the traditional parasite, Gelasimus, who brought about their bankruptcy in the first place and now wishes to prey upon them again. The major part of the play is taken up with monologues by Gelasimus on his insatiable hunger, by comical quarrels between Gelasimus and the servants of the sisters, and finally by an orgiastic drinking and dancing scene at the celebration of their homecoming by the slaves of the two brothers, Stichus and Sangarinus. The plot as such is little more than an excuse for a good carouse, and the play ends with an exhortation "ad spectatores" to go home and have a party of their own.

From what Lessing completed of *Weiber sind Weiber*, it is clear that he intended to emphasize whatever serious plot elements Plautus had provided, bringing the tone of the play away from the "Possenspiel" and closer to that of the "wahre Komödie", retaining many of the standard features of the Saxon comedy of character to provide humor. Apparently Plautus's *Stichus* was merely to provide the skeleton for the plot of a very different kind of play, a comedy of manners similar to *Die alte Jungfer*. In *Weiber sind Weiber*, Laura and Hilaria, two sisters, have for three years heard nothing from their hus-

[11] Kurt von Reinhardstoettner, *Plautus: spätere Bearbeitungen plautinischer Lustspiele* (Leipzig, 1886), pp. 742-45.

bands, who left them after having squandered their fortunes. Both their father, Herr Seltenarm, and Lisette urge them to forget the absent men. Hilaria, whose husband had devoted his riches to her enjoyment alone, is perfectly willing to have her marriage dissolved, if only she can have some proof of his death or infidelity. Laura, on the other hand, who had been treated badly by her husband, insists on remaining loyal to him. Thus, as in *Der Freygeist*, two opposing types of women are again stylized. Neither of the sisters is very keen on the suitors their father has found for them. These are Herr Wohlklang, a music teacher, who gives Seltenarm singing lessons, and Capitän von Segarin, a latter-day "miles gloriosus", who regales the old man with tales of his purported military exploits. Seltenarm wishes to marry his daughters off again so that he can more freely pursue Lisette. Presumably, to reconstruct briefly Lessing's further intentions for the plot, the two "Weiber" would agree to marry their suitors, Hilaria gladly, Laura reluctantly, both convinced by an impostor of the disloyalty of their husbands, who would probably appear in disguise in the third act, and reveal their identities after much comic by-play in the fifth, just in the nick of time to prevent the remarriage of their wives and assure the necessary happy ending.

The dialogue of *Weiber sind Weiber* is similar to that of Lessing's other plays of this period. Characterization, however, is by no means as subtle, and personages seem reduced to two-dimensional types, rather than resembling the somewhat more humanly individualized ones which Lessing had lately succeeded in creating. Lisette is the typical chaffering maid, Hilaria the flighty wife, Laura the faithful one, their father a mean and lecherous old man, and the musician and soldier completely defined by their professions.

Wohlklang and Segarin are stylistically characterized through their use of figures of speech from their professions. Thus, for example, Wohlklang will say:

Nun, mein Herr, werden die Entschlüßungen Ihrer Frau Tochter bald mit unsern Absichten harmoniren? Wie lange soll noch diese,

mir so widrige, Dißonanz anhalten? Wann wir Virtuosen uns
sonst einer Dißonanz bedienen, so geschieht es aus keiner andern
Absicht, als die übereinstimmenden Töne beßer ins Gehör fallen
zu laßen. Aber diese übereinstimmenden Töne, wann werden sie
mich einmal ergötzen?   (*LM*, III, 288.35-289.5)

Not to be outdone in the flaunting of his trade, Capitän von
Segarin says:

Wann ich Bergen op Zoom belagert hätte, so würde ich nicht so
lange haben darvor liegen müßen. Und eine Frau soll mich so
lange aufhalten? Wenn es noch eine Jungfer wäre. Und auch bey
der würde eine monatliche Belagerung schon ziemlich romanen-
hafft seyn. Ich muß also einen Sturm wagen, einen Generalsturm.
Du indeßen, Lisette, sollst versuchen ob du sie zur Capitulation
bewegen kanst.   (*LM*, III, 293.21-26)

Possibly because Lessing never revised this play for the stage
or for publication, Herr Seltenarm surpasses any of the old
men encountered in earlier comedies in sheer crassness and
questionable taste in his speech. In this passage, the old man
is making amorous overtures to Lisette:

SELTENARM. ... Aber Lisette, laß uns doch auch von unsrer Sache
etwas reden.
    LISETTE. Was ist das vor eine Sache?
    SELTENARM. Je, unsre Sache —
    LISETTE. Ich weiß nicht was Sie wollen.
    SELTENARM. Je Närrchen —
    LISETTE. Ha! ha! Aus dem Närrchen merke ich bald was es
seyn soll. Nein, damit schweigen Sie nur vor jezo stille —
    SELTENARM. Aber bist du nicht ein dummes Thier? —
    LISETTE. Das sind allerliebste Carreßen —
    SELTENARM. Alberne Hure, ich meyne es ja nicht so arg —
    LISETTE. O, immer beßer und beßer.
    SELTENARM. Nu, das ist wahr. Dümmer, alberner, und när-
rischer kan wohl auf der Gotteswelt kein Mädel seyn, als du bist.
Du siehst ja, daß alles zu deinem Besten seyn soll. Ich bin dem
Aase so gut, und gleichwohl —
    LISETTE. Und gleichwohl nennen Sie mich ein Aas.
    SELTENARM. Je, soll denn alles bey dir complimentirt seyn. Ich
rede wie mirs ins Maul kömmt. Die Complimente, der hunds-
füttsche Quark —

LISETTE. Kömmt Ihnen der auch ins Maul?

(*LM*, III, 287.14-33)

The relative simplicity and mechanical use of these character-izing devices is strongly reminiscent of *Der junge Gelehrte*, where Damis is constantly speaking in the terms of his vocation, though in a more credible way. This reversion to an earlier mode of characterization may have been brought about by Lessing's intensive study of Plautus at this time, and might be seen as an attempt to transfer into German the characteristics of Plautus' use of words, where a secondary meaning so fre-quently lurks behind the primary one. This may be seen in the examples of Wohlklang's and Segarin's speech quoted above. The transfer of "harmoniren" and "Dißonanz", "be-lagern" and "Generalsturm", for example, from their musical or military contexts to the field of love and courtship is a typical Plautine device, analogous to the puns made in *Captivi* on place names and various kinds of cooks. This sort of punning appears in Lessing's comedies in such concentration only during this period of interest in Plautus. The character of Seltenarm partakes very much of that of Antipho, his counterpart in *Stichus,* and he rants far more violently and vilely than do any of his contemporaries in Lessing's creative chronology, such as Lisidor or Wumshäter. Lessing was evidently trying to create here a colorful and vivid portrayal of the type of the lecherous old man, and perhaps the fact that the play was never completed indicates that Lessing could not draw this character without violating good taste more than the strictures of the regular theatre and his own sound judgment would allow.

The means used by Lessing to characterize the two sisters, Hilaria and Laura, resemble those used in depicting Henriette and Juliane in *Der Freygeist*. In the opening scene of *Stichus*, a similar contrast is made between the two sisters, but it is not as sharply drawn as in Lessing's version. A brief sample of the dialogue between Hilaria and Laura may suffice to display the differences between them as they are indicated in their language. The frivolous sister, Hilaria, is considering the

question of their suitors, and the apparently virtuous Laura
rebukes her:

HILARIA. Das ist es eben, was mir noch einigen Verdruß machen
könnte, wenn ich nur im geringsten darzu aufgelegt wäre. Ein
Frauenzimmer wie ich nur einen Freyer zu haben? Das kränkt;
das ist unerträglich. Und wo sich nicht bald wieder neue bey mir
melden, Schwester, Schwester, so wirst du deinen Herrn Wohlklang am längsten gehabt haben. Glaubst du nicht, daß ich reitzend
genug bin ihn dir abspänstig zu machen?
LAURA. O Hilaria, was verräthst du vor ein niederträchtiges
Gemüth! Ist das die Treue, die du deinem Manne an dem heiligen
Altare geschworen? Überlegst du denn gar nicht was die Welt von
dir sagen wird?
HILARIA. O, ich sage von der Welt was ich will, und die Welt
hat eben das Recht über mich.   (*LM*, III, 283.16-27)

Like Henriette in *Der Freygeist*, Hilaria speaks in a foolishly
saucy way. Not only is she ungrateful and hard-hearted
towards her absent husband; she is also vain and rapacious.
The impression of her flightiness and vanity is reinforced by
the way in which Hilaria expresses herself, quite aside from
the candid cattiness of the content of her speech. In comparison to her sister she is forceful in her style, which is frequently
elliptical, as in "Ein Frauenzimmer wie ich nur einen Freyer
zu haben?", or given to overstatement, "Das kränkt; das ist unerträglich." The teasingly threatening repetition, "Schwester,
Schwester" is also clearly intended to underline her ex-
citable temperament.

If Hilaria is a more malicious Henriette, her sister is a less
virtuous Juliane. Laura is made to mouth pious words about
fidelity and the holy altar, but betrays herself more than once
by seeming more concerned about what the world will say
about her than about the true nature of her loyalty to her
husband, which is as shaky as her sister's fidelity. Laura's
language, lacking those emphatic stylistic features which
enliven Hilaria's, has a hollow rhetorical quality.

Weiber sind Weiber shows signs of Lessing's attempt to adapt
the pungency of Plautine dialogue to his own uses. Given the
overdrawn and superficial characterizations which emerge

from the stylistic extravagances involved, only a comedy of manners, none of whose figures are to be taken seriously, can result. This form of comedy no longer held Lessing's interest. Small wonder and less loss, considering Lessing's ultimate progress in the poetics of drama and towards his ideal of true comedy, that this feeble farce should remain uncompleted.

Der Schatz

The only Plautine play which Lessing completed was *Der Schatz*, written in 1750. Evidently he was quite pleased with this adaptation, for it was published in the *Schriften* in 1755 and again in his collection of *Lustspiele* in 1767. In the inventory of Plautus' works appended to the biography, Lessing called *Trinummus*, the source for *Der Schatz*, "Nach den 'Gefangenen' des Plautus ... sein vortrefflichstes Stück."[12] Lessing was drawn to this comedy by the same elements which made *Captivi* so attractive; it is a comedy of friendship tried and triumphant, of prodigality punished, regretted, and forgiven, a situation comedy which, for all of its elements of humor and intrigue, has genuinely moving moments.

Trinummus is essentially a comedy of situation, whose plot is most strongly affected by the operation of coincidence on a given situation, only secondarily by intrigue, and only in a tertiary sense by character. Hence it was not so important for Lessing to concentrate on building up the individual characters in their relations to each other in his adaptation. The characters in *Der Schatz* are still very much the same types which Lessing found in *Trinummus*; the three old men, benevolent, stingy, or fatherly, the young wastrel, the rascally servant, the naive young lover. Lessing's main dramaturgic aim in constructing *Der Schatz* seems to have been to keep the play moving briskly from one scene to the next, through skillful use of various devices of pacing to establish an internal dynamism in this comedy and keep the very contrived plot alive and interesting to the audience. Dramaturgic considerations were

[12]   *LM*, IV, p. 81.

surely of greatest importance, for here Lessing produced the most tightly organized of his early comedies, already showing the strict sense for efficient structure which was later to reveal itself so impressively and variously in *Minna von Barnhelm* and *Emilia Galotti*. Not only has the plot of *Trinummus* been re-modelled to suit Lessing's purposes, but individual scenes are constructed with a sense of comic pacing which, if present at all in the earlier comedies, was not nearly as strongly in evidence. In *Der Schatz*, the larger units of dramaturgic organization, the scenes and their function in furthering the plot, are the main objects of the playwright's concentration. As an apparent result, the language of the individual roles is not strikingly demonstrative of differentiating features.

For a more convenient comparison of the structure of *Trinummus* with that of *Der Schatz*, the plots of both plays will be presented in the form of scene synopses, beginning with *Trinummus*.

Act I, Scene 1: Megaronides, an old gentleman, deplores the necessity of castigating his old friend, Callicles, but reasons that it is necessary if the city's already lax moral standards are to be upheld in any way.

Act I, Scene 2: Megaronides reproaches Callicles with dishonesty for having bought the house of their absent friend, Charmides, who had entrusted Callicles with the welfare of his son and daughter while he was away. Callicles defends himself by telling Megaronides the secret of the treasure which Charmides had hidden in the house to be used as a dowry for his daughter. Lesbonicus, Charmides' wastrel son, had offered the house for sale, and Callicles had bought it to preserve his friend's treasure for him.

Act II, Scene 1: Young Lysiteles weighs the disadvantages of lust and luxury with the advantages of devotion to right living.

Act II, Scene 2: Lysiteles asks his father, Philto, to let him marry the sister of Lesbonicus without asking a dowry in order to relieve Lesbonicus in his poverty. Philto agrees to go and arrange the marriage.

Act II, Scene 3: Philto monologizes briefly that parents should consider their children's wishes when handling their affairs and not act selfishly.

Act II, Scene 4: Lesbonicus and his slave, Stasimus, find that they have wasted almost all the money received from Callicles.

Philto enters and proposes that Lesbonicus' sister marry his son. Lesbonicus refuses, as he has no dowry to offer. Although Philto insists he desires none, the proud Lesbonicus offers him a farm, all that he has left. Philto seeming ready to accept out of politeness, Stasimus tells him of the calamitous condition of the farm and warns him not to take it. Philto wrests Lesbonicus' agreement to the marriage from him, leaving the matter of the dowry in abeyance.

Act III, Scene 1: Upon hearing of the betrothal from Stasimus, Callicles rushes to consult with Megaronides.

Act III, Scene 2: Lysiteles and Lesbonicus quarrel over the dowry which Lysiteles refuses to accept.

Act III, Scene 3: Megaronides and Callicles find a way to pay the dowry without arousing Lesbonicus' greed. A swindler (Sycophanta) hired by them is to go to Lesbonicus with the money and letters purportedly from his absent father.

Act IV, Scene 1: Charmides returns from abroad unbeknownst to all.

Act IV, Scene 2: The swindler asks Charmides the whereabouts of his own family and explains his mission. Charmides offers to complete in person the errand which he had supposedly entrusted to his "friend". The swindler, thinking that he is confronted with an even greater fraud, flees.

Act IV, Scene 3: Stasimus tells Charmides of the sale of the house. Just as the old man is bewailing the loss of his treasure,

Act IV, Scene 4: Callicles enters and begins to explain matters.

Act V, Scene 1: Lysiteles, exulting, enters and

Act V, Scene 2: introduces himself to Charmides, who is mollified by the explanations of what has occurred. Lesbonicus is forgiven by his father. Lysiteles shall marry the sister the next day and Lesbonicus the daughter of Callicles on the day after.

In terms of its fidelity to its Roman model, *Der Schatz* can be regarded as a mean between the extremes of the very faithful translation which Lessing gave *Captivi*, on the one hand, and the radically divergent adaptation of *Stichus* on the other. Many scenes in *Der Schatz* are little more than slightly paraphrased translations of the Plautine originals. Some of Plautus' names are retained, and other character names are taken from the common stock of European comedy. Thus, in *Der Schatz*, Plautus' Megaronides and Philto are merged in Staleno, who is the guardian of Leander (Lysiteles), who wants to marry Kamilla (the sister not named by Plautus). Lesbonicus has become Lelio and Callicles Philto. The Italian element is represented by Anselmo, the former Charmides, and Maskarill, a more high-handed, witty, and wicked mutation of Stasimus.

In his treatment of Plautus' plot, Lessing was more conservative than either of his predecessors in adapting *Trinummus* had been. In the sixteenth century, the prolific Italian writer of comedies, Gian Maria Cecchi (1518-1587), had written *La Dote* (The Dowry), which was mainly based on *Trinummus*. Aside from transforming the Latin names into contemporary Italian ones, Cecchi added a father who was not, like Plautus' Philto, willing to let his son marry without a dowry. This last is a change clearly taken over from Cecchi by Lessing. It is unlikely that he ever read Cecchi's play, but an outline of the plot was available to him in Riccoboni's *Théâtre Italien*, which had appeared in Paris in two parts in 1727 and 1731, and which was among the pieces published by Lessing in his *Theatralische Bibliothek* in 1754, thus very likely known to him in 1750. Lessing could not have known Destouches' *Le Trésor Caché* at the time, however. This play had been written in 1745, but performed only once. It was not published until 1758, after Destouches' death, as Lessing himself mentions in the *Hamburgische Dramaturgie*.[13]

In the same article, Lessing says of *Der Schatz* that it is an imitation of the Plautine *Trinummus* in which the author had tried to concentrate all of the comic scenes of the original into one act.[14] As has been indicated in the synopsis, the original play is divided into five acts, as are the adaptations of Cecchi and Destouches. But Plautus had not indicated a new scene each time one of the characters made an entrance or an exit, or at best he followed this convention, so strictly observed in the eighteenth century, only inconsistently. If one were to divide the five-act, fourteen-scene *Trinummus* according to the more rigorous usage of Lessing's time, it would have twenty-two scenes. How Lessing succeeded in concentrating these

13 *LM*, X, p. 222.
14 *LM*, X, p. 221.

into an eighteen-scene, one-act play may be seen from the following synopsis of *Der Schatz*. The functionally equivalent scenes of *Trinummus* are indicated in parentheses following the scene numbers.

Scene 1 (II, 2): Leander asks his guardian, Staleno, for permission to marry Kamilla, the sister of Lelio, despite the fact that she has no dowry. Staleno objects strongly, but promises to consider the matter.

Scene 2 (I, 1): Staleno determines to tell his old friend, Philto, the guardian of Lelio and Kamilla, what he thinks of him.

Scene 3 (I, 2; II, 4; III, 1; III, 3): Staleno first reproaches Philto for having bought the house from Lelio, but when he learns the reason, repents of his lack of trust. Then, having determined that there can be a dowry for his ward after all, Staleno proposes that Leander marry Kamilla. Philto agrees, and the two friends decide, as in *Trinummus*, to hire a swindler to bring the money.

Scene 4 (II, 4): Lelio and Maskarill try to account for the money which they have spent from the proceeds of the sale of the house, which have all but disappeared. Like Plautus, Lessing makes no scene division when Philto enters and tells Lelio that he has received an offer of marriage for Kamilla, but that it cannot be arranged for lack of a dowry. Lelio is overcome with remorse.

Scene 5 (no counterpart in *Trinummus*): Lelio unsuccessfully tries to borrow money for his sister's dowry from Maskarill.

Scene 6 (II, 4): Lelio offers Staleno the farm as a dowry for Kamilla. Staleno makes a show of accepting it, and Lelio goes off to have an inventory and transfer papers for the farm drawn up.

Scene 7 (II, 4): Like Stasimus, Maskarill wants to save the farm for his master and himself, and describes the horrors which have taken place on the farm. Merely to torment Maskarill, Staleno thanks Maskarill for his good advice, saying he will tell his ward to sell the farm again as soon as possible.

Scene 8 (no counterpart in *Trinummus*): Maskarill, in a transitional monologue, expresses his indifference to the fate of his master, for Maskarill has his fortune secure. He informs the audience of the approach of a traveler, to whom he will speak out of curiosity.

Scene 9 (IV, 5): The traveler is Anselmo, returned after an absence of nine years.

Scene 10 (no counterpart in *Trinummus*): Anselmo, waiting for Maskarill to return with Lelio, begins to count up his profits on his trip.

Scene 11 (IV, 2): This scene, between Anselmo and a rascally town-crier, Raps, is virtually a verbatim translation of the scene between Charmides and the swindler.

Scene 12 (IV, 3): A porter tells Anselmo the truth about his family, and just as Anselmo is about to despair of his affairs,

Scene 13 (IV, 4): Philto enters and welcomes him, saying that he will explain everything within the house. Together they carry in Anselmo's trunk, leaving the stage clear for

Scene 14 (no counterpart in *Trinummus*): Lelio, who fears his father's wrath, is reassured by Maskarill, who promises that he will arrange matters.

Scene 15 (IV, 4; V, 1: V, 2): Anselmo expresses his approval of Philto's stewardship.

Scene 16 (no counterpart in *Trinummus*): Staleno enters, and it is found that Leander is the son of a merchant, Pandolfo, now dead, to whom Anselmo had promised that Kamilla should marry his son.

Scene 17 (no counterpart in *Trinummus*): Through a series of artfully delivered build-ups and anticlimaxes, Maskarill makes Anselmo fear that harm has befallen Lelio, thus softening him up for

Scene 18 (No counterpart in *Trinummus*): in which Lelio falls to the feet of his father, who forgives him, bringing the play to a happy conclusion.

Lessing has succeeded in concentrating the comic scenes of the original and in strengthening them with elements of his own invention. *Der Schatz* is a highly selective adaptation, intended for a maximum comic effect. It is meant to be rapidly paced, and Lessing omitted all plot elements which could slow the progress of the play. The merging of Philto and Megaronides into one character, Staleno, which enables him, in Scene 3, to combine four important scenes, is a significant move in this direction. There is very little dialogue which does not contribute directly to the progress of the plot or to the humorous effect of the play. Most of Plautus' trenchant but lengthy passages deprecating the low moral standards of the society of his time and denouncing voluptuousness have been omitted. Thus, Megaronides' monologue (I, 1) has been shortened to only the most essential statement by Staleno in Scene 2. Most symptomatic is the handling of the character of Lysiteles. In *Trinummus*, Lysiteles is the model of the virtuous young man, and is given ample opportunity to expand on virtue and his reasons for embracing it in II, 1, II, 2, III, 2,

V, 1 and V, 2. Lessing, changing Lysiteles to a merely amorous Leander, has him appear only in the first scene. Almost all of the overt moralizing has been eliminated, leaving the action to speak for itself. Everything which is dramaturgically superfluous has been removed, and only those elements of the plot most important for theatrical and comic effect have been retained and augmented with Lessing's own comic inventions.

Although Lessing pruned the plot of *Trinummus* considerably, he followed the opposite procedure in his handling of individual scenes. Within the restricted plot structure, the element of humor is permitted to expand abundantly. Lessing recurrently achieves the effect of comic surprise through the device of building scenes to a false climax by a rapid and heated exchange of speeches, one character gulling, the other gulled, building suspense to a high level, only to have the whole elaborate structure collapse anticlimactically. The most deftly extravagant instance of this type of humor occurs in Scene 5, in which Lelio implores Maskarill to lend him money to supply a dowry for his sister:

LELIO. ... Höre, Maskarill! —
MASKARILL. Nun? — Aber denken kann ich Sie nicht hören; Sie müssen reden.
LELIO. — Willst du wohl alle deine an mir verübte Betriegereyen, durch eine einzige rechtschaffne That wieder gut machen?
MASKARILL. Eine seltsame Frage! Für was sehen Sie mich denn an? Für einen Betrieger, der ein rechtschaffner Mann ist, oder für einen rechtschaffnen Mann, der ein Betrieger ist?
LELIO. Mein lieber, ehrlicher Maskarill, ich sehe dich für einen Mann an, der mir wenigstens einige tausend Thaler leihen könnte, wenn er mir so viel leihen wollte, als er mir gestohlen hat.
MASKARILL. Du lieber ehrlicher Maskarill! — und was wollten Sie mit diesen einigen tausend Thalern machen?
LELIO. Sie meiner Schwester zu Aussteuer geben, und mich hernach — vor den Kopf schießen.
MASKARILL. Sich vor den Kopf schießen? — Es ist schon wahr, entlaufen würden Sie mir mit dem Gelde alsdann nicht. Aber doch — (als ob er nachdächte.)
LELIO. Du weißt es, Maskarill, ich liebe meine Schwester. Jetzt

also muß ich das Aeusserste für sie thun, wenn sie nicht Zeit Lebens mit Unwillen an ihren Bruder denken soll. — Sey großmüthig, und versage mir deinen Beystand nicht. —

MASKARILL. Sie fassen mich bey meiner Schwäche. Ich habe einen verteufelten Hang zur Großmuth, und Ihre brüderliche Liebe, Herr Lelio, — wirklich! bezaubert mich ganz. Sie ist etwas recht edles, etwas recht superbes! — Aber Ihre Jungfer Schwester verdient sie auch; gewiß! Und ich sehe mich gedrungen —

LELIO. O! so laß dich umarmen, liebster Maskarill. Gebe doch Gott, daß du mich um recht vieles betrogen hast, damit du mir recht viel leihen kannst! Hätte ich doch nie geglaubt, daß du ein so zärtliches Herz hättest. —Aber laß hören, wie viel kannst du mir leihen? —

MASKARILL. Ich leihe Ihnen, mein Herr, —

LELIO. Sage nicht: mein Herr. Nenne mich deinen Freund. Ich wenigstens will dich Zeit Lebens für meinen einzigen, besten Freund halten.

MASKARILL. Behüte der Himmel! Sollte ich, einer so kleinen nichtswürdigen Gefälligkeit wegen, den Respekt bey Seite setzen, den ich Ihnen schuldig bin?

LELIO. Wie? Maskarill, du bist nicht allein großmüthig, du bist auch bescheiden?

MASKARILL. Machen Sie meine Tugend nicht schamroth. — Ich leihe Ihnen also auf zehn Jahre —

LELIO. Auf zehn Jahr? Welche übermäßige Güte! Auf fünf Jahr ist genug, Maskarill; auf zwey Jahr, wenn du willst. Leihe mir nur, und setze den Termin zur Bezahlung so kurz, als es dir gefällt.

MASKARILL. Nun wohl, so leihe ich Ihnen auf funfzehn Jahr —

LELIO. Ich muß dir nur deinen Willen lassen, edelmüthiger Maskarill —

MASKARILL. Auf funfzehn Jahr leihe ich Ihnen, ohne Interessen -

LELIO. Ohne Interessen, das gehe ich nimmermehr ein. Ich will, was du mir leihest, nicht anders, als zu funfzig Procent —

MASKARILL. Ohne alle Interessen —

LELIO. Ich bin dankbar, Maskarill, und vierzig Procent mußt du wenigstens nehmen.

MASKARILL. Ohne alle Interessen —

LELIO. Denkst du, daß ich niederträchtig genug bin, deine Güte so zu mißbrauchen? Willst du mit dreyßig Procent zufrieden seyn, so will ich es als einen Beweis der größten Uneigennützigkeit ansehen.

MASKARILL. Ohne Interessen, sage ich. —

LELIO. Aber ich bitte dich, Maskarill; bedenke doch nur, zwanzig Procent nimmt der allerchristlichste Jude.

MASKARILL. Mit Einem Worte, ohne Interessen, oder —
LELIO. Sey doch nur —
MASKARILL. Oder es wird aus dem ganzen Darlehn nichts.
LELIO. Je nun! weil du denn deiner Freundschaft gegen mich
durchaus keine Schranken willst gesetzt wissen —
MASKARILL. Ohne Interessen! —
LELIO. Ohne Interessen! — Ich muß mich schämen! — Ohne
Interessen leihest du mir also auf funfzehn Jahr — was? wie viel?
MASKARILL. Ohne Interessen leihe ich Ihnen noch auf funfzehn
Jahr — die 175 Thaler, die ich für sieben Jahre Lohn bey Ihnen
stehn habe.
LELIO. Wie meynst du? die 175 Thaler, die ich dir schon schuldig
bin? —
MASKARILL. Machen mein ganz Vermögen aus, und ich will sie
Ihnen von Grund des Herzens gern noch funfzehn Jahr, ohne
Interessen, ohne Interessen lassen.
LELIO. Und das ist dein Ernst, Schlingel?
MASKARILL. Schlingel? Das klingt ja nicht ein Bißchen erkennt-
lich.   (*LM*, II, 144.13-146.24)

The burden of this passage could have been expressed by
Lelio and Maskarill in three speeches apiece. But efficiency
of communication is hardly the object in this scene. Rather,
using the counterforces of Maskarill's ironic magnanimity
and Lelio's extravagant credulity, Lessing inserts a gratuitous
comic episode by intensifying the suspense of the conversation
and staving off the anticlimax which must come as long as
possible. Attention is rapidly shifted from the question of
whether the loan will be granted at all to the question of its
duration, and from there to the terms of the loan, the nego-
tiations being stretched out ever more maddeningly as the end
approaches. As Maskarill's generosity reveals itself to have
been mere mockery at the end of the passage, so Lelio's
ardent protestations of friendship turn out to have been nothing
but manifestations of rank opportunism, Lelio's grasping at
the last possible straw. The whole scene serves to further the
progress of the plot not one whit. Rather, it is a delaying
action used to expand the comic element of the play as much
as possible in order to flesh out a relatively meagre plot, in
the same way in which Plautus had used the long moralizing

speeches which Lessing excised. The technical means employed in building this scene were already to be observed in *Der junge Gelehrte*, where scenes were often stretched by bounteous use of aposiopesis, the characters interrupting each other constantly to hinder the flow of the action. Doubtless Lessing had learned this from Molière, who had used it to great advantage. *Der Schatz* depends on this device of building and then destroying climaxes for its internal comic dynamism, for in its eighteen scenes, similar delaying devices are used nine distinct times.

Because of the concentration on the arrangement of the scenes, characterization through individualized style plays a markedly secondary role within the structure of the play. We do not find the care lavished on details of diction apparent in *Die Juden* and *Der Freygeist*, which were essentially comedies of character rather than comedies of situation. Lessing did not casually use his devices of stylistic characterization in every play, but was selective in applying them. In *Der Schatz*, these means of characterization might indeed enrich the texture of the play, but, for the total effect, they would do so superfluously. Aside from the actual content of their speeches, the ways in which the characters speak, their styles, are very much alike. There are no stylistic differences between young and old, between virtuous and rascally. Even the role of Maskarill, which Lessing would earlier have taken as a golden opportunity to insert all sorts of verbal pyrotechnics into the dialogue, displays none of these, expressing his roguish nature by the things he says and which are said about him rather than by the way in which he says them. Stasimus/Maskarill and Philto/Staleno speak in very much the same styles, using similar vocabulary. In the scene quoted earlier, too, Lelio and Maskarill are indistinguishable from each other in their manners of speech.

The one character whose speech is distinctive, as it is in *Trinummus*, is the swindler's equivalent, Raps, who, in Scene 11, looses a barrage of puns which is an exact reflection of that with which his Plautine counterpart bombards Charmides

(IV, 2). As was mentioned in Chapter I, this use of puns was a characterizing stylistic feature used by Plautus to differentiate the language of slaves and parasites from that of their social betters. In this one instance, Lessing followed Plautus' practice, although, as we have noted, he does not do so in the case of Maskarill, where this device might also have been expected. The lack of distinctive characterizing features of style among the characters other than Raps might also be attributed to the influence of Plautus, in whose plays the socially more elevated characters rarely display such features either. It seems to the writer, however, that this divergence from Lessing's usual means of characterization is due, rather, to the nature of the material offered by the original and the means which Lessing found necessary to use in order to adapt *Trinummus* into a play which could live on the stage of his time.

Der Schatz is an isolated instance of departure from the characteristic style which Lessing had developed in his earlier comedies and to which, as will be seen shortly, he soon returns. Considered in its totality, *Der Schatz* shows too much interest in virtuosity and sprightliness of form and the movement of scenes and relatively little creative use of the devices of language at Lessing's disposal. This is a temporary imbalance and one which Lessing will have overcome at the height of his powers.

DIE GLÜCKLICHE ERBIN

The outlines and sketches of comedies which Lessing produced desultorily between 1750 and 1767 strongly betray the waning of his interest in comedy as a meaningful form of expression for him. This interest flickered up again occasionally, and he would work on a comic invention for several days or even weeks, only to put it aside once more for the sake of another project. This sporadic enthusiasm reveals itself in other works of Lessing, so many of which were destined to remain uncompleted. Because the catholicity of Lessing's interests far overreached the time and concentration which he could devote to them, his intentions frequently exceeded his actual achievements. Against the background of so multifarious and unordered a productive life, especially in the area of comedy, *Minna von Barnhelm*, as a singularly rounded and perfect work, is thrown into even sharper relief. The remaining plays to be examined in this chapter suffered a fate far more typical for Lessing's ideas and plans during this turbulent period of his life. All strongly bear the marks of having been planned for a specific occasion and of having been laid aside when the occasion was past.

From Leipzig, on December 8, 1755, in a letter to his friend Moses Mendelssohn, in Berlin, Lessing wrote:

… Eine von meinen Hauptbeschäftigungen ist in Leipzig noch bis jetzt diese gewesen, daß ich die Lustspiele des Goldoni gelesen habe. Kennen Sie diesen Italiäner? Wenigstens dem Nahmen nach? Er lebt noch. Er ist Doktor der Rechte und prakticirte ehedem in Venedig. Jetzt aber ist er Direktor einer Bande von Schauspielern. Die Ausgabe seiner Werke von 1753 bestehet aus sieben Oktavbänden, welche 28 Komödien enthalten. Es ist fast in allen viel Gutes, und die meisten sind auch ziemlich regelmäßig. Ich will Ihnen nichts mehr davon schreiben, weil ich ehestens einen Auszug daraus nach Berlin schicken werde, welcher in das vierte Stück meiner theatralischen Bibliothek kommen soll. Eine von diesen Komödien *l'Erede fortunata* habe ich mir zugeeignet; indem ich ein Stück nach meiner Art daraus verfertigt. Sie sollen es ehestens gedruckt sehen. Koch aber wird es noch eher aufführen, und wenn das geschehen ist, will ich Ihnen schreiben, ob ich mir etwas darauf zu gute thue, oder nicht.   (*LM*, XVII, 46)

Lessing went on to say that he had five other plays "großenschontheils, auf dem Papier, größtentheils aber noch im Kopfe", which he planned to add to this play to compose a volume of comedies to be presented to the German public in the Spring of 1756. What follows this passage in the same letter is particularly revealing of Lessing's attitude towards comedy at this juncture of his career. He writes, concerning the projected collection of comedies, "Alles, was ich zu meiner Entschuldigung anführen kann, ist dieses, daß ich meine Kindereien vollends auszukramen eile."

This new preoccupation with comedies, then, was for Lessing only a temporary lapse to "childishness", one which he himself found difficult to justify. For some time already, his interests had most definitely lain elsewhere. Since 1750, comedy had interested Lessing chiefly in his function as a critic for the *Berlinische privilegirte Zeitung*, from which vantage point he had established himself as a respected and feared literary critic in Berlin and, despite his youth, a critical and literary power to be reckoned with in Germany. During this time, Lessing's creative interests had been concentrated chiefly upon tragedy. July 10, 1755 saw the triumphant first performance of *Miß Sara Sampson* in Frankfurt an der Oder, the fruits of Lessing's interest in the English middle-class tragedy. After this success, Lessing decided to devote himself to dramatic production once more. Since Berlin had no stage to offer him for the plays he planned, and since Frederick the Great looked with a jaundiced eye not only upon original compositions by Germans, but also, through past incidents, upon Lessing himself, the young playwright left his position in Berlin for the more congenial atmosphere of Leipzig. There, where *Der junge Gelehrte* had first been performed, Koch's theatrical company, the only one of any significance in Germany at the time, was once more active. Lessing arrived in Leipzig in October, 1755. Since he was anything but financially independent, having not only to support himself, but also partially to subsidize his poverty-stricken and ever-demanding family in Kamenz, Lessing accepted the offer of Johann Gottfried Winkler, a wealthy young Saxon gentleman of about his own age, that he should accompany him on a trip to England and other countries, beginning the following Spring and taking a total of three years. Until May, 1756 Lessing was supported in Leipzig by Winkler and was free to carry on his literary activities. One of these was the commission of the publisher Reich for him to assemble the abovementioned volume of comedies. The project came to naught, however, since Lessing was also occupied with other projects at the time. Seven scenes of the adaptation of Goldoni's *L'Erede fortunata*, *Die glückliche Erbin*,

are all of the materials in Lessing's literary estate that can
definitely be said to have been intended for this volume, except for the fragment of his own play, *Vor diesen!*. These
scenes had already been set up in type, which was broken up
by the enraged publisher when Lessing did not deliver more
material as promised, and it is merely through the fortuitous
circumstance that a sheet of proof was saved that we have
what we do of *Die glückliche Erbin*.

One of the "Kindereien" which Lessing dug out with a
view to including it in the collection was the fragment *Palaion*,
a projected one-act comedy in French which he had begun in
Berlin five years earlier. It is quite likely that Lessing hoped
to gain an entry to the Prussian court with this play. At the
time he began work on *Palaion*, he was still on good terms with
Voltaire and his secretary, Richier de Louvain, who, it is
thought, helped Lessing with the niceties of French in writing
the play. Only three scenes were ever completed, and when
Lessing broke with Voltaire over the acrimonious affair of the
page proofs of the latter's *Le siècle de Louis XIV*, *Palaion* was
temporarily abandoned among Lessing's papers.

From what there is of the piece, it is clear that *Palaion* was
to be an entirely conventional play in the French manner.
The main character, Palaion, has the comic eccentricity of
constantly praising times past at the expense of his own, a
characteristic more or less common to the old men of the
European comedy, but increased by several powers in Palaion.
The plot would have eventually involved Palaion's duping by
his daughter so that she could marry. M. Codex, a comical
lawyer, similar to Herr Solbit in *Der Misogyne*, enters in the
third scene, and the usual comic servants would inevitably
have put in their appearance. In 1756, finding this play
among the most advanced of his projects, Lessing set about
translating *Palaion* into German and completing it. In the
German version, the play received the title *Vor diesen!*, the
favorite expression of Willibald, the germanized Palaion. Lessing wrote a further scene, but evidently soon tired of this
piece, for he never returned to it again.

Stylistically, *Vor diesen!* is on a level with *Der Misogyne*, the characterization being, if anything, less penetrating than in that play. The individual speeches do not show the same craftsmanship in their linking to one another, in the creation of the illusion of actual colloquy, which we have come to know as the hallmark of Lessing's style in the comedies. Since *Palaion/Vor diesen!* is such a very short fragment, barely giving any firm notion of the style of the play, and since that dialogue which was written does not show anything significant that has not been observed before, the play will not be further considered here.

It is another significant indication of Lessing's attitude towards comedy during this period that he should write to Mendelssohn, concerning Goldoni's comedies, "Es ist fast in allen viel Gutes, und die meisten sind auch ziemlich regelmäßig." For Lessing, "regelmäßig" meant that the comedies followed the rules of form which Germany had adopted from the French regular comedy and which had been applied in his early comedies by Lessing himself. Goldoni's comedies fulfilled the criteria that small casts of characters be involved in fairly linear and morally salutary plots which move within the framework of the unities of time, place, and action. For however much Lessing was an innovator in the realm of tragedy in Germany in 1755, he was still in harmony with the traditional principles of form for comedy, and, indeed, was attempting to bring progressively more of the realistic and colloquial elements of comic form into tragedy. *Miß Sara Sampson*, for all that this play brought to Germany for the first time, shows many of the formal features to be found in the comedies; the characters speak in colloquial, if usually elevated prose, the play has but a single plot line in opposition to the English tendency towards complex sub-plots intertwined with the play's major action, and, with but few exceptions, the play generally observes the required unities, although this point was hotly disputed by purists at the time. Thus, just as the Plautine comedies had earlier been favored for their closeness to the theatrical standard of Lessing's time, for which they and their Greek predecessors had served as models, Goldoni's *L'Erede fortunata* could, in 1755, still be chosen chiefly on the basis of its "regularity" for adaptation into a play according to Lessing's own fashion.

A comparison of the plot of *L'Erede fortunata* and that intended by Lessing for *Die glückliche Erbin*, or, as an earlier version called it, *Die Klausel im Testament*, is once again instructive, for it seems to confirm the fact observed concerning Lessing's treatment of Plautus' *Trinummus*, that his interest in comedy at this time was chiefly formal, mainly an interest in organizing the action as efficiently as possible, with the omission of extraneous elements except insofar as they combine the virtues of heightening the comic effect of the play and furthering the plot's progress. The action of *L'Erede fortunata* is quite complex, and badly in need of such simplification as Lessing intended for it. As the curtain rises for the first act, the relatives of the recently deceased Petronio Balanzoni are gathered to hear the reading of his will. This document names Balanzoni's daughter and only child, Rosaura, his sole heiress on condition that she marry Pantalone Bisognosi, his aged business partner. If Rosaura should refuse these terms, the fortune would revert to her uncle, "il Dottore" Balanzoni and his nephew, Florindo Aretusi, in equal parts, Rosaura receiving only 4.000 ducats as her dowry. The doctor and his nephew, sure that Rosaura will recognize and follow her own best financial interests in the matter, vigorously protest the will, threatening to take the matter to court. Rosaura, however, loves and is loved by Ottavio, the son of Pantalone. Out of love and duty towards his father, Ottavio is prepared to renounce his Rosaura when he finds that Pantalone seems prepared to marry the girl as stipulated. Pantalone wishes to do this chiefly because it will keep the business concern, which he and Rosaura's father had built up, in the same hands. When Pantalone accidentally finds out, in an interview with Rosaura, that she loves Ottavio, he is ready to put his own interests to one side and let his son mary Rosaura. He tries to persuade Ottavio to go to Rosaura's room at once and ask for her hand, planning, for his part, to come shortly afterward and give his blessing in his triple function as Ottavio's father, Rosaura's guardian, and executor of the will. Unknown to Pantalone, however, Ottavio goes to his own room, and Florindo, who hopes to win Rosaura's hand, slips into her room with the aid of Brighella, a servant of Pantalone. In a scene clearly intended more for its effect onstage than for its contribution to the content of the play, Pantalone enters Rosaura's room with her, the only light being supplied by a candle, and gives her hand to Florindo, thinking he is Ottavio. When the lights come up again, the whole mistake is cleared up, but now Ottavio has doubts about Rosaura's love for him, thinking that Rosaura had invited Florindo to come to her. Brighella, moved by feelings of remorse for having made Ottavio doubt Rosaura's love, cuts the Gordian knot of the will which stands in the way of the young lovers. He shows Dottore Balanzoni letters which purport to inform Pantalone that the credit of his company is exhausted in various cities, and that the firm, which makes up the bulk of Rosaura's inheritance, is on the verge of bankruptcy. In reality, of course, the letters have been forged by Brighella. The doctor, panicked by this news, hastens to save something for himself, and resigns his rights under the terms of the will for a cash settlement, leaving Rosaura to marry whomever she wishes. No sooner is the agreement signed than Brighella reveals his ruse, and the doctor and the nephew must depart, defeated. Ottavio and Rosaura are reconciled, and she is indeed the fortunate heiress.

As comic sub-plots, there are the travails of a jealous wife, Beatrice, the daughter of Pantalone, and her husband, Lelio, who cures her of her jealousy, and the comic wooing of Colombina by Arlecchino.

How seriously Lessing took the standards of regularity in comedy current in his time may be seen from the revisions he intended for the plot of the Goldoni play. The main action was to remain more or less intact. The scene in Rosaura's room, however, which was chiefly theatrical in nature and did not

really serve to advance the action, was to be eliminated. The
motivation behind this omission was undoubtedly also dramaturgic, since the scene would have disturbed the unity of place
unnecessarily, a consideration which Goldoni did not always
observe with the requisite nicety, letting various settings appear within the same act. Lessing clearly intended to reduce
these settings to only one room, however much irony he might
have expressed earlier involving this sort of forced unity, and
however much he himself had violated it in *Miß Sara Sampson*.
Beatrice and Lelio were to be retained merely for comic effect,
it would seem, but were to be allotted a much smaller proportion of the total number of scenes in the adaptation than
in the original. The love intrigue of the servants was to be
handled in much the same compressed way, Arlecchino and
Brighella being merged in one character, Pasquin. The other
characters, equipped with the standard names of Goldoni's
comedies, were to receive the standard names of the Franco-
German tradition, as follows:

Goldoni	*Lessing*
Pantalone Bisognosi	Araspe
Ottavio	Lelio
Beatrice	Camilla
Lelio	Philibert
Rosaura	Juliane
Il Dottore Balanzoni	Panurg
Florindo Aretusi	Joachim
Brighella	Pasquin
Arlecchino	
Colombina	Lisette

Although Lessing completed the outline of *Die glückliche Erbin*,
only seven scenes of dialogue are preserved. Two of these
are entirely of Lessing's own invention, and one has been
considerably remodelled, but the other four are practically
direct translations from Goldoni. It seems fair to conclude
that this was to be the pattern of the balance of the adaptation,

and that Lessing did not intend to alter Goldoni's scenes except where he found them too slow-moving and clumsy for his purposes. An example of this sort of alteration shall be seen shortly. Lessing's style in translating Goldoni, however, can be observed in a comparison of the following speeches by Pantalone/Araspe to Ottavio/Lelio. The original speech shall be presented first:

Figlio mio, che dici tu di questa fortuna di casa nostra? Il signor Petronio, obbligando Rosaura a sposarmi, mi lascia erede di tutto il suo. Se avessi dovuto separar la sua parte dalla mia, e dar a Rosaura la porzione di sua padre, per noi sarebbe stato un gran tracollo. Non è tutt'oro quel che luce. Abbiamo un gran credito, abbiamo dei gran capitali, ma abbiamo ancora dei debiti. Così nessuno sa i fatti nostri, si tira avanti il negozio, continua l'istesso nome, e si fa l'istessa figura. Ma che hai tu che non parli? Tu guardi il cielo e sospiri? Ti dispiace che tuo padre abbia avuta questa fortuna? Hai forse paura che maritandomi non pensi più a maritari anche te? No, Ottavio, non dubitare; tu sai quanto ti amo; Penso a te più che a me medesimo; e se passo alle seconde nozze, lo fo piuttosto per migliorar la tua condizione, che per soddisfar il mio genio. Cercati una ragazza savia, e da par tuo; te la darò volentieri. Se vuoi esser padrone, ti farò padrone. Manderò fuori di casa quel ganimede di Lelio mio genero, e quella matta di mia figlia, gelosa di quel bel fusto. Se anche Rosaura tua matrigna ti darà soggezione, mi ritirerò con essa in campagna e ti lascierò in libertà; che vuoi di più? Tuo padre può far di più per te? Via, figlio mio, via, Ottavio, consolami, fatti vedere allegro, corrispondi con amore al tuo povere padre, che per te spargerebbe il sangue delle sue vene.[15]

(My son, what do you say to this happy event for our house? In obliging Rosaura to marry me, Signor Petronio left me heir to all of his property. If I were obliged to separate his part from mine, and to give her father's portion to Rosaura, it would be a great catastrophe for us. All that glitters is not gold. We have a large credit, we have a great capital, but we also have debts. This way, no one knows of our affairs. Business continues as before, the same name continues, and the same appearance is presented. But why do you not speak? You look to heaven and sigh? Does it displease you that your father has had this luck? Do you possibly fear that, marrying, I no longer think also of your marrying? No, Ottavio, do not fear; you know how much I love you; I think of you more

[15] Carlo Goldoni, *Tutte le opere* (Milan, 1936), II, p. 974.

than of myself; and if I marry again, I do it more to improve your circumstances than to satisfy my fancy. Look for a wise girl, who is fit for you; I will give her to you willingly. If you wish to be the master, I will make you the master. I will order my fop of a son-in-law, Lelio, out of the house, and also my crazy daughter, who is jealous of that pretty fruit. If your stepmother, Rosaura, causes you uneasiness, I will retire to the country with her, and leave you at liberty; what more do you want? Can your father do more for you? Go, my son, go, Ottavio, console me, go about your business cheerfully. Answer with love your poor father, who would spill the blood of his veins for you.)

As is the entire scene in the adaptation, Lessing's version of this speech will be seen to be virtually a direct translation of Goldoni. Araspe is speaking:

Sieh da, mein Sohn! — Was sagst du, Lelio, zu dem Glücke deines Vaters? Der rechtschaffene Pancraz! Es würde mit mir, und also auch mit dir, nicht zum besten ausgesehen haben, wenn ich mich mit Julianen hätte abfinden müssen. Es ist nicht alles Gold, was glänzet. Wir haben einen großen Credit, wir haben große Kapitale; aber wir haben auch große Schulden! Wie gut ist es, daß nunmehr alles in seiner Ordnung bleibt, und unsre Handlung, unter ihrem alten Namen, mit gleichem Nachdrucke fortgeführet werden kann! — Aber was ist das? Warum sprichst du nicht? — Du siehst gen Himmel? Du seufzest? Gönnest du mir mein Glück nicht? Oder befürchtest du, ich möchte in einer neuen Ehe weniger auf deine Versorgung bedacht seyn? Fürchte nichts, mein Sohn. Du weißt, wie sehr ich dich liebe; ich denke weniger an mich selbst, als an dich, und wenn ich zu einer zweyten Verbindung schreite, so thu ich es, weil ich muß, und mehr um deine Umstände zu verbessern, als etwa einer mir nunmehr unanständigen Neigung zu willfahren. Suche dir ein Frauenzimmer, das dir gefällt; hier hast du meine Einwilligung im Voraus. Du sollst, so bald du willst, dein eigner Herr seyn. Mein Eidam, das Stutzerchen, soll mir aus dem Hause, sammt meiner närrischen eifersüchtigen Tochter. Ist dir auch deine Stiefmutter Juliane lästig, so will ich mich mit ihr aufs Land begeben, und dich allein hier lassen. Was willst du mehr? Kann dein Vater mehr für dich thun? Drum sey auch wieder heiter und fröhlich, mein Sohn. Erwiedre die Liebe deines Vaters mit Liebe. Mein Blut wollte ich für dich vergießen. (*LM*, III, 344.12-34)

By contrast, the stilted and overly literal English translation should be an index to the way Lessing translated the Italian speech, which is colloquial and intimate in its tone, into equally colloquial and intimate German. As he did in his translation of Plautus' *Captivi*, Lessing here avoided the pitfalls of attempting to translate idiomatic elements too literally. The passage in which Pantalone is discussing the further progress of the business, for example, is strongly idiomatic, making very awkward sense in the literal translation. Lessing has recast the statement into idiomatic German, retaining the essential meaning, but departing from the literal sense for the sake of clarity. Sensitivity to idioms is again demonstrated in the rendering of the terms which Pantalone applies to his son-in-law and daughter. The "ganimede" becomes a "Stutzerchen", and "matta di mia figlia, gelosa di quel bel fusto" becomes merely "meine närrische eifersüchtige Tochter", Lessing realizing that "quel bel fusto" is quite untransferrable in its literal sense. It is evident, however, that, aside from alterations dictated by linguistic necessity, Lessing was content to leave Goldoni's style largely intact in transferring those scenes which met his approval.

The second scene of *Die glückliche Erbin*, on the other hand, shows how much Lessing could rearrange a scene if he found it too long and laden down with unnecessary matter, just as he could radically prune the plot for the same reason. The equivalent scene in the original is the first scene in the play, thus carrying the full weight of the exposition. In this scene, accompanied by the counterpoint of the comments of the expectant relatives, the Notary first reads the will, and then the Doctor and Pantalone quarrel over it, establishing the situation for the action which is to follow. Lessing divides the burden of the exposition between two scenes, the first between Pasquin and Lisette, which is a comic servants' love scene, with ironical overtones and comments on the main action, and the second scene, which begins only after the will has been read, thus showing the audience only the significant reactions of the characters to the document, and leaving the actual provisions to be revealed gradually. In building up this scene, Lessing reverted very much to his own style. He differentiated the characters' styles of speaking far more sharply than did Goldoni, or than he himself did in *Der Schatz*. Whereas Florindo, for example, is a reasonably urbane and well-spoken young man in *L'Erede fortunata*, similar in speech and bearing to Ottavio, Joachim, his counterpart in *Die glückliche Erbin*, is represented as a half-witted clod who occasionally spouts bad Latin tags which he has picked up from his blustering uncle, Panurg. The following passage is taken from this second scene, and occurs just before Panurg and Joachim, enraged, leave. Again, this passage accurately reflects the general style of the scene:

PANURG. ... O ich bin durch die Schulen durch. Ich weiß es aus der Erfahrung, wie dergleichen Sachen laufen können. Und wissen Sie, was ein Falsarius für Strafe zu erwarten hat? Sie werden sich noch zu gratuliren haben, wenn Sie den Galgen abkauffen können. Der Notarius aber, der sich dazu hat brauchen lassen, der muß dran glauben. Da ist keine Gnade! Er muß hängen; und ich seh ihn, ich sehe ihn schon hängen.

ARASPE. (lächelnd.) Der arme Mann!

PANURG. Sie lachen noch? Nun hab ich genug. An dem Rande seines Verderbens zu lachen —

JOACHIM. Per risum multum —

PANURG. Tum! Wo du noch einmal reden wirst, Junge — Hören Sie, Araspe, damit ich zeige, daß ich Menschenliebe habe, und daß ich einmal Ihr guter Freund gewesen bin; entsagen Sie sich im guten aller Ansprüche auf die Verlassenschaft meines Bruders. Wenn Sie das wollen, so wollen wir den ganzen Plunder begraben; ich will nichts aufrühren, sondern zufrieden seyn, daß Juliane die einzige Erbin quasi ab intestato bleibe, nur mit der Bedingung, daß sie Vetter Jochen heyrathet.

JOACHIM. Mich, Herr Araspe, mich! O ja, thun Sie es doch!

PANURG. Erklären Sie sich bald; wollen Sie, oder wollen Sie nicht?

ARASPE. Aber was kann das werden? Der arme Notar hängt ja doch einmal am Galgen.

PANURG. Sie spotten, glaub ich, gar?

JOACHIM. Herr Araspe, ich bitte, ich bitte —

PANURG. Du bittest, Schurke? Und er sollte uns bitten, daß wir seine Streiche nur noch vertuschen möchten? Esel von einem Jungen! Willst du denn nie klug werden? Ich rüffle doch an dir, und rüffle — Komm fort! Wissen Sie, Herr Bräutigam, Herr Erbe,

auch Herr Vormund zugleich, wo ich nun spornstreichs hingehe?
Zum Advocaten! Zum Advocaten!
    ARASPE. So werde ich wohl immer das Geld, mich vom Galgen
los zu kauffen, bereit halten müssen?
    PANURG. Ja; Herr Bräutigam, Herr Erbe, Herr Vormund zu-
gleich — Wirst du dich drollen, Junge? (Geht ab, indem er Jochen
voranstößt.)   (*LM*, III, 343.4-36)

Waldemar Oehlke's observation that *Die glückliche Erbin* shows
no indication that Lessing was capable of producing a work
of the caliber of *Minna von Barnhelm*[16] is true not only of the
contents of the play, but largely also of the style. While in
general the language is comparable to that of *Der junge Gelehrte*
or *Der Misogyne*, what we have of *Die glückliche Erbin* shows
little of the talent for pacing and characterization in dialogue
which were to be found in those early plays. Lessing clearly
planned to make *Die glückliche Erbin* into a comedy of character
as well as intrigue, whereas the stress in Goldoni's version lay
on the latter. Panurg and Jochen were to be stupid and malicious, while Araspe and the other characters on his side were
to be modest and virtuous, treating their opponents with
gentle irony. The obvious and heavy-handed devices which
Lessing employed in his earliest comedies, but soon improved
upon, are in evidence again eight years later. Jochen's use of
Latin tags, Panurg's rhetorical bombast, his double use of the
phrase, "Herr Bräutigam, Herr Erbe, Herr Vormund zugleich", portends that it would have turned up as a characterizing tag a good deal more often if Lessing had completed the
play.

    Die glückliche Erbin seems to represent the doldrums of Les-
sing's career as a writer of comedies. Perhaps the fact that the
play was part of a commissioned anthology, and thus had to be
completed quickly, if at all, had to do with the evident lack
of enthusiasm with which Lessing set to work on the adaptation.
Despite Lessing's respect for Goldoni as a playwright, the style
of *Die glückliche Erbin*, as far as we can determine, does not
display any great zest for the task of adaptation. It is lack-

[16] *PO*, X, p. 163.

luster, fluctuating between translations of whole scenes which, however good they may be, add little of Lessing's own creative personality to the play, and mechanical recastings of scenes and characters according to formulas which Lessing had perfected years before, and which are in no way extended or broadened. If anything, *Die glückliche Erbin* shows a retrogression in its style to the plays which were written before *Die Juden*. Except for isolated outlines, *Die glückliche Erbin* is Lessing's last attempt at writing a comedy before 1763, when, after a long silence caused by his intense occupation with other literary and personal interests, Lessing wrote the play which was doubtless still beyond his reach in 1755, *Minna von Barnhelm*.

DER SCHLAFTRUNK

The remaining comic fragments from which anything of consequence concerning Lessing's use of language in comedy can be inferred were written after the publication of *Minna von Barnhelm*. At that time, Lessing was in Hamburg and just beginning his activities for the "Nationaltheater". *Der Schlaftrunk* and *Die Matrone von Ephesus* reflect the rejuvenation of Lessing's interest in comedy and the theatre in general which was apparently brought about by his early optimism about the venture with which he was connected. Each demonstrates in its own way that Lessing, even after the success of *Minna*, was still experimenting with new possibilities for comedy.

In content and style, the two fragments are most dissimilar. *Der Schlaftrunk*, set in Germany, very likely in Hamburg, might almost be termed a realistic portrait of contemporary German middle-class life. *Die Matrone von Ephesus*, on the other hand, is set in a tomb in Asia Minor, in a time in the indefinite past. The contrast between these plays may serve to demonstrate that, despite his preoccupation with weightier matters, despite his earlier dismissal of comedies as "Kindereien", Lessing was once more inexorably drawn to the medium and actively engaged in exploring its limits.

The way in which *Der Schlaftrunk* was conceived provides an anecdote attesting to Lessing's desultory but constant interest in comedy. In his introduction to his brother's theatrical "Nachlaß", Karl Lessing writes, concerning *Der Schlaftrunk:*

Die Entstehung dieser Komödie ist sonderbar genug. Mein Bruder machte schon 1766, als er noch in Berlin war, den ersten Entwurf. In einer Gesellschaft guter Freunde, wo er und Professor Ramler auch waren, kam die Rede auf die Stoffe, welche zu einer Komödie am besten paßten. Mein Bruder behauptete, man könne aus allem eine Komödie oder Tragödie machen, indem es mehr auf die Bearbeitung des Stoffes als auf den Stoff selbst ankäme: der Stoff wäre nur arm, wenn es der Dichter wäre. Dieses schien der Gesellschaft etwas paradox, und Herr Professor Ramler fragte ihn, ob er es selbst mit der Tat beweisen wollte. "Warum nicht?" erwiderte mein Bruder. "Nun, so machen Sie", versetzte jener, "ein Lustspiel, wo ein Schlaftrunk die Katastrophe ist, und benennen Sie es darnach!" Die ganze Gesellschaft billigte es einmütiglich, und mein Bruder versprach's.   (*PO*, X, 242)

Lessing is supposed to have worked out the main plot elements within the following few days, and to have taken the manuscript which he had begun with him to Hamburg when the offer from the theatrical syndicate came. Apparently Lessing intended to finish the play with a view toward having it produced by the company, for he had the completed scenes of *Der Schlaftrunk* printed.

Der Schlaftrunk displays little of that inventive virtuosity which, on the convivial evening described above, Lessing claimed was necessary for the molding of any kind of plot material into a good play. He tried to make *Der Schlaftrunk* into a comedy of character into which he could credibly bring an intrigue involving a sleeping potion. The story, as far as the sketchy outline tells it, concerns Samuel Richard, an old and extremely forgetful merchant, who is the guardian of his young niece, Charlotte. Herr Berthold, the father of Karl, to whom Charlotte is engaged, is bringing suit against Samuel for a debt supposedly unpaid, which the old man claims has long since been settled. Through his forgetfulness, Samuel has already missed the first two days on which he was to defend himself in court. The play begins on the eve of the third and last possible day. If Samuel forgets to go to court again, he loses the suit by default. Samuel is reminded of this fact successively by his niece and his brother, but seems to forget each time. When Berthold and Karl come to visit him, Samuel, suddenly alert, quarrels with Berthold, and each of the old men swears that if he loses the lawsuit, he will prevent the marriage of Karl and Charlotte. It is clear that Samuel must be made to miss his day in court. He will lose nothing by doing so, for Berthold merely means to bring his own absent-mindedness home to Samuel, who always insists that his memory is excellent, and Berthold will not make Samuel pay when he loses. Thus, Samuel is drugged with a sleeping potion by Karl Berthold, wakes up late the next morning and is furious at having missed his day in court. Samuel is mollified, however, when Berthold arrives and tells him that he will not have to pay. Both men then consent to the marriage of Karl and Charlotte, and the play reaches the conventional comedy conclusion. The comic villain of the piece, although a most ineffectual one, is Samuel's younger brother, Philipp Richard, who is a scapegrace in his fifties, and has already undergone several bankruptcies. Apparently it is intended that Philipp try to persuade Finette, the maid, to bring Samuel, through flattery, to change his will from Charlotte's favor to Philipp's, in exchange for which, Philipp promises, he will marry Finette. The main elements of the plot as given above, however, are merely deduced from Lessing's outline, since the fragment breaks off in the seventh scene of the second act.

The possibility that *Der Schlaftrunk* would be produced fairly shortly after its completion had an unmistakable impact on Lessing's plans for the work. It is one of the few manuscripts in which very explicit stage directions are indicated. Furthermore, the names of the characters in the latest and most complete execution of the fragment are German names, as we have seen, whereas in the earlier outline, made in Berlin, the names had been those of more typical comedy characters, Berthold, Celiante, Lysidor, Dorante. Evidently

Lessing had found this formula for the naming of characters, which is more characteristic of middle-class tragedy than of comedy, effective in *Minna von Barnhelm* and decided to utilize it again in *Der Schlaftrunk*. This play, partly for these reasons and partly for reasons to be mentioned below, has a texture which is more realistic than that of any of Lessing's previous plays, including, despite its wealth of concretely real detail and contemporary references, *Minna von Barnhelm*.

In reviewing the succession of Lessing's comedies written prior to *Der Schlaftrunk*, it will be noted that, while all of them involve an intrigue of some sort in their plots, all of them also have some internally rooted traits of personality of the various characters as the motive force of the play, some comic flaw which must be overcome and which can be discussed and disputed in the play. Thus, these earlier plays do not rely solely upon external action for their effect or for the matter of the dialogue. This is not the case in *Der Schlaftrunk*. The absent-mindedness of an old man is not ridiculous in the same way as is the precocious pedantry of a Damis, the compulsive misogyny of a Wumshäter, or even, on occasion, the unbending honorableness of a Tellheim. Samuel Richard's forgetfulness is a pathological fact. It has its impact on the workings of the play, but it is not an error of reason which can be discussed, overcome, or defeated in the same sense that the traits just cited can. At best, Samuel's failure to acknowledge his forgetfulness could be a surrogate for such an error, but it is only a very weak one. According to the definition of characters to be presented in the comedy, Samuel Richard does not really belong on stage at all. Possibly it is because *Der Schlaftrunk* was to revolve around such a character that the play was fated to remain incomplete. Lessing's strong sense of the theatre and for regularity in comedy, for exactly what types of characters should be depicted, must have shown him that the play could not be successfully concluded.

Because the nature of Samuel's flaw leaves nothing to be said about him once his forgetfulness and age have been made clear, the play concerns itself with external matters to a greater extent than do the earlier comedies. Old Samuel's will and Berthold's lawsuit, far from being mere engines to overcome the ridiculous vagaries of a character, become, though quite uninteresting in themselves, the central concerns of all of the characters. In addition, entirely extraneous aspects of everyday life enter into the movement of the play. Samuel's comically detailed preparations for his ride to his weekly "Kränzchen" are shown fully on stage, as is a scene, probably topical and funny at the time, in which Charlotte and Lucinde, Karl's sister, discuss with Finette what kind of wine they will have, rejecting the sweet wine which women were supposed to drink for headier stuff. Philipp Richard, the bumbling intriguer, also serves to pad the action with his occasionally acerbic and dissolute humor. Because of the inclusion of such elements, which were more restricted in earlier plays and carefully subordinated in the interests of a more engrossing main action, *Der Schlaftrunk* has an intimate and realistic atmosphere. The classical comedy situation is still the same, but there is much of the humdrum tone of urban middle-class life to be gleaned in the lines of this play. The following passage from the opening scene will serve to demonstrate this:

(Scene, eine Wohnstube; wo [Samuel] Richard, in einem Lehnstuhle, vor einem Schreibepulte sitzt, und durch die Brille in Zieglers Schauplatze der Zeit, einem Folianten lieset. Charlotte sitzt am Fenster, auf einem Taburet, und macht Filet.)
CHARLOTTE. Legen Sie doch das Buch weg, lieber Onkel —
S. RICHARD. (indem er immer fortlieset.) Warum denn, Lottchen?
CHARLOTTE. Der Besuch wird gleich da seyn.
S. RICHARD. Ich muß erst meine tägliche Geschichte auslesen.
CHARLOTTE. Sie schwächen sich ja nur Ihre Augen noch mehr.
S. RICHARD. Du hast wohl recht.
CHARLOTTE. Und strengen Ihr Gedächniß an.
S. RICHARD. Es ist wohl wahr.
CHARLOTTE. Da Ihnen Ihr Gedächniß ohnehin so sehr ablegt.
S. RICHARD. (indem er die Brille abnimmt, und das Buch zumacht.) Nein, Lottchen, nein; das sage nicht. Mein Gedächniß ist noch recht sehr gut. Ich wollte dir wohl die Geschichte, die

ich itzt gelesen habe, von Wort zu Wort wieder erzehlen. Leg deine
Arbeit weg, und höre mir zu. — Es war einmal ein König von
Frankreich — nein, ein König von England war es —ja, ein König
von England, der führte einen schweren Krieg wider die Mohren —
wider die Mohren — Sagte ich ein König von England, Lottchen?
Nein, siehst du, man kann sich irren; es war ein König von
Spanien; denn er führte Krieg mit den Mohren — dieser König —

CHARLOTTE. Ich höre wohl, lieber Onkel, daß Sie alles recht
wohl behalten haben. Aber Sie haben es auch, nur erst diesen
Augenblick, gelesen. Wenn Sie es auf den Abend wieder erzehlen
sollten —

S. RICHARD. Nun gut, gut; erinnere mich auf den Abend
wieder daran. Ich will dirs auf den Abend erzehlen —

CHARLOTTE. Wohl, lieber Onkel —

S. RICHARD. Sprachst du nicht vorhin von Besuche? Wer will
uns denn besuchen?

CHARLOTTE. Ihr alter guter Freund, Herr Berthold, und sein
Herr Sohn —

S. RICHARD. Der junge Herr Berthold? Nu, nu, der kömmt nicht
so wohl zu mir, als zu dir, und der mag immer kommen. Aber was
der Vater mit will? —

CHARLOTTE. Der Vater? Ist der nicht Ihr ältester, bester Freund?

S. RICHARD. Gewesen, Lottchen, gewesen! Sieh, wie vergeßlich
du bist. Hat mich nicht dieser älteste, beste Freund verklagt? Um
eine Post verklagt, die ich längst richtig gemacht habe? Bin ich
nicht —? Potz Stern! gut, daß ich daran gedenke! — Lottchen,
geschwind gieb mir den Kalender her.

CHARLOTTE. (vor sich.) Ah, nun erinnert er sich an den unglücklichen Termin.

S. RICHARD. Hörst du nicht, Lottchen? den Kalender —

CHARLOTTE. Wir schreiben den sechszehnten, lieber Onkel. —

S. RICHARD. Den Kalender, Lottchen!

CHARLOTTE. Den sechszehnten September, lieber Onkel —

S. RICHARD. Lange mir ihn doch nur her, Lottchen; er steckt
hinter dem Spiegel. Ich habe mir was darinne notirt. Wenn dichs
zwar inkommodirt — (er rückt mit seinem Lehnstuhle, als ob er
aufstehen wollte.)

CHARLOTTE. Nicht doch! lieber Onkel; bleiben Sie doch sitzen.
(sie hohlt ihm den Kalender.) Hier ist er!

S. RICHARD. Ich danke, Lottchen. Was für einen Monat haben
wir?

CHARLOTTE. September.

S. RICHARD. Und den wie vielten, sagst du, schreiben wir?

CHARLOTTE. Den sechszehnten.

S. RICHARD. Den sechszehnten September! — Da ist er! Richtig!
richtig! Lieber Gott! was habe ich für vergeßliche Leute in
meinem Hause! Kein Mensch erinnert mich an was! Und wenn es
vergessen ist, so soll ichs vergessen haben!

(*LM*, III, 415.3-417.17)

Whether with realistic intention or merely as a by-product of
the establishment of Samuel Richard as a forgetful, crotchety
old man, Lessing has succeeded to a remarkable extent in
bringing to the stage what must have been the day-to-day
atmosphere in a household like Richard's. The directions at
the beginning of the scene are unusually detailed for Lessing,
and are instrumental in setting the scene in the mind's eye.
Previously, if stage directions have been given at all, they have
specified merely the neutral common ground of comedy, a
"Saal". Both through the initial stage directions and the allusions of the characters, the room seems fairly crammed with
objects. The things surrounding the characters, their chairs,
their handiwork, calendars, mirrors, are apparently far more
on their minds than in earlier plays. In *Minna von Barnhelm*,
there was a trend in this direction, various beverages, meals,
police reports, rings, poodles, and pistols being drawn into the
dialogue. Whereas these objects, which give *Minna von Barnhelm* so much of its concreteness and immediacy, are an integral and vital part of the plot, the use of such detail in *Der
Schlaftrunk* seems to serve chiefly to give characters who do
not have very much to say to each other something to talk
about.

Aside from this device, which heightens the colloquial
character of the language by bringing into it allusions to
objects and topics of middle-class life, Lessing's style in this
play is the familiar one. Old Samuel's language is like that of
Wumshäter, the language of the characterization of such old
men, reinforced by oaths and frequent exclamatory expressions. The desultory tone of the old man's responses, so
strongly at variance with the epigrammatic bite we have observed in the dialogue of earlier plays, calls to mind more
strongly than ever the humdrum tone of ordinary speech, and

not only an artistic approximation of it, although Samuel's protests against Charlotte's implication that his memory is slipping are more reminiscent of Lessing's other old men. Repetition, such as with the matter of the guests, the date, and the calendar, is used to emphasize Samuel's absentmindedness. Later on in the play, Samuel must be told twice that he is still drinking his first cup of coffee that afternoon, and it is to be presumed that, had the play been completed, such repetitions would have been used several times more.

The chief characteristic setting *Der Schlaftrunk* apart from the earlier plays, then, is its greater concreteness and realism of atmosphere. Otherwise, in its use of stereotyped characters, its contrived plot, and its consistent use of one structural feature, it does not rise above Lessing's efforts of the period before *Minna* in any way. The best that can be said of *Der Schlaftrunk* is that it reveals to us how Lessing was still experimenting, even if only with slight success, for the development of more satisfactory forms of the traditional comedy.

DIE MATRONE VON EPHESUS

Lessing's attempt to base a viable comedy on the bitter Petronian fable of the widow of Ephesus has heretofore been depicted as an embarrassing lapse in his taste and dramaturgic instinct. The repugnant nature of the subject matter, making a decorous and credible execution of Lessing's plan impossible, is adduced by Erich Schmidt[17] and Th. C. van Stockum[18] to explain the unfinished state in which the play was left. Both critics associate the origins and intentions of this attempt at a comedy almost exclusively with Lessing's theoretical objections to earlier treatments of the theme. They regard *Die Matrone von Ephesus* as an insufficient proof of the idea that skillful handling can vindicate even the most im-

[17] Schmidt, *Lessing*, I, pp. 559-60.
[18] Th. C. van Stockum, "Lessings Dramenentwurf 'Die Matrone von Ephesus'", *Neophilologus*, XLVI (1962), pp. 125-33.

possible subject. Seen only in the light of Lessing's dramatic theory, such judgments appear sound enough. They wholly disregard, however, the decided departure in this play from the conventional and traditional appraisal of the widow's behavior. In relation to the customary image of her character, Lessing's conception of the widow is novel, indeed revolutionary. This conclusion is justified not only by Lessing's careful timing and motivation of the widow's actions, but also by the unusually expressive way in which he lets her speak, with a richness of diction unprecedented in his dramas. The play, as a result of these innovations, has a remarkable temperamental and thematic affinity with certain of his earlier comedies, particularly *Minna von Barnhelm*. Rather than a misguided display of dramaturgic skill, *Die Matrone von Ephesus* is an approach to yet another realization of what Lessing termed "die wahre Komödie": the comedy which should both amuse its audience *and* arouse their emotions.

The story of the matron of Ephesus appears in the *Satyricon* of Petronius, where it is told with wit and forthrightness. A young widow is determined to die of grief and starvation in the tomb of her husband. A soldier, guarding crucified thieves lest they be stolen for burial, enters the tomb and quickly gains the widow's love, rekindling her will to live. When, during their dalliance, one of the bodies is stolen from its cross, the widow has her husband's corpse strung up in its place in order to save her new lover.

Variations on this tale seem to be as old as storytelling itself. Eduard Grisebach[19] says that the story originated in India, whence it spread to China and westward via Asia Minor to Europe. The version of Petronius began an almost unbroken chronology of the topic in Western European literature and remained the most popular model, despite the later im-

---

[19]   Eduard Grisebach, *Die Wanderung der Novelle von der treulosen Wittwe durch die Weltlitteratur*, 5th edn. (Berlin, 1886). Also see Peter Ure, "The Widow of Ephesus: Some Reflections on an International Theme", *The Durham University Journal*, New Series, Vol. XVIII, No. 1 (December, 1956), pp. 1-9.

portation of a similar Chinese story. Each epoch treated the fable according to its own lights. In the Middle Ages it was told in a tone of moral indignation. Jean de Salisbéry (d. 1183) faithfully copied the story from Petronius in his *Policraticus de nugis curialium et vestigiis philosophorum*, putting it under the heading, "De molestiis Conjugiorum, ... et de pernicii libidinis, de mulieris Ephesiae & similium fide", and appending the righteous comment, "Mulieremque tradit impietatis suae et sceleris parricidalis et adulterii poenas luisse."[20] The *Historia septem sapientum*, translated throughout Western Europe during the fifteenth century, added grisly mutilations of the dead husband's body, usually carried out by the widow herself, giving the wry Petronian story a macabre and brutally wanton twist. One German version, a metrical adaptation, *Diocletianus Leben* (1412) by the Alsatian Hans von Bühel, had her lover cut off the widow's head after she has eagerly disfigured her husband's corpse to make it match that of the stolen thief more exactly.[21]

In the following centuries, the savage condemnation of the widow's infidelity evident in the medieval versions was tempered by a more tolerant attitude, not seldom accompanied by a degree of psychological insight and philosophical reasoning. Attention began to shift from the gruesome betrayal of the dead husband to the widow herself. Her vow to die in her husband's tomb, praiseworthy and fitting to the earlier adaptors of the tale, gradually came to be regarded as an erroneous exaggeration, as a hypocritical attempt to prove that there can be even one exception to the inconstancy of women, to their frailty in the face of the temptations of love. An English vindication of the widow's need and right to love was Walter Charleton's *The Ephesian Matron* (1659). The cynical and satirical tolerance, the worldly wisdom with which the widow was viewed by most French, English, and German writers who treated the old story in the 17th and 18th

---

[20] Grisebach, *op. cit.*, p. 38.
[21] Grisebach, *op. cit.*, 102-8.

centuries is best caught in the last lines of Jean de la Fontaine's
tale, *La Matrone d'Éphèse* (1682):

> Cette veuve n'eut tort qu'au bruit qu'on lui vit faire,
> Qu'au dessein de mourir, mal conçu, mal formé:
>   Car de mettre au patibulaire
>   Le corps d'un mari tant aimé,
> Ce n'étoit pas peut-être une si grande affaire
> Cela lui sauvoit l'autre: et tout considéré,
> Mieux vaut goujat debout qu'empereur enterré.[22]

The two comedies most pertinent to Lessing's adaptation were
written in the spirit of La Fontaine: *Die Matrone von Ephesus* by
Christian Felix Weiße[23] and *La Matrone d'Ephese* by Antoine
Houdar de la Motte.[24] When, in 1748, Lessing read Weiße's
alexandrine comedy, he was inspired to attempt a play on the
same theme which would, according to Karl Lessing, deal
more gently with the widow than had Weiße.[25] Although all
traces of Lessing's early Leipzig version of *Die Matrone von
Ephesus* have been lost, the obvious parallels between his later
sketches and the play written in 1744 by Weiße indicate the
probable survival in the later version of major elements of
Lessing's early ideas for a dramatic adaptation of the ancient
story.

Although Weiße otherwise followed the Petronian tale
closely in the plot of his one-act comedy, he departed from it
in two significant details; firstly, as in most contemporary
treatments of the fable, the action takes place within the time
required to act out the play instead of over three days as
specified by Petronius; secondly, the widow's confession of love
for the soldier occurs only *after* the theft of the body instead of

---

[22] Jean de la Fontaine, *Œuvres*, 12 vols. (Paris, 1890), VI, pp. 85-6.

[23] In: Christian Felix Weiße, *Beytrag zum deutschen Theater*, 5 vols.
(Leipzig, 1768), V. *Die Matrone von Ephesus* is bound in at the end of this
volume (from the Library of Princeton University) and is paginated
separately — hereafter cited as *MvE*.

[24] In: Antoine Houdar de la Motte, *Œuvres...*, 10 vols. (Paris, 1754),
V, pp. 466-510. — *La Matrone d'Ephese* is hereafter cited as *MdE*.

[25] Waldemar Oehlke, *Lessing und seine Zeit*, 2 vols. (Munich, 1919), I,
p. 265.

three days before. The first of these changes, necessary to the dramatic adaptation, is obviously a concession to the requirement of the unity of time. The second change, however, is as significant as it is original. Quite possibly Weiße introduced it in order to alleviate the impression of an unduly hasty change in the widow, which is necessarily caused by the sharply restricted time in which the action must take place. The young widow, Antiphila, has been persuaded by the soldier, Carion, to live in order to better mourn her husband. Outwardly, however, Antiphila steadfastly resists Carion's attempts to gain her love. Indeed, while Carion is outside discovering the theft of the corpse, Antiphila seems ready to rebuff him severely for his presumption. In the second version (1783), in fact, Weiße, as if to reinforce the fact of Antiphila's resistance, has her ready a dagger for Carion's breast.[26] It is only the widow's fear of losing the young soldier which makes her express the love she has had such difficulty in subduing. Obviously, Weiße was trying to exculpate the widow to an extent, explaining her shocking act as a sign of the power of love rather than as an example of the treachery of wantonness. Nonetheless, the alteration is unseemly in its speed. At the beginning of the play, Antiphila lovingly remembered her husband and had been willing to die for the sake of his memory:

> Entfärbt Euch, jugendliche Wangen;
> Der Mund der vormals mit Verlangen
> Euch sanft geküßt, ist nun erblaßt:
> Und jeder Mund ist mir verhaßt.
> Verhaßt ist mir die Lust der Erden,
> Drum will ich, meinem Gatten treu,
> Hier neben ihm zur Asche werden;
> O Tod, steh meinen Wünschen bey.   (*MvE*, p. 3)

Now, like the Petronian widow, moved by love for the soldier and fear of losing him by his own hand, she says:

> Halt! — trauriges Geschicke!
> Umwölkst Du stets für mich die schönsten Augenblicke!

---

[26]   Christian Felix Weiße, *Lustspiele*, 3 vols. (Leipzig, 1783), I, p. 415.

Kaum stirbt mir armen Frau ein lieber junger Mann,
So greift das Unglück schnell auch meinen Tröster an.
Zween Männer auf einmal? daran kann ich nicht denken!
Laßt uns den todten Mann dafür an Galgen henken!

(*MvE*, p. 40)

Dorias, the maid, surely echoing La Fontaine, has the last word:

Der Einfall ist geschickt: Ich henk ihn mit hinan.
Ein Mann, der lebt, gilt mehr, als ein gestorbner Mann.

(*MvE.*, p. 40)

It was surely the brash haste with which the substitution was decided upon, falling so harshly into the tenderly amorous and gently ironic tone of the play that challenged Lessing to improve upon Weiße's version of the subject. What flawed Weiße's adroit and sensible handling of the plot was shallowness and inconsistency in characterization. It was precisely in respect to the problem of characterization that Lessing departed most distinctively from Weiße's conception, giving an entirely different motivation to the widow's actions.

For nearly twenty years after leaving Leipzig, Weiße, and his early sketches for *Die Matrone von Ephesus* behind him, Lessing showed no further interest in the theme, although most of his comedies were written during those two decades. The apparent spur to Lessing's renewed interest was the one-act comedy, *La Matrone d'Ephese* by Antoine Houdar de la Motte, first performed in 1702, but not published until 1754. La Motte padded the spare story unabashedly. Euphemie, the young widow, is first courted by old Chrisante, the father of her future lover, Sostrate, who is in command of the soldiers guarding the hanged criminal. Euphemie's rejection of the old man's suit, her adamant insistence upon dying in the tomb of her husband send the lovesick Chrisante tottering off to bed. Frosine, the widow's maid, explains, however, that Euphemie is more pliable than she seems. A young man would have a better chance than Chrisante: "Je connois Euphemie; la jeunesse & la bonne mine la mettroient cent fois mieux à

la raison, que les plus beaux discours du monde." Euphemie
had vowed to devote her life to the service of Diana, from
which the tears and pleas of her family could not keep her,
but "... lorsquelle apperçut un jeune homme qui, d'un clin
d'æil, lui coupa la parole; ... elle sentit qu'elle n'étoit point
faite pour Diane; il fallut la marier huit jours après" (*MdE*,
p. 470). Sostrate and Euphemie finally meet in the eighth
scene, and by the fourteenth, after a minimum of protest and
one scene spent backstage with the young officer, Euphemie
confirms Frosine's prognosis, sighing; "Ah, Sostrate! à quoi
sçavezvous me réduire? Par quel enchantement puis-je con-
sentir a vivre, & à vivre pour vous?" (*MdE*, p. 497). The
news of the stolen body comes during Chrisante's bitter
denunciation of the widow and his son, and it is Chrisante,
moved by his son's peril, who wrests from Euphemie her
mute consent to Frosine's suggestion of the substitution.

This strange mixture of harlequinade, amorous comedy, and
sentiment drew Lessing's critical fire in the thirty-sixth article
of the *Hamburgische Dramaturgie* (September 1, 1767), which
was surely written after Lessing had once more begun work
on his own *Matrone von Ephesus*. In this article, Lessing discusses
the general problem of transferring to the stage materials
which have been effective as narratives, choosing Petronius's
tale of the Ephesian widow as an especially apt illustration.
In the tale, says Lessing, the widow has a certain charm and
arouses no more than a not unpleasureable scornful smile for
the overconfidence of conjugal love in the reader. On the
stage, however, at least in such versions as de la Motte's, the
ghastly betrayal, which had been only a possibility for the
imagination to contemplate in the story, becomes horrible
actuality to the beholder. We no longer have an image of
feminine weakness in general, but rather one of a particular,
especially vicious and depraved woman. Lessing refers to
the comment of one of the tale's hearers in the *Satyricon*, that
the widow should have been strung up on the cross instead
of her husband, and states that, in the previous dramatizations
of the tale, the audience agrees with this verdict: "... Und

diese Strafe scheinet sie uns um so viel mehr zu verdienen, je weniger Kunst der Dichter bey ihrer Verführung angewendet; ... – Kurz, die petronische Fabel glücklich auf das Theater zu bringen, müßte sie den nehmlichen Ausgang behalten, und auch nicht behalten; müßte die Matrone so weit gehen, und auch nicht so weit gehen. – Die Erklärung hierüber anderwärts!" (*LM*, IX, 334).

What we have of the play thus heralded are two sketches of the plot, the more elaborate of which describes the complete action in eight scenes, and two virtually identical drafts of completed dialogue, of which the longer, though still incomplete draft covers eight scenes. Lessing evidently was not following his original scenario when writing the dialogue, for in the eighth scene of the latest draft, no mention of the theft has been made as yet. Thus, the play would require at least one, if not two more scenes to complete the action. The earliest fragments of Lessing's *Die Matrone von Ephesus* which have been preserved date from 1767, and the latest handwriting in any of the manuscripts seems to have originated in 1771, when, as Muncker surmises, Lessing dropped the entire project because he was absorbed in his work on *Emilia Galotti*.[27]

Lessing did plan to show on stage those aspects of the widow's character which he perceived in the story, to make the action have the same outcome and yet not have it, to have the widow go so far and yet not go so far, solving the paradox he proposed in the *Hamburgische Dramaturgie*. Like the widow in Weiße's version, Lessing's heroine is called Antiphila. She, too, is not to confess her love for the officer, Philokrates, until the report of the theft. These borrowings from Weiße's *Matrone* are probably the only remnants of Lessing's Leipzig plan in the later fragment. In all other respects, Lessing's *Matrone von Ephesus* bears the stamp of the more mature artist. Like de la Motte, and following the tradition of European comedy, Lessing accompanies the main characters with servants of a specifically comic cast; Mysis, Antiphila's maid, and

---

[27] *LM*, III, xiii.

Dromo, a soldier serving under Philokrates.[28] Lessing's major innovations in the plot of the fable are two deceptions in the manner of the comedy of intrigue. Philokrates deceives Antiphila into letting him remain in the tomb by claiming to have known her husband, using information he has merely read on the epitaph as proof. The crucial ruse, which lets the plot fulfill the author's paradoxical specification, is Dromo's spurious report that the body of one of the hanged prisoners has been stolen. This is indicated in the scenario. Lessing never wrote the dialogue for this action or for Antiphila's confession of love and consent to the substitution. There is dialogue in the longer scenario, however, in which Dromo announces that the story was just a trick contrived by him, presumably without the knowledge of Philokrates, to make the widow reveal her true feelings.

What distinguishes Lessing's *Matrone von Ephesus* from earlier versions, including Weiße's, is not his handling of the plot, but rather the characterization and motivation of the widow. Weiße's Antiphila mourns the loss of her husband, recalling the sweet dalliances of their brief life together and longing for death as the release from her grief. She is entirely human and comprehensible in her suffering, to which she gives tenderly lyrical expression. Her very humanity makes her rapid change of heart all too inhuman, spoiling the play's design. The grief of Lessing's Antiphila has very different dimensions. She is portrayed as a woman not merely superficially in mourning, like de la Motte's Euphemie, but so mad with grief as to be ready to leave this life, which apparently has nothing left to offer her but mockery for being alive any longer. Yet, in her less conscious moments, the young woman is very much alive and cannot, much as she would, escape the bondage of the flesh and its imperatives. For all of

---

[28] Lessing's choices of names for his characters seem to support the interpretation offered here. Following the European comedy tradition and, in the matter of the widow's name, Weiße, of naming characters according to their prevalent humors, "Antiphila" can clearly be taken to mean "against love", "Philokrates" "the power of love", or, "indeed, the love of power".

this, however, Antiphila is radically disturbed, not only out of grief for her dead husband, but also through a violent sense of having been wronged and cheated by the fact of his death. She is at odds not only with her immediate society, as have been the central figures of Lessing's earlier comedies, but with her gods, with the entire universe.

When we first encounter Antiphila in the third scene (*LM*, III, 450-54), she cannot accept her husband's death and hopes that he can still be revived. With the cry, "O ich wahnsinnige!", Antiphila gives up this hope. In her derangement she reasons that, since she had not seen him die, her husband cannot really be dead, and that a gruesome joke is being played on her. The death of her husband is unnatural, impossible to her, for why did not her heart break, which was so attuned, so one with his? She vows to serve the goddess Diana, who could let such a thing happen, no longer, and makes the terrible pledge to follow her husband: "Bey allem, was in jener Welt schrecklich und heilig ist, bey ihm, bey dem die Götter zu schwören sich scheuen, – schwöre ich, daß ich nie, nie diesen Ort, ohne dem [sic] Geliebten meiner Seele, verlaßen will." Ironical as this will turn out to have been in the light of the later events of the play, the vow, at the time Antiphila speaks it, is entirely in earnest. It is the utterance of a woman whose gods have deserted her, who cannot comprehend a natural order which lets her heart live on though broken. Lessing's Antiphila is certainly the most genuinely and radically distraught widow in the history of the old fable.

Lessing has created in Philokrates, the officer, a character at once noble and ingenious, worthy of Antiphila and yet possessed of the loving craft to prevail in the task of winning her. The officer emerges as a unified, consistent character, sensitive to each situation in which he finds himself and responding fittingly to each. In his adaptability, his liveliness and wit, he is the healthy contrast to the seemingly inflexible Antiphila and can thus return her to the world she has so stubbornly abandoned. In the intensity of his feeling, on the other hand, he is a worthy counterpart to the passionate widow.

Erich Schmidt, who accorded this comedy its fullest critical treatment to date, dismisses it as an attempt at a witty farce, "das Experiment einer bohrenden und tüftelnden Lustspielsprache", doomed at the outset by the highly questionable choice of subject matter. "'Die Matrone von Ephesus'", concludes Schmidt, "ein geistreiches aber unmögliches Stück, ist eine Stilübung nach, neben, und vor den verschiedenen Fassungen der 'Emilia Galotti'."[29] Schmidt sees Lessing as motivated here merely by the desire to improve technically upon the earlier dramatic adaptations of the theme. Although this was certainly part of Lessing's intention, it is very much open to question whether he meant *Die Matrone von Ephesus* to be just another witty satire on the vagaries and weaknesses of women, like *Die alte Jungfer* and *Weiber sind Weiber*. Antiphila hardly can be compared to the "heroines" of these farces. Neither is she, however, merely an Ur-Emilia, but a fully-rounded dramatic personage in her own right, motivated by her own griefs and speaking with a passion uniquely hers.

On the basis of his extremely individual and anti-traditional treatment of the characters of the two protagonists of the old fable, Lessing's *Die Matrone von Ephesus* should be considered as the work of the playwright who had written *Minna von Barnhelm* only four years earlier, and not as that of the aspiring young author who, two decades previously, had produced brittle farces on the fickleness of women. Externally, in terms of setting and plot, the differences between the two plays could hardly be greater. Internally, however, *Die Matrone von Ephesus* and *Minna von Barnhelm* have a striking affinity with each other, the fragment continuing and supplementing in a remarkable way the essential theme of the earlier comedy. Both plays, within the terms of their worlds of action, involve characters who are brought back through the loving ruse of another to an affirmation of that which they have

---

[29]   Schmidt, *Lessing*, I, p. 560.

renounced. As we see Tellheim in the later scenes of Act IV
in *Minna von Barnhelm*, he wishes to renounce not only Minna
but apparently even life itself for the sake of his desire for
justice and the recognition of his honor. Thus, when he
thinks that his freedom of movement has been restored by the
authorities without a complete vindication of his good name,
Tellheim says: "Man wird mich wollen lauffen lassen. Allein
man irrt sich; ich werde nicht lauffen. Eher soll mich hier
das äusserste Elend, vor den Augen meiner Verleumder, ver-
zehren –" (*LM*, II, 242). It is only Minna's pretense at having
been disowned, only Tellheim's belief that she now needs
him which gives new motive power to his soul, making him
ready to undertake anything for Minna.

In her way, Antiphila is as absolute in her turning from the
world because of a wrong done her by life as is Tellheim in
his. She is ready to give up her life not only out of love for her
husband, but also because the gods have wronged her in
letting him die, a point which is strongly emphasized. The
widow's initial inflexibility, her absoluteness in her wish to
destroy herself, do not arouse the admiration of the other
characters, any more than does Tellheim's stubborn, almost
inhuman insistence on his honor in *Minna*. Mysis and Dromo
are sarcastic about Antiphila's exaggerated fidelity, so admired
by the citizens of Ephesus in the original tale. Like Tellheim's sense of his own honor, Antiphila's fidelity, a virtue
in itself, becomes a dangerous vice in its extremity. When
Philokrates enters the tomb, forthright and natural in his
zest for life, the stage is set for the overwhelming of the widow's
unnatural stubbornness, her aggrieved revolt against the gods,
her perverse pleasure in the contemplation of her grief. She is
forced to admit, speaking of her broken heart, "– solche Wun-
den weigern sich aller Linderung. Nur in ihnen wühlen, ist
Wollust" (*LM*, III, 465). Her heart, which did not stop
beating with that of her husband, had a greater wisdom than
she herself, and, as in *Minna*, it is this wisdom of the heart
which, for Lessing, is to prevail at the end. The contrast in
character between Antiphila and Philokrates is certainly

reminiscent of that between Tellheim and Minna in Act II of *Minna von Barnhelm*. Judging from what we have of the play, Philokrates is to be to Antiphila the redeemer from extremeness that Minna was for Tellheim. The ruse of the stolen body in *Die Matrone von Ephesus*, without which Lessing's Antiphila, like Weiße's, evidently would not have been turned from her path to self-destruction, would not have confessed her sudden passion, can be regarded as a parallel to Minna's ruse. Antiphila's rapid alteration would certainly be reminiscent of Tellheim's restoration from his morbid preoccupation with his honor. The solution of so extreme a situation as Antiphila's must necessarily also be extreme. Just as the vindication of his honor becomes of secondary importance to Tellheim, when he thinks that Minna's happiness and honor are imperilled, so Antiphila's fancied duty to the dead would be ignored, the dead even sacrificed, when she believes the life of Philokrates to be at stake as a penalty for the neglect of his duty. In *Die Matrone von Ephesus*, then, as in *Minna von Barnhelm*, the substitution of duty to another, an answer to an ethical imperative, for a personal grievance, brings forth the true personality and feeling of the character and redeems that character from a dangerous, potentially tragic involvement to an extreme degree in personal, ultimately illusory concerns.

Lessing rang an entirely new set of changes on the Petronian fable. The widow's initial radical loyalty to her husband, a great virtue in the Roman tale, becomes, in this version, an irrational extremeness, a "Wahnsinn" which must be healed. Her attraction to the soldier, on the other hand, and her simultaneous offer of her husband's corpse to save his life, the bitter proof of the fickleness of women for all tellers of the story before Lessing, become the emblem of her having been healed. As the actual theft, however, is merely a ruse, the widow's humanity would be redeemed for the audience through her release from the burden of actually having the grisly deed performed. Thus, as Lessing specified, the story would have the same outcome as the tale and yet not have it. Antiphila's salvation from her own radical loyalty would be accomplished, and this would seem to be the true import of the play. Such an intention on Lessing's part is not diminished in its merits by his unwillingness or supposed inability to complete the play, credibly depicting Antiphila's transformation. That the widow should live to love again rather than die for the sake of an illusory duty to the dead is certainly more consonant with reason and the ideas of humanity which the Enlightenment and Lessing himself espoused than the traditional interpretation of the tale.

The stylistic evidence provided by the fragment seems to make even clearer Lessing's intention of recasting the story as outlined above. The way the widow is presented – not only what she says, but how she says it – is essential, in the writer's opinion, to a full understanding of this fragment. When we first encounter Antiphila, she has just awakened from a restless sleep. After a brief moment in which she does not know quite where she is, she gives free rein to her grief:

ANTIPHILA. ... — Ah, dieser Sarg — (indem sie aufspringt) dieses schaudernde Gewölbe — diese verlöschende Lampe — sie erinnern mich, wo ich bin! wer ich bin! — Und mein Unglück stehet ganz wieder vor mir! Mysis, Zeuginn meiner Verzweiflung — (sie bey der Hand ergreiffend)

MYSIS. Laßen Sie mich; ehe die Lampe verlöscht. Ich will Oel aufgießen — (welches sie thut)

ANTIPHILA. Laß sie verlöschen! — Laß die Sonne und alle Gestirne des Himmels mit ihr verlöschen! — Alles werde um mir so Dunkel und Nacht, als es in mir ist! — Sieh, Mysis! Es wird heller; die Flamme lodert neu auf! — Komm her, wie hast du das gemacht?

MYSIS. Ich habe Oel zugegoßen und den Dacht gereiniget —

ANTIPHILA. Kannst du das? — O, so wirst du mehr können. — Kannst du eine sterbende Flamme erwecken — komm, so must du mir auch meinen Mann erwecken! —Komm, — gieß neues Leben in seine Adern, — reinige seine Nerven von dem Moder der Verwesung — Komm! (zieht sie gegen den Sarg) Du mußt, du mußt! — (sie wieder loslaßend) O ich wahnsinnige!

MYSIS. Wie jammern Sie mich!

ANTIPHILA. Aus den eisernen Armen des Todes ist keine Rettung. Er ist dahin, unwiederbringlich dahin! — Und doch, je öftrer ich mir es sage, je unglaublicher wird es mir. — Er, er, mein Telamon todt? — Sage, Mysis, blühte er nicht noch vor sieben Tagen, gleich einer Rose? Als ich ihn vor sieben Tagen verließ, wie verließ ich ihn? Rede, wie du es weißt! Und gestern, wie fand ich ihn wieder? — Reime mir das zusammen, wenn du kanst! Wie ich ihn verließ, und wie ich ihn wiederfand! — Nein, da ist Betrug dahinter! Er ist nicht todt; er ist nicht todt! — Gesteh es mir, Mysis, daß er nicht todt ist! Sage: er lebt! und nimm deine Freyheit dafür, und nimm mein Geschmeide, nimm alles, was ich habe!

MYSIS. Und wenn ich es sagte? —

ANTIPHILA. So wäre es darum doch nicht wahr? So wäre er doch todt? — Wo bin ich denn indeß gewesen? Fern über Land und Meer? Warum hohlte man mich nicht? — Bin ich weiter als in der Stadt gewesen? Hätte ich nicht den Augenblick hier seyn können? Er hätte in meiner Abwesenheit sterben wollen? — Das macht die ganze Sache verdächtig. — Sage, habe ich ihn sterben sehen?

MYSIS. Freylich nicht.

ANTIPHILA. Aber ich hätte ihn sehen können? Sage —

MYSIS. Allerdings.

ANTIPHILA. So? Ich hätte ihn können sterben sehen? und habe ihn nicht gesehen? — O, so ist er auch nicht gestorben! — Und wo war ich in der Stadt? — Ein neuer Beweiß, daß ihr mich betrügt, daß ihr mich zum Besten habt! — Wo war ich? In dem Wirbel der leichtsinnigen Welt? Jugendlichen Zerstreuungen, verführerischen Ergötzlichkeiten überlaßen? Ich nehme dich selbst zum Zeugen, Göttinn Diana, ob mich etwas anders als dein Fest da beschäftigte? Täglich und stündlich in deinem Tempel, wo ich zu dir betete, dir Hymnen sang, dir opferte, und deine Priester beschenkte — und du hättest indeß diß Unglück von mir nicht abgewandt? Du hättest ihn sterben laßen — O so wärest du nicht die große Diana von Ephesus —

MYSIS. Wo gerathen Sie hin, meine Frau? —

ANTIPHILA. Nein, so ist sie es nicht! So will ich nie mehr zu ihr beten, nie mehr ihr Hymnen singen, nie mehr ihr opfern, nie mehr ihre Priester beschenken!

MYSIS. Die Göttinn wird Ihren Schmerz ansehen, und Ihnen verzeihen.

ANTIPHILA. Und laß auch die Göttinn nichts beweisen! Sie mag nicht gewollt oder nicht gekonnt haben! — Was hier, hier noch klopft, (auf ihr Herz) ist mir glaubwürdiger, als alle Götter. Mein Herz, das mit seinem Herze so innig verwandt, so gleich gestimmt, so völlig nur ein Herz mit ihm war, diß Herz wäre nicht zugleich mit seinem gebrochen? Reiße die Blume am Bache von ihrem Stengel, und ihr Bild im Waßer verschwindet zugleich. Verdunkle

die Sonne, und der Mond hört auf zu scheinen — Nein, nichts kann
sich selbst überleben. Und nur mein Herz überlebte sich selbst?
überlebte das Herz, in welchem es lebte, durch das allein es lebte?
— Widersprich mir das, wenn du kannst! Widersprich mir
das, Mysis! Wie stumm und beschämt du da stehst! Habe
ich dich ertappt? — Nun gut, ihr habt mich aufgezogen, grausam aufgezogen. Aber macht auch einmal dem unmenschlichen
Scherze ein Ende! — Komm, hilf mir den Sarg aufmachen. Ich
wette mit dir, der Sarg ist leer — Telamon ist nicht darinn; oder
wenn er darinn ist, so wird er plötzlich auffahren, und mir lachend
in die Arme fallen. — Ich werde auch lachen wollen, aber das
Weinen wird mir näher seyn. — Nun, komm doch, Mysis; wenn
er allzulange so liegt, sich allzulange so zwingt und verstellt —
es könnte ihm schaden.   (*LM*, III, 451.4-453.12)

For the representation of this unusual character, Lessing has
employed what are, for him, unusual means. The most striking
feature is the use made of images, similes, and metaphors,
which are rare in Lessing's previous comedies in this degree of
concentration, although they play a much more significant
role in his critical prose works, as has been pointed out by
Lehmann.[30] Such figures of speech give a greater pathos to
the widow's language and enlarge the frame of reference of the
play. Her use of images is limited chiefly to the scene just
quoted, which represents an instance of concentrated metaphoric language rarely to be found in Lessing's dramas.
Thus, the widow wants Mysis to cleanse her husband's body
of the decay of death, just as she cleans and replenishes the
lamp. Then she asks Mysis whether she had not left her husband in blooming good health, "gleich einer Rose". In an
eloquent double simile which ranges in one leap from a flower
and a brook to the sun and moon, which had been mentioned
earlier in an imprecation, the widow expresses her feeling of
being out of joint with both the least and greatest orders of
magnitude in the universe. Lessing further reinforces her inner
agitation with a copious use of repetitions. Sometimes this
repetition is simple, such as "er, er", "nein, nein". Sometimes,
however, it is more involved, a single repeated phrase forming

[30]   August Lehmann, *Forschungen über Lessings Sprache*, pp. 21-99.

the framework around which an entire speech is organized. Thus, the triple use of "Komm", with the final repetition introducing the double use of "Du mußt", gives the passage from line 15 to 19 above, an insistent, compelling force seldom equalled in Lessing's comedies. Repetitions have the same effect in the passages from lines 48-54 and 56-58, above. In the first of these passages, Antiphila describes her devotions to Diana in an apostrophe to the goddess. "Täglich und stündlich in deinem Tempel, wo ich zu dir betete, dir Hymnen sang, dir opferte, und deine Priester beschenkte." Since Diana could not keep misfortune from her servant, Antiphila concludes that she could not be the great goddess Diana of Ephesus, and in a series of emphatic repetitions of the recital of the ways in which she had served the goddess, resolves to serve her no longer. "So will ich nie mehr zu ihr beten, nie mehr ihr Hymnen singen, nie mehr ihre Priester beschenken." In the incantatory style of this negating echo to the earlier cataloguing of her deeds, Antiphila shows a ritual-like rigidity. This gives the speech something of the force of a prayer and a curse.

The use of repetition to convey Antiphila's agitation is supported by the use of extremely short periods, with interrogatives and imperatives predominating. The occasional use of verb ellipsis ("Er, er, mein Telamon todt?") further adds to the frenetic quality of her style. Aposiopesis appears with relative rarity. The syntactic structure is intact throughout.

The language of Philokrates shifts subtly through many phases. When he first enters the tomb, it is with a sarcastic jest on his lips, aimed at the somewhat craven Dromo, who tells his captain not to be afraid. Philokrates answers, "O, den tapfern Dromo an seiner Seite, wer sollte sich fürchten?" This sharpness of tone is further emphasized by his epigrammatic response when Mysis assures him that Antiphila is a widow who does not want to be consoled. Philokrates answers, "O, wenn sie getröstet seyn wollte, so wäre sie schon getröstet! Die nicht getröstet seyn wollen, denen ist eben der Trost am nöthigsten. Die andern trösten sich selbst –" In saying this,

Philokrates has perhaps expressed the keynote for the entire play. Lest his interest and his idea of consolation seem too innocent, too humanitarian, however, he is made to say, when Mysis tells him that Antiphila is asleep, "Desto beßer! So kann ich erst sehen, ob sie des Tröstens werth ist" (*LM*, III, 455).

When he sees Antiphila, however, Philokrates's tone changes, and he gives a rhapsodic description of the charms of the beautiful widow:

PHILOKRATES. ... Venus, als sie ihren Adonis beweinte, war nicht rührender!

MYSIS. Nun haben Sie Ihre Neugierde gestillt, Herr Hauptmann! — Nun entfernen Sie sich wieder! Verlaßen Sie uns.

PHILOKRATES. Was sagst du? — Komm her, glückliche beneidenswürdige Sklavin! Denn du gehörst ihr zu. — Komm her; wie heißt deine Gebietherin?

MYSIS. Antiphila.

PHILOKRATES. Antiphila? Ein lieblicher, schmeichelnder Name! — Wie alt ist sie?

MYSIS. Vier und zwanzig Jahr —

PHILOKRATES. Nicht doch; das weis ich beßer. Aber meine Frage war auch so abgeschmackt. Es ist Hebe, die Göttinn der Jugend, die keine Jahre zählt. — Und hier, neben ihr, in diesem Sarge? —

MYSIS. Ruht ihr entseelter Gemahl.

PHILOKRATES. Wie lange hat er sie gehabt?

MYSIS. Ins fünfte Jahr.

PHILOKRATES. Wie alt starb er?

MYSIS. Im dreyßigsten.

PHILOKRATES. Und er liebte sie? Verstehe mich recht; es ist eine Unmöglichkeit, sie nicht zu lieben. — Ich frage: er liebte sie doch so sehr, so innig, mit der Liebe, der inbrünstigen Liebe? —

MYSIS. O ja; wie Sie aus ihrer Trostlosigkeit leicht schließen können.

PHILOKRATES. Hat sie Kinder von ihm?

MYSIS. Nein.

PHILOKRATES. Nein? (Antiphila wendet sich hier, um ihr Gesicht zu verbergen) Sieh, sie regt sich! Itzt wird sie erwachen. — Ich zittere vor Erwartung. — Nein, sie legt sich nur anders — und entzieht uns ihr Antlitz. Das holdseligste Antlitz! — Aber unendliche Reitze sind über den ganzen Körper verbreitet. Auch so könnte ich ein Jahr hier stehen, und sie anstaunen. — Dieses Haar,

so lockicht und wild! — Dieser Hals, mit seiner abfallenden
Schulter! — Diese Brust! Diese Hüfte! — dieser Fuß, so frey über
den andern geschlagen! Dieser Arm, so weiß, so rund! — Diese
Hand, so nachläßig im Schooße! — Diese ganze Stellung, so
mahlerisch hingeworffen! — Ah, diese Hand, — meinen Mund
auf diese Hand zu drücken, — da sie noch schläft — (er ergreift
sie)   (*LM*, III, 456.25-457.26)

Especially in the last passage, in which Philokrates describes
Antiphila's charms, Lessing's style shows how much he was involved with the visual arts at the time he was working on this
play. *Wie die Alten den Tod gebildet* possibly was a project
parallel to *Die Matrone von Ephesus*. This is especially evident
in Philokrates's mention of the fact that Antiphila's foot is
crossed over the other, which, as Lessing sought to demonstrate
in the abovementioned essay, was the sign in the art of antiquity that the sleeper was enjoying a peaceful sleep. At any
rate, Lessing's visual sense, as opposed to the abstract play of
ideas, is more strongly in evidence than in any previous piece.
Lessing puts these observations into the mouth of Philokrates
to define his character further, to motivate properly his actions
when the widow is awake. As he becomes more and more en-
raptured with what he sees, Philokrates's syntax, so firm and
epigrammatic at first, falls apart before the reader's very eyes.
His agitation at the sight of Antiphila becomes apparent at the
very first moment, when he first compares her to Venus mourning Adonis, then to Hebe, the eternally youthful cupbearer of
the gods. When he asks Mysis about Antiphila's relationship
with her husband, his speech becomes halting, and in his
excitement, he must constantly qualify and clarify his statements. He finally cannot bring his thought to the resolution
which it should find in a relative clause following the prepositional phrase, "... mit der Liebe, der inbrünstigen Liebe?
—". As his anticipation grows of seeing Antiphila awake and
speaking to her, and as he nears her resting place, Philokrates
becomes more and more agitated, which fact is clearly reflected in the further unraveling of his syntax (lines 30-34,
above). He follows her every movement with rapt admiration,

breaking into superlatives ("Das holdseligste Antlitz") and hyperbole ("... unendliche Reitze..."; "Auch so könnte ich ein Jahr hier stehen und sie anstaunen"). Again, repetitions with only slight variations are used, which reinforces Philokrates's trancelike style, an effect already created by the elliptical quality of his clauses, which trail off in adjectival phrases (lines 35-39, above). Thus, in differentiating between the ways the officer speaks before and after he has seen the widow, Lessing emphasizes how instantaneously smitten Philokrates is.

When he is actually speaking with Antiphila, we see another side of Philokrates's character, and therefore of his style. Now he is once again sure of himself and his goals, which are to gain the widow's confidence by claiming to have known her husband, and finally, by his own merits, to win her love. The following passage will show how Philokrates's style can be parodistically controlled, modelling itself to that of Antiphila's grief. Here, Antiphila is trying, for the last time, to persuade the officer not to spend the night in the tomb, although it is cold and raining outside, as he claims:

ANTIPHILA. Die Götter wißen es, wie gern immer unser Dach den Fremdling, den Schutzlosen aufgenommen! Ganz Ephesus nannte Cassandern[31] den Gastfreyen. — Aber wer fodert in einem Grabmahle das Gastrecht?

PHILOKRATES. Cassander? — Wen nennen Sie da, Madame?

ANTIPHILA. Wen sonst, als ihn?

PHILOKRATES. Ihren Gemahl? — Aber doch nicht Cassandern, des Metrophanes Sohn?

ANTIPHILA. Des Metrophanes Sohn.

PHILOKRATES. Des Metrophanes Sohn, den Phylarchen?

ANTIPHILA. Den Phylarchen.

PHILOKRATES. Den Phylarchen? den großmüthigen bey allen Bedürfnißen des Staats sich selbst erbietenden Liturgen?

ANTIPHILA. Ihn! eben ihn!

---

[31] There is a discrepancy in the names given Antiphila's husband. In the early scenes, he is Telamon, in the later, Cassander.

PHILOKRATES. Und dieser Cassander ist todt? Und dieser Cassander war Ihr Gemahl?

ANTIPHILA. Und Sie haben ihn gekannt?

PHILOKRATES. Ob ich ihn gekannt habe? Diesen tapfersten, edelsten, besten aller Männer von Ephesus!

ANTIPHILA. Besten aller Männer! Dieß war er! — war er! (indem sie sich wendet, und mit gerungnen Händen nach den Särgen geht.)

PHILOKRATES. (der ihr folgen will.) Ob ich ihn gekannt?

MYSIS. (ihn zurückhaltend) Ein Wort, Herr Hauptmann —

PHILOKRATES. Was willst du, Mysis?

MYSIS. Im Vertrauen, Herr Hauptmann — Sie können doch lesen?

PHILOKRATES. Warum nicht?

MYSIS. Geschriebnes, und in Stein Gehauenes?

PHILOKRATES. Beides.

MYSIS. Und haben ein gutes Gedächtniß, Herr Hauptmann?

PHILOKRATES. So ziemlich. Aber mach ein Ende: was willst du? —

MYSIS. Nun so wette ich, daß Sie unsern Todten nicht gekannt haben —

PHILOKRATES. Aber du hörst es ja —

MYSIS. Sondern daß Sie, bey dem Scheine Ihrer Fackel, das Epitaph draußen über dem Eingange gelesen haben.

PHILOKRATES. Verleumderinn! — Aber, liebe Mysis, wette was du willst; du sollst alles gewinnen: nur sey mir nicht zu wider — Unterstütze mich —

MYSIS. Nur frisch! Das Eisen glüht; folgen Sie ihr —

PHILOKRATES. (der ihr in der Vertiefung nachgcht) Ob ich Cassandern gekannt? — Wir thaten zusammen unsern ersten Feldzug. In so feurigen Jahren knüpft gemeinschaftliche Gefahr die zärtlichsten Freundschaften. Die unsere ward durch meinen Aufenthalt an dem Persischen Hofe unterbrochen. Darauf entstand dieser Krieg mit den Kolophoniern. Ich mußte zu meinem Phalanx, ohne Cassandern vorher umarmen zu dürfen. Und indeß — indeß hat ihn die grausame Parze abgefodert! O ich Unglücklicher! — Doch mein Schmerz, Madame, hat kein Recht, sich neben dem Ihrigen zu äußern. (*LM*, III, 463.3-464.12)

Philokrates, for all of his serious designs on Antiphila, is here parodistically reciting the epitaph of the dead Cassander, as the participial extended adjectival phrase "den großmüthigen, bey allen Bedürfnißen des Staats sich selbst erbietenden

Liturgen" shows, which seems stilted and out of place in the otherwise colloquial tone of the dialogue. Antiphila, however, does not hear this discrepancy, although Mysis does, and calls the attention of Philokrates (and the audience) to it. His brusque, natural tone when talking to Mysis serves to heighten the contrast between this tone and his tone when speaking again with Antiphila, where he takes on the pathos of her mourning very adeptly, ornamenting his discourse with comparatively vivid adjectives, ("In so feurigen Jahren knüpft gemeinschaftliche Gefahr die zärtlichsten Freundschaften"), and mythological figures, ("die grausame Parze"). Although Philokrates's language shows these three distinct styles, epigrammatic, emotional, and parodistic, on three distinct levels of colloquial and even semi-poetic discourse, he still appears as a unified character, sensitive and responsive to each situation in which he finds himself.

The farcical element in *Die Matrone von Ephesus* is constituted, of course, by Mysis and Dromo. More than providing a gratuitous comic touch, however, they comment epigrammatically on the central matter of the play. While they distinctly lead their own lives as characters, they are more thoroughly integrated into the structure of the play than most of the servants encountered thus far. As the following excerpt from the second scene shows, the style of Dromo and Mysis, despite the macabre environment in which their conversation takes place, is still very much that of Lessing's earlier and more conventional comic servants. In this scene, Dromo has stumbled into the tomb and, at first, takes Mysis for a ghost. When he lights his torch from her lamp, he is more convinced of her corporeality, but wishes to convince himself further, to which Mysis's objections are only moderate:

MYSIS. Wie ich nun sehe, so ist Er ja wohl gar ein Soldat.
   DROMO. Zu dienen, mein freundliches Gespenst —
   MYSIS. Aber für einen Soldaten ist Er auch verzweifelt furchtsam.
   DROMO. Ja, ich bin nicht Soldat, mich mit dem Teufel zu balgen
— Diß gesagt, ohne dich erzürnen zu wollen, lieber Geist —

Mysis. Er ist nicht klug mit Seinem Geiste! Noch leib ich, und leb ich.

Dromo. Wie? im Ernst? — Mit Erlaubniß! (indem er sie mit der flachen Hand hier und da behutsam betastet) Gewiß, das Ding ist doch ziemlich compact (geht mit der Laterne rund um sie herum, und leuchtet ihr endlich ins Gesicht) Ey! ein allerliebstes Gesichtchen! Nein das Gesichtchen gehört wohl keinem Gespenste. Welch ein Paar Augen! Was für ein Mündchen! Was für ein Paar Bäckchen! (indem er sie in den einen Backen kneift.)

Mysis. Nun? was soll das? — Weg doch!

Dromo. Ich muß mich ja wohl überzeugen, daß es wirkliches Fleisch ist. — Wahrhaftig, wirkliches Fleisch! Und gesundes, derbes Fleisch. (indem er sie auch in den andern kneift) — Wird mir doch wieder ganz wohl ums Herze! — Was sagte Sie denn, mein schönes Kind, ich wäre im Grabe? bey Todten?

Mysis. Das ist er dem ohngeachtet doch!

Dromo. Doch? (sieht sich mit der Laterne um) — Ah! Särge? — Und was sitzt denn auf dem einen? —

Mysis. St! geh Er nicht zu nahe! Er möchte sie aufwecken.

Dromo. Schläfts nur? Was ist es denn?

Mysis. Es ist meine arme Frau; eine unglückliche junge Wittwe.

Dromo. Junge Wittwe? Und was macht ihr denn hier zusammen?

Mysis. Ist das noch zu fragen? Sie hat ihren Gatten verloren.

Dromo. So muß sie sich einen andern nehmen. Aber hier wird sie ihn schwerlich finden.

Mysis. Einen andern? Sein Glück, mein Freund, daß sie schläft, und diese Lästerung nicht hört. Einen zweyten Gatten! O Gott, über die Weiber, die einen zweyten Mann nehmen können!

Dromo. Nun? warum nicht? Einen zweyten, einen dritten, einen vierten — Nur nicht alle auf einmal! —

Mysis. Weil ihr Männer es mit den Weibern so haltet! — Nein, weiß Er, daß meine Frau eine tugendhafte Frau ist.

Dromo. Welche Frau wäre das nicht!

Mysis. Sie ist keine von denen die ihr Herz verschenken, und wieder nehmen und wieder verschenken —

Dromo. Giebt es dergleichen?

Mysis. Wer es einmal beseßen, soll es ewig besitzen.

Dromo. Ey!

Mysis. Sie hat ihren Mann über alles in der Welt geliebt —

Dromo. Das ist viel!

Mysis. Und liebt ihn noch über alles!

Dromo. Das ist gar zu viel! Er ist ja gestorben.

Mysis. Drum will sie auch sterben.

Dromo. O geh Sie, Kind; mach Sie mir nichts weiß.

MYSIS. Wie könnte sie einen solchen Verlust auch ertragen? Ihre Verzweiflung ist aufs äußerste gestiegen. Wenn Gram und Hunger tödten können, so wird sie es nicht lange mehr machen. Hier, neben dem Sarge ihres geliebten Mannes, will sie den Geist aufgeben. Schon haben sie alle Kräfte verlaßen. Nachdem sie zwey-mal vier und zwanzig Stunden nichts als gejammert, und geweint, und geschrieen, und die Hände gerungen, und die Haare zerrißen, ist sie vor Ermüdung eingeschlaffen —

DROMO. Und schläft ziemlich fest. Gut; Schlaf bringt auf beßere Gedanken. Wenn sie wieder aufwacht, wird alles vorbey seyn. Ich kenne das!

MYSIS. (bitter) Ich kenne das? Was kennt Er denn, Herr Soldat? Er mag viel kennen! — So? ist der Herr auch von den abgeschmakten Spöttern, die an die Treue der Frauen nicht glauben?

DROMO. Ich? behüte! Ich glaube ja an Gespenster — wie Sie gesehen hat, mein Kind —, warum sollte ich an die Treue der Frauen nicht glauben? Ich glaube an alles, was nicht so recht glaublich ist.   (*LM*, III, 447.24-449.28)

Compared to the relatively highly-charged, frequently almost poetic language of Philokrates and Antiphila, this dialogue between Mysis and Dromo fairly bubbles with a colloquial common sense which belies the background against which it takes place. At first, Mysis is the one to bring Dromo, who believes she is a ghost, to his senses. When he addresses her as "lieber Geist", she deflates him with a wicked little pun, "Er ist nicht klug mit Seinem Geiste". Dromo's direct way of convincing himself that Mysis is indeed no ghost is an anti-cipation on a lower level of the way in which Philokrates will lovingly observe and ecstatically describe the charms of Mysis's mistress. The use of diminutives adds to the colloquial in-formality of the description. When Dromo finally apprehends where he is, and with whom, his healthy equilibrium returns, and, with heavy epigrammatic irony, he comments on Mysis's exposition. When he sees that his direct suggestions that Antiphila remarry have no effect, he pretends to believe Mysis, his answers to her statements becoming shorter and shorter, until he finally bursts out in irritation: "O geh Sie, Kind, mach Sie mir nichts weiß!" When Mysis does not

respond even to this outburst, and still disagrees with him,
Dromo again becomes very matter-of-fact; "Schlaf bringt auf
beßre Gedanken.", and finally coldly ironical: "Ich glaube ja
an Gespenster – ... – warum sollte ich an die Treue der
Frauen nicht glauben? Ich glaube an alles, was nicht so recht
glaublich ist." Dromo's comments on Antiphila's vow are
those of humane rationality sense, and might be said to reflect
the attitude of Lessing to the entire idea. As Dromo is a parody
of his commander, so Mysis is a parody of her mistress, and
uses, in this dialogue with Dromo, phrases which she has
obviously picked up from Antiphila, and in which she herself
does not really believe. Thus, as on lines 32-33 and 36-37,
above, Mysis will make statements quite out of line with her
normally skeptical and rational character, which corresponds,
as the later action of the play reveals, far more to that of Dromo
than to that of her mistress.

The general characteristics of the style of such a scene have
not changed essentially in twenty years. In this scene, the use
of anadiplotic links, a device favored by Lessing throughout
his career as a dramatist, can be observed clearly, used in the
last of his comedies as it had been in the first. Again, the lines
are short, exclamations and interrogatives being favored.
The effect here, as it was in *Der junge Gelehrte*, is to give the
dialogue a sprightly tone. What *Die Matrone von Ephesus* has
stylistically in common with *Minna von Barnhelm* is the range of
possible styles in which a character can move, according to
situation and mood. The language is thus more supple in its
possibilities. The differences between the various styles, the
directly epigrammatic or colloquial, the emotionally poetic or
the parodistic, are patently present.

The setting of *Die Matrone von Ephesus* already indicates a
movement on Lessing's part away from the standard mold
of regular European comedy. The intellectual content of the
play and especially its stylistic richness reinforce this impression. It might be speculated that Lessing was moving towards
a new conception of comedy, dissolved from the immediate
social context, thus breaking away from the theoretical excuse

for comedy as a literary form, and concerned with more general human problems, treated in an exotic setting. In this respect, albeit in hardly any other, *Die Matrone von Ephesus* might be seen as a forerunner not so much of *Emilia Galotti* as of *Nathan der Weise*.

The purpose of this chapter has been to trace the progress of Lessing's language in the comedies and comic fragments written between 1749 and 1771. They represent sporadic and minor efforts on Lessing's part, treated almost furtively as "Kindereien" in a turbulent period of his life when, in the main, more important matters by far moved him. Yet for all of that, these pieces show Lessing in his step-by-step development, experimenting with and discarding various possibilities for comedy. Neither the model of Roman comedy, represented by Plautus, nor that of Goldoni's Italian regular comedy could ultimately hold his attention very long, and Lessing's conventional treatment of the plays of these masters of the comic form, technically ingenious as it often may have been, betrays his waning enthusiasm for comedy as an outlet for his creative energies before he went to Breslau. It is significant, too, that we should find indications of new directions, a few in *Der Schlaftrunk*, many more in *Die Matrone von Ephesus*, only in the plays begun after Lessing completed his comic masterpiece, *Minna von Barnhelm*.

V. MINNA VON BARNHELM

It is generally acknowledged that *Minna von Barnhelm* is the crowning achievement of Lessing's career as a writer of comedies. The circumstances surrounding the creation of the play, analyses of the plot and structure, the relationship of its matter to the life of Lessing's time; all of these have been subjects of various studies and unlike these facts about the lesser-known comedies do not require further mention here, except as they may relate to the language of the play. The purpose of this chapter shall be to demonstrate the significance of language in *Minna von Barnhelm* as an element contributing to its total success as a work of art and to its legendary durability upon the German stage. The chapter is also to show that the use of certain stylistic devices of characterization is not new or peculiar to this comedy, but rather that, in respect to its language, *Minna von Barnhelm* is the culmination of a long development in Lessing's use of language.

Since *Minna* is the best-known of Lessing's comedies, having received by far the most critical attention, it is the comedy in which the role of language has been most generally recognized. Erich Schmidt, for example, speaks of the way in which characters are contrasted according to social station and character through devices of language, of the grace and strength of the dialogue, and of its spontaneous and energetic quality.

... Wohl sind einige Stellen der letzten Akte künstlich, doch die Abtönung nach Stand, Charakter und Geschlecht verdient das höchste Lob. Wie artig weicht Franziskas Geplauder von Minnas sicherer Haltung und Gewandtheit ab; wie stark strömt das lang

niedergepreßte Pathos Tellheims hervor; wie munter kontrastiert
der Schwall des geschmeidigen Wirtes, der gleich anfangs auch
volkstümliche Trinksprüchlein auskramt, mit Justs Gebrumm, und
wie viel vulgärer als der Wachtmeister darf der Reitknecht
sprechen! ... In der 'Minna' erreicht Lessings Gesprächskunst
ihren Gipfel, ... Wie ein Ball wird der Dialog in verschiedenem
Ton, Tempo und Ausmaß hin und her geschlagen. Was das
Fräulein sagt, schwatzt der Wirt als seine Weisheit nach; was
Tellheim zu Minna äußert, spielt diese dann gegen ihn selbst aus;
was Werner leicht hinwirft, hält Franciska ihm später neckisch vor.
Die leisesten Winke werden aufgefaßt, Reden und Gegenreden
wechseln behend, so daß ausgesponnenes oder zu Berechnetes
dagegen verschwindet. Ueberall bietet sich eine Fülle frischer, an-
mutiger, derber, nachdenklicher, geistreicher Wendungen dar,
ohne den Eindruck, als seien sie mühsam gesucht, denn 'macht
man das, was einem so einfällt?' [1]

This is perhaps the most concise summation of the features of
the language of *Minna von Barnhelm* which such commentators
as Paul Böckmann and Otto Mann have singled out. None of
them, however, describes precisely how the effects mentioned
by Schmidt are achieved. [2] Of course, none of these critics was
primarily interested in the language of the play, but rather in
interpreting its action or analyzing its structure. The studies of
Mohri and Schuchmann, which treat the dramaturgic technique of Lessing's dialogue, do not directly discuss the problem
of Lessing's style, although, as has been mentioned, Mohri
touches upon it when problems of dramaturgy and style
intersect. [3] Thus, both as a climax to the present study and as a

---

[1] Schmidt, *Lessing*, I, p. 464.
[2] See Paul Böckmann, *op. cit.*, I, pp. 540-46 and Otto Mann, *Lessing,
Sein und Leistung*, 2nd edn. (Hamburg, 1961), pp. 209-13. Bockmann sees
the language of *Minna von Barnhelm* as a function of Lessing's penetration
beyond the forming principle of "Witz". The language of "Witz" in
Minna is employed as an essential prelude to the language of the heart, and
the purely intellectual function of comedy is overcome. Mann discusses
Lessing's combination of the characterizing and expressive functions of
language in *Minna*. As has already been observed in Chapter II, language
had this dual function in Lessing's comedies far earlier.
[3] Hans Schuchmann, *Studien zum Dialog im Drama Lessings und Schillers;*
Wilhelm Mohri, *Die Technik des Dialoges in Lessings Dramen.*

contribution to the literature specifically dealing with *Minna*, it seems fitting to examine closely the language of this greatest of Lessing's comedies.

A most pertinent and analytical comment on the style of *Minna* was made in the very year of its publication, 1767, in *Unterhaltungen*, a periodical appearing in Hamburg, where, in the course of a long and not altogether laudatory article on *Minna*, the anonymous critic said:

> Ein besonderes Lob verdient noch der Dialog des Herrn Leßings. Es herrschet darinn allenthalben der wahre ungekünstelte Ton des Umgangs; er hat die verschiednen Redensarten des höhern und niedern Standes, die eigenthümlichen Wendungen der Sprache überhaupt, und die besondern Inversionen und Ausdrücke der Leidenschaft und der Laune vollkommen in seiner Gewalt; seine Personen reden beständig munter, unterhaltend, charakteristisch; alles was sie sagen, hängt ohne ängstliche Verbindung, in der verschönerten Unordnung wirklicher Gespräche, an einander; sie locken sich die Antworten ab, unterbrechen sich oft, und zwar beständig da, wo sie es sollen; und endlich die episodischen Einfälle, die zum Hauptzweck der Scene entbehrlich wären, aber die Charaktere nach ihren feinsten Zügen auszubilden dienen, sind sehr natürlich ins Ganze hineingeflochten.[4]

This description lends support to the thesis put forth in this study; that there is a continuity of style from the beginning of Lessing's career to its climax. For here we find in a nutshell the stylistic elements present in the first play examined, *Der junge Gelehrte*, whose language C. H. Schmid had described even more concisely as being "Natürlich und dennoch gewählt, familiär und dennoch witzig, körnigt und dennoch geschmeidig" (cf. p. 29, above). The language of *Minna*, says the writer, has the tone of natural colloquial conversation, the level which was found to prevail in *Der junge Gelehrte*, and within this wide range, the various modes of colloquial language graded in shading from elevated conversation to ordinary slang. *Der junge Gelehrte* was also found to employ inversions, oaths,

---

[4]   Quoted in Julius Braun, *Lessing im Urtheile seiner Zeitgenossen*, 3 vols. (Berlin, 1884-97), I, p. 192.

exclamations, "die eigenthümlichen Wendungen der Sprache überhaupt". In that first play, the characters also spoke "charakteristisch", each with his own particular tone and sometimes with a characteristic speech tag, traces of which feature will still be found in *Minna*. The colloquial indirectness and leisureliness of dialogue, enlivened by a liberal use of ellipsis, which was noted in *Der junge Gelehrte* is also observed by our writer in *Minna*, where, as in *Der junge Gelehrte*, the disorder of colloquial speech, despite its vividly lifelike effect, is still definitely purposive, is "verschönert". Clearly, Lessing's device of linking the speeches through anadiplosis, thus achieving a connection which is not "ängstlich" is meant by the critic's statement, "sie locken sich die Antworten ab". Aposiopesis, which Lessing could use to such good effect at the start of his career, was evidently also observed by our commentator, for he says that the characters interrupt their speeches frequently, and always at the proper point.

To illustrate the stylistic features which this early critic found in *Minna* and to relate them to those found in earlier comedies, let us examine an excerpt from one of the best-loved scenes in the play, that between Just and the Innkeeper in Act I, Scene 2:

DER WIRTH. Ey, Herr Just! ich will doch nicht hoffen, Herr Just, daß Er noch von gestern her böse ist? Wer wird seinen Zorn über Nacht behalten?

JUST. Ich; und über alle folgende Nächte.

DER WIRTH. Ist das christlich?

JUST. Eben so christlich, als einen ehrlichen Mann, der nicht gleich bezahlen kann, aus dem Hause stoßen, auf die Straße werfen.

DER WIRTH. Pfuy, wer könnte so gottlos seyn?

JUST. Ein christlicher Gastwirth. — Meinen Herrn! so einen Mann! so einen Officier!

DER WIRTH. Den hätte ich aus dem Hause gestoßen? auf die Straße geworfen? Dazu habe ich viel zu viel Achtung für einen Officier, und viel zu viel Mitleid mit einem abgedankten! Ich habe ihm aus Noth ein ander Zimmer einräumen müssen. — Denke Er nicht mehr daran, Herr Just. (Er rufft in die Scene:) Holla! — Ich wills auf andere Weise wieder gut machen. (Ein Junge kömmt)

Bring ein Gläßchen; Herr Just will ein Gläßchen haben; und was gutes!

JUST. Mache Er sich keine Mühe, Herr Wirth. Der Tropfen soll zu Gift werden, den — Doch ich will nicht schwören; ich bin noch nüchtern!

DER WIRTH. (zu dem Jungen, der eine Flasche Liqueur und ein Glaß bringt) Gieb her; geh! — Nun, Herr Just; was ganz vortreffliches; stark, lieblich, gesund. (er füllt, und reicht ihm zu) Das kann einen überwachten Magen wieder in Ordnung bringen!

JUST. Bald dürfte ich nicht! — Doch warum soll ich meiner Gesundheit seine Grobheit entgelten lassen? — (er nimmt und trinkt)

DER WIRTH. Wohl bekomms, Herr Just!

JUST. (indem er das Gläßchen wieder zurück giebt) Nicht übel! — Aber Herr Wirth, Er ist doch ein Grobian!

DER WIRTH. Nicht doch, nicht doch! — Geschwind noch eins; auf einem Beine ist nicht gut stehen.

JUST. (nachdem er getrunken) Das muß ich sagen: gut, sehr gut! — Selbst gemacht, Herr Wirth? —

DER WIRTH. Behüte! veritabler Danziger! echter, doppelter Lachs!

JUST. Sieht Er, Herr Wirth; wenn ich heucheln könnte, so würde ich für so was heucheln; aber ich kann nicht; es muß raus: — Er ist doch ein Grobian, Herr Wirth!

DER WIRTH. In meinem Leben hat mir das noch niemand gesagt. — Noch eins, Herr Just; aller guten Dinge sind drey!

JUST. Meinetwegen! (er trinkt) Gut Ding, wahrlich gut Ding! — Aber auch die Wahrheit ist gut Ding. — Herr Wirth, Er ist doch ein Grobian!

DER WIRTH. Wenn ich es wäre, würde ich das wohl so mit anhören?

JUST. O ja, denn selten hat ein Grobian Galle.

DER WIRTH. Nicht noch eins, Herr Just? Eine vierfache Schnur hält desto besser.

JUST. Nein, zu viel ist zu viel! Und was hilfts Ihm, Herr Wirth? Bis auf den letzten Tropfen in der Flasche würde ich bey meiner Rede bleiben. Pfuy, Herr Wirth; so guten Danziger zu haben, und so schlechte Mores! — Einem Manne, wie meinem Herrn, der Jahr und Tag bey Ihm gewohnt, von dem Er schon so manchen schönen Thaler gezogen, der in seinem Leben keinen Heller schuldig geblieben ist; weil er ein Paar Monate her nicht prompt bezahlt, weil er nicht mehr so viel aufgehen läßt, — in der Abwesenheit das Zimmer auszuräumen!

DER WIRTH. Da ich aber das Zimmer nothwendig brauchte?

da ich voraus sahe, daß der Herr Major es selbst gutwillig würde geräumt haben, wenn wir nur lange auf seine Zurückkunft hätten warten können? Sollte ich denn so eine fremde Herrschaft wieder von meiner Thüre wegfahren lassen? Sollte ich einem andern Wirthe so einen Verdienst muthwillig in den Rachen jagen? Und ich glaube nicht einmal, daß sie sonst wo unterkommen wäre. Die Wirthshäuser sind jetzt alle stark besetzt. Sollte eine so junge, schöne, liebenswürdige Dame, auf der Straße bleiben? Dazu ist Sein Herr viel zu galant! Und was verliert er denn dabey? Habe ich ihm nicht ein anderes Zimmer dafür eingeräumt?

JUST. Hinten an dem Taubenschlage; die Aussicht zwischen des Nachbars Feuermauren —

DER WIRTH. Die Aussicht war wohl sehr schön, ehe sie der verzweifelte Nachbar verbaute. Das Zimmer ist doch sonst galant, und tapezirt —

JUST. Gewesen!

DER WIRTH. Nicht doch, die eine Wand ist es noch. Und Sein Stübchen darneben, Herr Just; was fehlt dem Stübchen? Es hat einen Kamin; der zwar im Winter ein wenig raucht —

JUST. Aber doch im Sommer recht hübsch läßt. —

(LM, II, 174.6-176.9)

This scene is a model example of Lessing's technique for embedding leisurely exposition in a scene in which the main objects seem to be to exploit the humor of a situation embellished by characterizing episodic touches. Here, in contrast to the splitting of the functions of exposition and characterization so evident in Lessing's earliest plays, we see the perfect blending of these functions. More importantly, we can find in this passage once again the features already present and fully and consciously used in *Der junge Gelehrte.* Again, the clauses are terse, running, as befits such an agitated scene, to exclamatory, interrogative, and imperative clauses, rather than to more involved normal declarative clauses. Interjections abound, such as "Ey", "Pfuy", "Holla", "Behüte!", "O ja". Vulgar pejoratives are used by the appropriate characters, chiefly Just, who here restricts himself to a triple use of the mild term "Grobian", but in the previous scene has availed himself of "Schurke", and in the course of the first act will use "des hämischen, unbarmherzigen Rackers", and finally, in Act I, Scene 12, his famous and, at the time, controversial line, "Wie wärs ... wenn wir ihm seine Tochter zur Hure machten?" As the critic of the *Unterhaltungen* mentioned, inversions are used in *Minna*, as they were in *Der junge Gelehrte*. Thus we find: "Den hätte ich aus dem Hause gestoßen? ... Dazu habe ich viel zu viel Achtung für einen Officier, ...", "Bald dürfte ich nicht!", "In meinem Leben hat mir das noch niemand gesagt!", "O ja, denn selten hat ein Grobian Galle", "Bis auf den letzten Tropfen in der Flasche würde ich bey meiner Rede bleiben." These inversions again lend a free and natural flavor to the dialogue by re-creating the pattern of shifting word order and emphasis found in colloquial speech.

The dialogue is also given its spontaneous flavor by the liberal use of ellipsis. Just's speech is full of it. In his anger, he expresses himself extensively in minor clauses, and, as in ordinary conversation, his meaning is perfectly clear within the given context. Thus, at the beginning of the passage, when the Innkeeper asks, "Wer wird seinen Zorn über Nacht behalten?" Just answers elliptically, "Ich; und über alle folgende Nächte." His response to the Innkeeper's next question is similar in tone, sputtering by his third speech only in disconnected, albeit perfectly comprehensible phrases, "Ein christlicher Gastwirt. – Meinen Herrn! so einen Mann! so einen Officier!" A striking feature of Just's language in this passage is his frequent use of what Curme, in his *A Grammar of the German Language*, terms the absolute infinitive, illustrating again Lessing's willful loosening of grammatical cohesion in dialogue in order to create the illusion of colloquial speech. Thus, when the Innkeeper asks him, "Ist das christlich?", referring to Just's stubborn rage, Just replies with the absolute infinitive; "Eben so christlich, als einen ehrlichen Mann, der nicht gleich bezahlen kann, aus dem Hause stoßen, auf die Straße werfen." This gives a spontaneous terseness and vividness, for example, to Just's antithetical reproach: "Pfuy, Herr Wirth; so guten Danziger zu haben, und so schlechte Mores!". The absolute infinitive here stands at once as a connective between the two comically opposite poles of the antithesis, the good "Danziger" and the bad "Mores", and as a factor momentarily delaying and making more comical their coming into contrast with each other. Hard on the heels of this comes Just's most spectacular use of the absolute infinitive in this passage (lines 55-60, above). Just begins with the object of a verbal construction as yet indefinite, vehemently follows this up with relative clauses, and then, apparently not sure any longer of how he began his sentence, closes it with an accusative and the absolute infinitive. In this passage in particular, we see how smoothly Lessing can now combine the dialogue's functions of exposition and characterization through the conscious use of stylistic devices.

Aposiopesis, another important element in creating the illusion of colloquial language, is used to a lesser extent here than in *Der junge Gelehrte*, where it appeared occasionally in excessive concentration. Just judiciously interrupts himself in the act of refusing a drink: "Der Tropfen soll zu Gift werden, den – Doch ich will nicht schwören; ..." Again, when the Innkeeper is trying to convince him of the quality of his new room; "Das Zimmer ist doch sonst galant, und tapezirt –", Just sharply cuts him off; "Gewesen!". Other instances of the effective use of this device shall be cited below. Suffice it to say here that aposiopesis is still a pertinent feature of Lessing's comic style.

The passage is intricately held together by anadiplotic links, another of Lessing's favorite devices. Just picks up the Innkeeper's "über Nacht" on line 3, and varies and intensifies it to "und über alle folgenden Nächte" (line 4, above). He belabors the In-keeper with his own reproachful adjective "christlich", using it as an ironic cudgel on lines 6 and 10, above. The Innkeeper indignantly picks up Just's phrases, "aus dem Hause stoßen, auf die Straße werfen" (lines 7-8, above), and returns them in the interrogative two speeches later on lines 12-13, above. In rationalizing his acceptance of the offer of a drink, Just slyly picks up and intensifies a word from the Innkeeper's description of the Danziger as "stark, lieblich, gesund", saying, "Warum soll ich meiner Gesundheit seine Grobheit entgelten lassen?" This use of the stem "Grob-" is echoed by Just's threefold repetition of the pejorative "Grobian", with which he parries the Innkeeper's encouragements to drink more. At the end of the passage, the device is varied by having Just, with comic deflation, finish the Innkeeper's praise of the room which he has given Just: "WIRTH. Es hat einen Kamin, der zwar im Winter ein wenig raucht – / JUST. Aber doch im Sommer recht hübsch läßt." This use of anadiplotic links, coupled with an effective antithesis, makes the actors seem more attuned to each other, makes them, in the words of the critic of *Unterhaltungen*, "snatch the answers from each other".

We have seen that the devices for creating a lively dialogue, one which cleaves close to the reality of colloquial speech, are, in *Minna von Barnhelm*, still basically the same ones which Lessing developed during his dramatic apprenticeship in Leipzig. What makes the difference in *Minna* is the masterful way in which Lessing has handled these devices in creating a characteristic pattern of language for each of the various roles he has written. If *Minna von Barnhelm* can be considered the apotheosis of the Franco-German comedy of the eighteenth century, incorporating the best possibilities of that very specialized medium, then the language of *Minna* can be seen as the summation of the best qualities of its language. Let us consider the ways in which Lessing applies his mastery of comic language in creating the characters of *Minna von Barnhelm*.

Many commentators have mentioned the way in which the characters are distinguished in their language from each other according to the social or professional class which each represents. Erich Schmidt's comment, quoted on pages 188-9, above, is once again fairly representative. The hierarchy of male characters is more elaborate and covers a wider range than that of the female characters. At the top of the social scale stands Tellheim. Below him, in descending order, are Riccaut de la Marlinière, Werner, the Innkeeper, and Just. The occasional servants who appear have such small parts as to be extraneous to our present considerations. The social scale ou the female side embraces Minna, Frau Marloff, and Franciska. Thus, minor nobility, a middle class newly prosperous through the war, male and female servants, and especially various levels of soldiery are represented. Each is characterized not only by traits of character and action, but definitely set off from the others by the way the representative of each of these classes speaks. In our analysis, we will begin with the characters most extraneous to the central action of the play, with Riccaut and the Innkeeper, proceeding to Just, Werner, and Franciska, and culminating in an examination of the ways in which the characters of Tellheim and Minna are stylistically developed as the play proceeds.

Lessing has made particularly conscious and successful use of personal pronouns of direct address in *Minna von Barnhelm*. These pronouns establish parallel hierarchies of social gradation and degrees of intimacy in an apparently precise and realistic manner. Among the ten characters appearing in the play, we can distinguish twenty-two dialogue relationships; that is, instances in which two characters are involved in a dialogue in such a way that their social relationship can be established. In terms of the pronouns of personal address they use in speaking with each other, these relationships can be divided into six distinct groups as follows. The character using the form is entered in the appropriate column:

I. *"du" answered with "du"*
    (1) Just   : Werner
II. *"Er" answered mit "Er" or "Sie"* (*3rd person singular*)
    (2) Franciska   : Just
    (3) Franciska   : Werner
    (4) Just   : Wirth
    (5) Just   : Ein Bedienter
III. *"Sie" answered with "Sie"* (*3rd person plural*)
    (6) Tellheim   : Minna
    (7) Tellheim   : Frau Marloff
    (8) Tellheim   : Wirth

    (9) Tellheim   : Graf Bruchsall
   (10) Tellheim   : Feldjäger
   (11) Minna   : Riccaut
   (12) Minna   : Wirth

IV. *"du" answered with "Sie" (3rd person plural)*
   (13) Graf Bruchsall   : Minna
   (14) Minna   : Franciska
   (15) Tellheim   : Franciska
   (16) Tellheim   : Just
   (17) Tellheim   : Werner

V. *"Er" or "Sie" (3rd person singular) answered with "Sie" (3rd person plural) or "Ihro Gnaden" (3rd person plural)*
   (18) Wirth   : Franciska
   (19) Minna   : Just
   (20) Minna   : Werner
   (21) Werner   : Wirth

VI. *"Ihr" (2nd person plural) to be answered with "Sie" (3rd person plural)*
   (22) Tellheim   : Ein Bedienter

Discussing the state of these forms of address in Lessing's own time, George O. Curme writes: "Towards the third quarter of the eighteenth century, *Sie* (with the verb in the 3rd pers. pl.) was the very polite form used to persons of high rank or as a special mark of respect. *Er* and *Sie* (with verb in 3rd pers. sing.) were the ordinary polite forms for ordinary people not well acquainted, for older people in addressing respectfully those younger, for those in higher station for addressing in respectful tone those in lower station, or for young people who desired to be respectful to older people but not coldly formal. *Ihr* was still less formal, and *du* with its plural *ihr* was used towards intimate friends or towards young people. This state of things can be seen in Lessing's play *Minna von Barnhelm*"[5]. Thus, categories I-III represent relationships between social equals or people on a familiar basis; the last three categories

---

[5] George O. Curme, *A Grammar of the German Language*, 2nd rev. edn. (New York, 1952), p. 178.

represent progressively wider disparities in social rank and familiarity between the characters involved. Both Tellheim and Minna are addressed with "Sie" by all of the characters in this microcosm of society with one exception for each; for Minna, that of Graf Bruchsall, who, since he is her uncle, properly calls her "du", and for Tellheim, that of the epistolary king, who addresses him with "Euch". Standing thus at the top of the social order of this world, Minna and Tellheim have the widest range of forms of address at their command, calling other characters "Sie", "Er", "Ihr", or "du" as the relationship warrants. Just, to take the other extreme, is called variously "du" or "Er". Franciska's situation is analogous to Just's. The Innkeeper, socially in a commercial class, to which the vocabulary of polite forms of address has still not adapted itself, occupies an anomalous position. Thus, though clearly not on a social level with Tellheim and Minna, he is addressed by both as "Sie", the form of greatest respect. Yet he is addressed as "Er" by Werner and Just, and returns the compliment. Since Franciska is obviously considerably younger than the Innkeeper, she addresses him as "Sie" (3rd pers. pl.) and must content herself with a "Sie" (3rd pers. sing.) from him, since she clearly does not have the same prerogatives in this respect as does her mistress who is, of course, as old as Franciska. The character of the Innkeeper, sycophantic and ingratiating to all, is thus reinforced by his being accepted on all social strata. By being placed on no particular level, he is at home on all of them. The apparent precision of these forms can be deceptive, however. Just and Werner, evidently old friends from the war, address each other as "du", despite the present disparity in their fortunes and ranks. Although Tellheim calls both "du", and both address him as "Sie", the reasons behind these appellations are different. Just uses the form out of deference to his master, who has the right to call him "du" through the same convention which allows Minna to address Franciska as "du", who also calls her mistress "Sie". In contrast to the "Feldjäger" who delivers the letter to Tellheim, and with whom Tellheim is on a "Sie-Sie" basis, Werner is on a "Sie-du" basis with his former commander, still calling him "Sie" out of respect for his noble birth and higher military rank, but, for his friendship in battle, enjoying what is apparently the honor of being addressed with the more familiar form by his superior. The relationships of Werner and Just to Tellheim, which appear to be similar if judged by the forms of address alone, take on different forms when seen as they must be, in the light of the actual relationships of the characters involved within the world of the play. But otherwise, Lessing's subtly graded use of these forms of address gives clear indications of the social and personal distance between the characters, who address each other as would their counterparts in the world outside the play, further adding to the colloquial and realistic quality of its language. The realistic use of conventional forms of address forms a rigid, socially imposed framework within which the interaction of the characters, who are so very much alive, is even more vivid by contrast.

Riccaut de la Marlinière, the French soldier of ill-fortune who appears briefly but spectacularly in Act IV, Scene 2, is the character in the play drawn with the fewest and simplest strokes. His chief qualities are his love of dishonest gambling, his elaborately wounded pride and his pompous defense of both of these. Far from being merely a comical episodic figure, Riccaut serves a definite function within the economy of the play by bringing into even sharper relief the qualities of the play's two chief actors. Erich Schmidt[6] has already pointed out how Riccaut does this for Tellheim by embodying all that Tellheim is not; morally weak, complaining, dishonest, a man whose only response to misfortune is to attempt to recoup his losses by more or less reprehensible means. Riccaut

[6] "Diese Kontrastszene des bettelhaften, ehrlosen Renommisten, des 'Spitzbuben', des abgedankten Kapitäns in demselben Akt, wo das Ehrgefühl des abgedankten Majors seinen vollsten Ausdruck erhält, ist mit dem ganzen, wenn nicht unlöslich, doch fest genug verknüpft, als daß sie ohne weiteres ausgeschieden werden könnte." Schmidt, *Lessing*, I, p. 456.

also serves to emphasize Minna's innocence and generosity by arousing her indignation through his confession that he is about to gamble dishonestly with her money. In Riccaut, Minna is confronted with a grotesque caricature. He actually is in the state of dishonored beggary to which Tellheim, in his worst moments, claims to have sunken. Minna's only reaction to such a man can be pity, and certainly cannot include respect, not to mention love. Tellheim's determination not to confront Minna as a disgraced beggar, as far from the truth as this self-description may be, gains reinforcement through Minna's reaction to Riccaut.

Lessing's stylistic characterization of Riccaut involves techniques which recall those found in *Der junge Gelehrte*, namely the identification of a character with a comical pattern of speech, in this case his mangling of the German language both phonologically and grammatically, and his use of French phrases. Although the characterization of Riccaut represents a more generalized use of this device than has heretofore been the case, it does not, as it might have earlier, completely exhaust Riccaut's character. The mannerism is not merely a tag, monotonously repeated, but pervades Riccaut's entire speech pattern. We have seen earlier such figures as Christoph in *Die Juden*, who intersperse their speech with clumsy French phrases, but this is the first time that Lessing has made such broad use of this device. There are many precedents for this technique of characterization. Schmidt lists various ancestors of Riccaut.[7] Lessing does not content himself with merely letting Riccaut intersperse his German with French phrases, but achieves an amazingly accurate total re-creation of a Frenchman trying to speak German:

Mein Namen wünscht Ihro Gnad? — Vous voyés en moi — Ihro Gnad seh in mik le Chevalier Riccaut de la Marliniere, Seigneur de Pret-au-vol, de la Branche de Prensd'or. — Ihro Gnad steh verwundert, mik aus so ein groß, groß Familie zu hören, qui est

---

[7] Schmidt, *Lessing*, I, p. 455. Schmidt traces the character of Riccaut to the Marquis of Hazard in Mrs. Centlivre's *The Gamester* and to Tout-á-bas, maître de tric trac in Regnard's *Le Joueur*.

veritablement du sang Royal. — Il faut le dire; je suis sans doute
le Cadet le plus aventureux, que la maison a jamais eu — Ik dien
von meiner elfte Jahr. Ein Affaire d'honneur makte mik fliehen.
Darauf haben ik gedienet Sr. Päbstliken Eilikheit, der Republick
St. Marino, der Kron Pohlen, und den Staaten-General, bis ik
endlik bin worden gezogen hierher. Ah, Mademoiselle, que je
voudrais n'avoir jamais vû ce pais-la! Hätte man mik gelaß im
Dienst von den Staaten-General, so müßt ik nun seyn, auf wenikst
Oberst. Aber so hier immer und ewik Capitaine geblieben, und
nun gar seyn ein abgedankte Capitaine —.

(LM, II, 229.29-230.11)

From apparently first-hand observations of the difficulties of
Frenchmen with the German language, Lessing included
various phonological features in his linguistic characterization
of Riccaut. Like many speakers of French, Riccaut is unable
to pronounce the voiceless dorso-palatal and dorso-velar
spirants, thus saying "ik" and "mik" rather than "ich" and
"mich"; "makte" rather than "machte". His claim to having
served "Sr. Päbstliken Eilikheit" seems to indicate the
characteristic problem with the velar spirant /h/ in initial
position, although Lessing seems to have been less consistent
about indicating it, letting Riccaut say "hören", "haben",
"hierher", "hätte". Noun inflection fares equally badly at
the hands of Riccaut, and we find, among other comical er-
rors, "Mein Namen", "ein groß, groß Familie", "meiner elfte
Jahr", etc. Verb endings find no mercy either, to which such
forms as "Ihro Gnad seh in mik–", "Ihro Gnad steh verwundert...", "Darauf haben ik gedient...", etc., attest. Riccaut
represents Lessing's most sophisticated use of broadly characterizing stylistic features in the language of a single character,
a device which we have seen develop from the earliest of
Lessing's plays.

The Innkeeper represents a more subtle but equally clear-
cut type. He appears in various stylistic guises, once speaking
the convivial language of the tapster, then with the pompously
official tone of the representative of the very exact police, and
last of all, probably his true tone, with that of the cynically
calculating merchant, awaiting the opportunity to squeeze

the last grain of gold from his victim. This technique of making a character speak on various stylistic levels, depending on which character he is involved with at a given moment, is also one which we have encountered already, notably in *Die Juden*, where Martin Krumm was found to be clumsily servile and boorishly rude by turns. Of course, the Innkeeper is no Martin Krumm, and has been equipped by Lessing with a larger and more refined variety of stylistic masks, none of which, however, contradicts the central characterization. In the passage from Act I, Scene 2 quoted above, we already saw the first of the styles in the Innkeeper's repertoire. In this scene, he ingratiatingly tries to soothe Just's ire with his "veritabler Danziger". His tone is a mixture of homespun piety ("Wer wird seinen Zorn über Nacht behalten?", "Ist das christlich?") and of convivial licentiousness (his use of drinking proverbs). As has been mentioned, he puts himself on the same level with Just, on an "Er-Er" basis. His apparently pretended indignation at Just's accusations is reinforced by his dramatic inversion and occasionally pathetic vocabulary; "Dazu habe ich viel zu viel Achtung für einen Officier und viel zu viel Mitleid mit einem abgedankten!", with which he simultaneously defends his moral posture and puts Just in his place by reminding him that his master is "abgedankt".

The Innkeeper next appears in an entirely different light, when he must, both for the sake of his own curiosity and the requirements of the Prussian police, find out Minna's identity and business in Berlin:

DER WIRTH. (den Kopf voransteckend) Ist es erlaubt, meine gnädige Herrschaft? —

FRANCISKA. Unser Herr Wirth? — Nur vollends herein.

DER WIRTH. (mit einer Feder hinter dem Ohre, ein Blatt Papier und Schreibzeug in der Hand) Ich komme, gnädiges Fräulein, Ihnen einen unterthänigen guten Morgen zu wünschen ,— (zur Franciska) und auch Ihr, mein schönes Kind, —

FRANCISKA. Ein höflicher Mann!

DAS FRÄULEIN. Wir bedanken uns.

FRANCISKA. Und wünschen Ihm auch einen guten Morgen.

DER WIRTH. Darf ich mich unterstehen zu fragen, wie Ihro Gnaden die erste Nacht unter meinem schlechten Dache geruhet?

FRANCISKA. Das Dach ist so schlecht nicht, Herr Wirth; aber die Betten hätten besser seyn können.

DER WIRTH. Was höre ich? Nicht wohl geruht? Vielleicht, daß die gar zu große Ermüdung von der Reise —

DAS FRÄULEIN. Es kann seyn.

DER WIRTH. Gewiß, gewiß! denn sonst — Indeß sollte etwas nicht vollkommen nach Ihro Gnaden Bequemlichkeit gewesen seyn, so geruhen Ihro Gnaden, nur zu befehlen.

FRANCISKA. Gut, Herr Wirth, gut! Wir sind auch nicht blöde; und am wenigsten muß man im Gasthofe blöde seyn. Wir wollen schon sagen, wie wir es gern hätten.

DER WIRTH. Hiernächst komme ich zugleich — (indem er die Feder hinter dem Ohr hervorzieht)

FRANCISKA. Nun? —

DER WIRTH. Ohne Zweifel kennen Ihro Gnaden schon die weisen Verordnungen unserer Policey. —

DAS FRÄULEIN. Nicht im geringsten, Herr Wirth —

DER WIRTH. Wir Wirthe sind angewiesen, keinen Fremden, weß Standes und Geschlechts er auch sey, vier und zwanzig Stunden zu behausen, ohne seinen Namen, Heymath, Charakter, hiesige Geschäfte, vermuthliche Dauer des Aufenthalts, und so weiter, gehörigen Orts schriftlich einzureichen.

DAS FRÄULEIN. Sehr wohl.

DER WIRTH. Ihro Gnaden werden also Sich gefallen lassen — (indem er an einen Tisch tritt, und sich fertig macht, zu schreiben)

DAS FRÄULEIN. Sehr gern. — Ich heiße —

DER WIRTH. Einen kleinen Augenblick Geduld! — (er schreibt) "Dato, den 22. August a.c. allhier zum Könige von Spanien angelangt" — Nun Dero Namen, gnädiges Fräulein?

DAS FRÄULEIN. Das Fräulein von Barnhelm.

DER WIRTH. (schreibt) "von Barnhelm" — Kommend? woher, gnädiges Fräulein?

DAS FRÄULEIN. Von meinen Gütern aus Sachsen.

DER WIRTH. (schreibt) "Gütern aus Sachsen" — Aus Sachsen! Ey, ey, aus Sachsen, gnädiges Fräulein? aus Sachsen?

FRANCISKA. Nun? warum nicht? Es ist doch wohl hier zu Lande keine Sünde, aus Sachsen zu seyn?

DER WIRTH. Eine Sünde? behüte! das wäre ja eine ganz neue Sünde! — Aus Sachsen also? Ey, ey! aus Sachsen! das liebe Sachsen! — Aber wo mir recht ist, gnädiges Fräulein, Sachsen ist nicht klein, und hat mehrere, — wie soll ich es nennen? — Dis-

trickte, Provinzen. — Unsere Policey ist sehr exackt, gnädiges
Fräulein. —   (*LM*, II, 191,32-193.19)

In this scene, the Innkeeper, seen in the previous act as a
congenial and ingratiating host, is shown as a self-important
unofficial representative of the Prussian state. His appearance,
with the quill stuck behind his ear and laden with the not
inconsiderable paraphernalia of writing, already indicate a
partial comic intention for this scene. The Innkeeper reminds
us, in his attempts to speak like his social betters, not only of
Martin Krumm, but also, in his earnest emulation of chancery
style, of the pompous Herr Solbit in *Der Misogyne*. As we see
from that early example of a parodistic use of chancery style,
Lessing had always found it a convenient butt of stylistic
humor, and used it to good effect once more in creating the
figure of the Innkeeper. Lessing's awareness of this kind of
language was, of course, sharpened by his experiences during
the Seven Years' War as the secretary to the Prussian general
Bogumil Friedrich von Tauentzien, for whom Lessing was
almost daily obliged to write letters like the following to his
sovereign, Frederick the Great (*LM*, XVIII, 405):

Allerdurchlauchtigster, Großmächtigster König,
Allergnädigster König und Herr,

Wegen des hiesigen Magazins habe Ewr. Königlichen Majestät
allerunterthänigst zu melden, daß es bereits auf jener Seite der
Oder stehet, und wüßte ich in der ganzen Gegend keinen beßern
Ort für selbiges ausfündig au machen. Die übrigen Punkte an-
belangend, werde ich alles Mögliche thun, Ewr. Königlichen
Majestät allerhöchste Intention darunter zu erfüllen, und wird
der Capitaine Goetz die Gnade haben, Allerhöchstdenenselben
mündlich das mehrere davon zu referiren.
    Der ich in tiefster Devotion ersterbe,
                            Ewr. Königlichen Majestät,
                        allerunterthänigster und gehorsamster
                                Knecht
                                B F Tauentzien
Breslau den 7 Octobr.
    1761.

The Innkeeper's style in the passage previously quoted above
is clearly derived from this formal epistolary style of official
reports. What creates a comic effect is precisely the fact that
this style was otherwise restricted in use only to formal letters
and was rarely heard in colloquial speech. What the Innkeeper's style here particularly has in common with that of the
chancery is the use of archaic and elaborate forms of address,
such as "Ihro Gnaden" "Dero Namen", etc. Then, too, there is
the use of self-deprecating adjectives, particularly when
the Innkeeper wishes Franciska and Minna "einen unterthänigen guten Morgen", and asks whether he may dare
inquire how they have slept under his poor roof. The comic
effect of the scene is heightened by Franciska's naively
straightforward reaction to these pompous formalities ("Ein
höflicher Mann") and her assertion that the roof was not
so bad, but the beds could have been better. The Innkeeper's closest approximation to the language of the chancery comes in lines 30-34 of the scene quoted, where he
seems to be quoting verbatim the statute which obliges him
to interrogate Minna. The genitive phrase, "weß Standes und
Geschlechts er auch sey" and the adverbial phrase of manner,
"gehörigen Orts", help give legalistic flavor, as does the long
suspension of the infinitive "einzureichen". The Innkeeper, however, is not long able to keep up his formal façade
and, under the impact of the fact that the two young ladies
are from Saxony, he reverts to his more accustomed tone,
interspersing his speech with interjections ("Ey, ey"), and
calling Minna "gnädiges Fräulein" instead of "Ihro Gnaden".
By the time he tries to sell Minna the ring, and is telling her
of the officer from whom he had received it, who is, of
course, Tellheim, the Innkeeper has once again taken on the
smug and somewhat coarser tone of a man who has battened
on the fortunes of war. Here he is no longer sycophantic and
humble, neither in his language, nor in his bearing:

DAS FRÄULEIN. Ich höre, daß der Officier, welcher durch uns
verdrengt worden —

DER WIRTH. Ja nur ein abgedankter Officier ist, gnädiges Fräulein. —
DAS FRÄULEIN. Wenn schon! —
DER WIRTH. Mit dem es zu Ende geht. —
DAS FRÄULEIN. Desto schlimmer! Es soll ein sehr verdienter Mann seyn.
DER WIRTH. Ich sage Ihnen ja, daß er abgedankt ist.
DAS FRÄULEIN. Der König kann nicht alle verdiente Männer kennen.
DER WIRTH. O gewiß, er kennt sie, er kennt sie alle. —
DAS FRÄULEIN. So kann er sie nicht alle belohnen.
DER WIRTH. Sie wären alle belohnt, wenn sie darnach gelebt hätten. Aber so lebten die Herren, währendes Krieges, als ob ewig Krieg bleiben würde; als ob das Dein und Mein ewig aufgehoben seyn würde. Jetzt liegen alle Wirthshäuser und Gasthöfe von ihnen voll; und ein Wirth hat sich wohl mit ihnen in Acht zu nehmen. Ich bin mit diesem noch so ziemlich weggekommen. Hatte er gleich kein Geld mehr, so hatte er doch noch Geldeswerth; und zwey, drey Monate hätte ich ihn freylich noch ruhig können sitzen lassen. Doch besser ist besser. — A propos, gnädiges Fräulein; Sie verstehen sich doch auf Juwelen? —   (*LM*, II, 195.28-196.13)

Here, for the first time, the Innkeeper shows his true colors, inadvertently taking Minna and Franciska into his confidence. He is no longer the merry host of Act I, Scene 2, nor does he really have the respect which he seems to show for Tellheim when he is so elaborately apologetic to the officer in Act I, Scene 3. His style is now straightforwardly colloquial, quite different from the pompously respectful tone in which he first addressed Minna. Since he thinks that the discharged officer cannot possibly have any significance for Minna, the Innkeeper is most direct, calling Tellheim, "nur ein abgedankter Officier ... mit dem es zu Ende geht", as scornfully idiomatic a comment as possible. All of the polite periphrasis has left the Innkeeper's language now, and, irritated by Minna's defense of the officer whom he had turned out of the room, he launches into a diatribe against the behavior of the officers during the war in general. Spontaneous and colloquial is his vigorously figurative use of verbs, such as "Jetzt liegen alle Wirtshäuser ... mit ihnen voll", and "Ich bin mit diesem noch so ziemlich weggekommen", and the idiomatic use, again, of "sitzen lassen". The Innkeeper's state of upset is also shown by his use of the colloquialism "Doch besser ist besser", incomprehensible in itself, but quite clear within the context, an echo of the drinking proverbs which he used in talking with Just. The Innkeeper, then, is characterized chiefly by his chameleon-like ability to alter his tone as the situation warrants, although, as we have just seen, Lessing causes him to betray himself when it is advantageous to the exposition of the play. The contrasts between the various registers in which he plays, from one scene to the next, and even within the scene, make the Innkeeper, in spite of his marginal function, one of the most effective comic creations of the play.

Just, Tellheim's gruff and touchingly loyal servant, occupies the lowest rung on the play's social and stylistic ladder. Like that of the other servants before him in Lessing's comedies, Just's language is straightforward and, at best, on the common colloquial level. In his dialogue with the Innkeeper in Act I, Scene 2, we have already seen *in nuce* the typical traits of his style. His sentences are short, frequently highly elliptical and full of exclamatory and interrogative phrases. His tone is generally surly. His vocabulary is shared by none of the characters who belong or pretend to higher social station. Just freely uses such terms as "Schurke", "Grobian", "des unbarmherzigen Rackers", "Hure" (all in Act 1), "ein lüderliches Mensch", "Rummel" (both in Act III, Scene 2). Just's tone, however, is subject to certain modulations, such as the calculatedly pathetic scene in Act 1, Scene 8, where he presents Tellheim with his "bill", or the equally effective scene in Act III, Scene 2, in which he, with sarcastic ambiguity, informs Franciska of the fates of Tellheim's former servants. His style, despite these variations, is still not essentially distinguishable from that of a host of earlier servants in Lessing's comedies. Through his splenetic nature, so much in contrast to the ebullient Werner, through his disinclination to be a witty or playfully critical manservant, Just's characterization is more realistic than those of such highly stylized manservants as Maskarill in *Der Schatz* or Christoph in *Die Juden*, although his language is, in its significant aspects, much like theirs.

The "Wachtmeister" Paul Werner shows more decorum in his speech than does his intimate friend and social equal, Just. He does not descend to any of the pejoratives which Just uses, and the only undecorous term which Werner uses is the adjective "hundsföttisch" ("Ich werde sagen, … daß es eine hundsföttsche Sache ums Lügen ist, weil man darüber ertappt werden kann" [*LM*, II, 217.33-35]). Werner's character is different from Just's. This is revealed not only in Werner's actions, which are noble and generous in intent, whereas Just's are generally governed by anger, sullenness, or a wish for revenge, but also in the style in which Werner speaks. Lessing has given Werner a characterizing speech tag, the "Frauenzimmerchen, Frauenzimmerchen" with which he addresses Franciska throughout, and which, while it has about it a teasing quality, also carries the element of comic inflexibility provided by such repetitive devices. The exuberance of Werner's style is perhaps most concentrated in the following passage from Act V, Scene 2, where Tellheim, having learned of Minna's supposed distress and determined to marry her, ostensibly against the wishes of her uncle, finally consents to borrow money from Werner:

v. TELLHEIM. … Aber wo wirst du mehr hernehmen, Werner? — Ich brauche weit mehr.

WERNER. Dafür lassen Sie mich sorgen. — Der Mann, der mein Gut gekauft hat, wohnt in der Stadt. Der Zahlungstermin wäre zwar erst in vierzehn Tagen; aber das Geld liegt parat, und ein halb Procentchen Abzug —

v. TELLHEIM. Nun ja, lieber Werner! — Siehst du, daß ich meine einzige Zuflucht zu dir nehme? — Ich muß dir auch alles vertrauen. Das Fräulein hier, — du hast sie gesehn, — ist unglücklich —

WERNER. O Jammer!

v. TELLHEIM. Aber morgen ist sie meine Frau —

WERNER. O Freude!

v. TELLHEIM. Und übermorgen, geh ich mit ihr fort. Ich darf fort; ich will fort. Lieber hier alles im Stiche gelassen! Wer weiß,

wo mir sonst ein Glück aufgehoben ist. Wenn du willst, Werner,
so komm mit. Wir wollen wieder Dienste nehmen.
    WERNER. Wahrhaftig? — Aber doch wos Krieg giebt, Herr
Major?
    v. TELLHEIM. Wo sonst? — Geh, lieber Werner, wir sprechen
davon weiter.
    WERNER. O Herzensmajor! — Übermorgen? Warum nicht
lieber morgen? — Ich will schon alles zusammenbringen — In
Persien, Herr Major, giebts einen trefflichen Krieg; was meynen
Sie?
    v. TELLHEIM. Wir wollen das überlegen; geh nur, Werner! —
    WERNER. Juchhe! es lebe der Prinz Heraklius!
                                            (*LM*, II, 246.1-24)

The disparaging way in which Werner speaks of money, referring here to "ein halb Procentchen Abzug" is a key feature of
his characterization. Earlier, imploring Tellheim to take his
money, he had said, "Bey meiner armen Seele, wenn ein Trunk
faules Wasser damals nicht oft mehr werth war, als alle der
Quark! Nehmen Sie, lieber Major! Bilden Sie Sich ein, es ist
Wasser. Auch das hat Gott für alle geschaffen" (Act III,
Scene 7).
    Werner's generous actions and his apparent unconcern
about money are given verbal confirmation through such
statements, and he is thus sharply distinguished, for example, from the Innkeeper, who attempts to cheat Minna
over the price of the ring. Lessing further underlines Werner's
impulsive and exuberant character by the contrasting exclamations "O Jammer!" and "O Freude!" with which he reacts
to Tellheim's news. The unique compound noun "Herzens-
major", whose two parts come from such divergent realms of
expression, further emphasizes Werner's lively imagination
and his joy at the prospect of going to war again. The same
effect of emphasis through antithesis is achieved in the yoking
of the adjective "trefflich" to "Krieg". Finally, through the
use of the interjection "Juchhe!", and the characteristic
reference to the admired Prince Heraklius, Werner exits on a
high note. Lessing has created in Werner and Just, who are
on the same social level of style, two contrasting character-

izations, much in the same way in which, fourteen years earlier, in *Der Freygeist*, he had brought Adrast and Theophan into clear stylistic contrast corresponding to the contrast in their characters, although they, too, were speaking within the same range of colloquial style.

Franciska, Minna's maid, companion, and confidante since girlhood, represents the final stage of development of the saucy maid, who, whether called Lisette, Finette, or Mysis, is a standard figure in all of Lessing's comedies. Franciska, however, has been endowed with warmth, charm, and grace, qualities granted to none of her predecessors. Yet her function within the economy of the play is certainly similar to theirs. She is a commentator upon the main action and a participant in it, and she is an actor in a liaison taking place on a lower level parallel to the main action. Although she often expresses herself on a more exalted level of sentiment than did the conventional Lisette, Franciska's speech is not essentially different from hers, just as Just's general style still resembles that of earlier manservants. To illustrate this fact, let us examine Franciska's style in Act II, Scene 1:

DAS FRÄULEIN. (im Negligee, nach ihrer Uhr sehend) Franciska, wir sind auch sehr früh aufgestanden. Die Zeit wird uns lang werden.

FRANCISKA. Wer kann in den verzweifelten großen Städten schlafen? Die Karossen, die Nachtwächter, die Trommeln, die Katzen, die Korporals — das hört nicht auf zu rasseln, zu schreyen, zu wirbeln, zu mauen, zu fluchen; gerade, als ob die Nacht zu nichts weniger wäre, als zur Ruhe. — Eine Tasse Thee, gnädiges Fräulein?

DAS FRÄULEIN. Der Thee schmeckt mir nicht. —

FRANCISKA. Ich will von unserer Schokolate machen lassen.

DAS FRÄULEIN. Laß machen, für dich!

FRANCISKA. Für mich? Ich wollte eben so gern für mich allein plaudern, als für mich allein trinken. — Freylich wird uns die Zeit so lang werden. — Wir werden, vor langer Weile, uns putzen müssen, und das Kleid versuchen, in welchem wir den ersten Sturm geben wollen.

DAS FRÄULEIN. Was redest du von Stürmen, da ich bloß herkomme, die Haltung der Kapitulation zu fordern?

FRANCISKA. Und der Herr Officier, den wir vertrieben, und dem wir das Kompliment darüber machen lassen; er muß auch nicht die feinste Lebensart haben; sonst hätte er wohl um die Ehre können bitten lassen, uns seine Aufwartung machen zu dürfen. —

DAS FRÄULEIN. Es sind nicht alle Officiere Tellheims. Die Wahrheit zu sagen, ich ließ ihm das Kompliment auch blos machen, um Gelegenheit zu haben, mich nach diesem bey ihm zu erkundigen. — Franciska, mein Herz sagt es mir, daß meine Reise glücklich seyn wird, daß ich ihn finden werde. —

FRANCISKA. Das Herz, gnädiges Fräulein? Man traue doch ja seinem Herzen nicht zu viel. Das Herz redet uns gewaltig gern nach dem Maule. Wenn das Maul eben so geneigt wäre, nach dem Herzen zu reden, so wäre die Mode längst aufgekommen, die Mäuler unterm Schlosse zu tragen.

DAS FRÄULEIN. Ha! ha! mit deinen Mäulern unterm Schlosse! Die Mode wäre mir eben recht!

FRANCISKA. Lieber die schönsten Zähne nicht gezeigt, als alle Augenblicke das Herz darüber springen lassen!

DAS FRÄULEIN Was? bist du so zurückhaltend? —

FRANCISKA. Nein, gnädiges Fräulein; sondern ich wollte es gern mehr seyn. Man spricht selten von der Tugend, die man hat; aber desto öftrer von der, die uns fehlt.

DAS FRÄULEIN. Siehst du, Franciska? da hast du eine sehr gute Anmerkung gemacht. —

FRANCISKA. Gemacht? macht man das, was einem so einfällt?

DAS FRÄULEIN. Und weißt du, warum ich eigentlich diese Anmerkung so gut finde? Sie hat viele Beziehung auf meinen Tellheim.

FRANCISKA. Was hätte bey Ihnen nicht auch Beziehung auf ihn?

(*LM*, II, 189.5-190.21)

Franciska's very first speech typifies her lively style and her strong resemblance to her predecessors in Lessing's comedies. She is apparently in the habit of answering any statement with a question.

As we have seen in the style of such characters as "Das Fräulein" in *Die Juden* and of Lisettes in general, a heavy concentration of interrogatives results in an effect of liveliness, impulsiveness, and spontaneity. In Franciska's case, this is further reinforced by a number of devices which serve to make her speech even more vivid. In her first speech, an accumulation of nouns is used, "Die Karossen, die Nachtwächter, die Trommeln, die Korporals" each asyndetically associated with its sometimes onomatopoetic sound, "zu rasseln, zu schreyen, zu mauen, zu fluchen", in order to convey the random quality of the noises which have kept Franciska awake during the night just past. This passage already conveys her very expressive manner of speech, which is associative and emotional rather than logical.

To establish Franciska's relation to Minna properly, her tirade against the night noises of the city is cut short as she offers her mistress a cup of tea in a far more formal tone. This alternation of styles between almost teasing familiarity and the formality proper to a servant is parallel to the external relationship between Minna and Franciska, who, although they have grown up together and are close friends, are nonetheless mistress and servant, and are accordingly obliged to observe the proper forms.

In general, Franciska's language, while not deviating far from the stylistic level of Minna's, is more colloquial in its quality. The word "Maul" would not be used by Minna except as here, in a moment of relaxed familiarity, and as an echo to Franciska's jibe. Nor would this sort of conceit be characteristic of Minna.

Such earthy expressiveness is a characterizing quality reserved for Franciska alone. Contributing much to the spontaneous and flippant quality of Franciska's style is the strong concentration of absolute, general, almost aphoristic statements in her speech. Minna and Tellheim are also given many such statements, but Franciska's language exhibits an especially great number of them, delivered in an apodictic formulation usually involving a generalized third-person-singular subject. Thus she will say: "Man traue doch ja seinem Herzen nicht zu viel. Das Herz redet uns gewaltig nach dem Maule", or, like Just, employing an absolute infinitive, "Lieber die schönsten Zähne nicht gezeigt, als alle Augenblicke das Herz darüber springen lassen!", or "Man spricht selten von der Tugend, die man hat; desto öftrer von der, die uns fehlt." In the directness and vividness of her expression, in the self-assured absoluteness of her speech, Franciska is the perfect counterpart to the male characters on her social level.

Minna von Barnhelm is the first of Lessing's comedies in which the relationship between the two lovers is the play's central concern. In the earlier plays, the lovers played only an accessory role in relation to the main action. Even in *Der Freygeist*, where love plays a fairly important part, the center of interest is Adrast as a freethinker, rather than as a lover. Appropriately to their central roles in the play, Minna and Tellheim are on stage together longer than any of the other characters. Through the effective use of episodic elements, such as the various scenes between the minor characters, Lessing delays the resolution and relaxes the tension of the situation, simultaneously leading on the audience's interest in how, through a combination of internal and external circumstances, the situation will be resolved. The first encounter of Tellheim and Minna in the play comes at the end of Act II, and serves chiefly to lay down the lines of the play's central problem; Tellheim's wounded pride, which, for him, prevents him from claiming Minna's hand, as she would have him do. Tellheim must be tricked into leaping this hurdle, into acting according to the dictates of his heart, rather than of his mind, which is preoccupied with the external question of his honor. It is this "mustard seed of action", as Otto Ludwig has called it,[8] which is expanded and elaborated upon, explored, even if only hypothetically, in its implications for both the man and the woman, and which forms the dialectical basis for the play. Act II, Scene 9 is a prelude for this. The significant encounters between Minna and Tellheim take place in Act IV, Scene 6 and the first scenes of the fifth act, and it is on these scenes that we shall concentrate in our examination of the language of Minna and Tellheim.

Both Minna and Tellheim speak in an elevated colloquial style. Unlike such characters as the Innkeeper and Werner, they are at home on this level, and commit no solecisms of the

---

[8] Quoted in Heinrich Meyer-Benfey, *Lessings Minna von Barnhelm* (Göttingen, 1915), p. 180.

kind mentioned earlier. What distinguishes their styles from those of all of the characters of Lessing's comedies to come before them is that their speech is delicately nuanced in tonal levels to suit the individual situation. How important this concept of tone is to the economy of the play may be seen in the frequency with which the word "Ton", referring to the tone of voice, the choice of words, occurs in the play, either in the dialogue itself or in stage directions. The significance of this element is already evident in Act II, Scene 8, in the highly critical moment in which Minna asks Tellheim whether he still loves her and refuses to let him qualify his affirmative answer, when Minna says:

> Geduld! — Sie lieben mich noch: genug für mich. — In was für einen Ton bin ich mit Ihnen gefallen! Ein widriger, melancholischer, ansteckender Ton. — Ich nehme den meinigen wieder an.
>
> *(LM*, II, 204.21-23)

How Minna reverts to her own tone, and what constitutes it, shall be analyzed below. Suffice it to say that not only words are caught, remembered, and echoed at decisive moments, but that the very tone in which Minna and Tellheim speak to each other adds to the communication between them, and is an integral part of the style of the play. Again, when Tellheim, at the beginning of Act IV, Scene 6, enters, behaving stiffly and formally, Minna immediately senses his tone and tries to lighten it;

> v. TELLHEIM. Gnädiges Fräulein, Sie werden mein Verweilen entschuldigen —
> DAS FRÄULEIN. O, Herr Major, so gar militairisch wollen wir es mit einander nicht nehmen. Sie sind ja da!
>
> *(LM*, II, 236.8-11)

Although the word "Ton" is not mentioned here, it is evidently Tellheim's tone which is overly "militairisch" here, and not so much his words, which are not much more formal than his normally polite way of speaking. How important tone must have been to Lessing in the creation of these characters is implicit in the fact that he not only indicates, through the words of a speech, or through the emphatic reaction to a tone of voice, how the speech is to be spoken, but that he also includes stage directions for the delivery of a line, a phenomenon almost unique in *Minna von Barnhelm* among Lessing's comedies. When Minna pretends that she has been cast out by her uncle, her tone towards Tellheim changes radically, which Lessing would not have the actress miss:

> v. TELLHEIM. (der sie zu unterbrechen kömmt) Sie sind ungehalten, mein Fräulein —
> DAS FRÄULEIN. (höhnisch) Ich? im geringsten nicht.
> v. TELLHEIM. Wenn ich Sie weniger liebte, mein Fräulein —
> DAS FRÄULEIN. (noch in diesem Tone) O gewiß, es wäre mein Unglück!...   (*LM*, II, 242.33-243.3)

Both through having the characters react to each other's tones of voice at significant instances, and through his occasional stage directions, which consciously and specifically make tone an integral part of the language of Minna and Tellheim, Lessing has added a significant new dimension to his stylistic devices. How Lessing creates the nuances of tone within the level of elevated colloquial language shall be the object of our investigation of the language of Minna and Tellheim.

Before their first encounter in Act II, Scene 8, Tellheim and Minna are exhibited to the audience in a wide range of situations, and thus in a wide range of tonal nuances in Acts I and II, respectively. This is done not so much for the sake of plot exposition, for what is dramaturgically necessary before the encounter of Minna and Tellheim can take place could be established in a far smaller scope. Rather, Acts I and II, interspersed with essentially episodic elements, in which each of the two main characters is confronted with almost every other character in the play (Tellheim with the Innkeeper, Just, Frau Marloff; Minna with Franciska, the Innkeeper, and Just) serve to outline the essential characteristics of Tellheim and Minna, to establish the *donnée* from which the healing of a character like Tellheim's, which is the business of the play, can take place. In the case of Minna, in Act II, the woman is being shown who is Tellheim's equal, worthy of his love, and who is capable of redeeming Tellheim from a bitter self-negation to which external circumstances and his own pride have brought him.

In Act I, Tellheim is given various opportunities to demonstrate to the audience large parts of the range of his tonal scale, whose extremes are reached later in the scenes with Minna. Many of Tellheim's qualities in the more significant later acts are anticipated in the first. Thus, in Act I, Scene 3, Tellheim is stiffly polite, "militairisch" with the Innkeeper:

DER WIRTH. Es ist wahr, Herr Just spricht für seinen Herrn, und ein wenig hitzig. Aber daran thut er recht; ich schätze ihn um so viel höher; ich liebe ihn darum. —

JUST. Daß ich ihm nicht die Zähne austreten soll!

DER WIRTH. Nur Schade, daß er sich umsonst erhitzet. Denn ich bin gewiß versichert, daß Ihro Gnaden keine Ungnade deswegen auf mich geworfen haben, weil — die Noth — mich nothwendig —

v. TELLHEIM. Schon zu viel, mein Herr! Ich bin Ihnen schuldig; Sie räumen mir, in meiner Abwesenheit, das Zimmer aus; Sie müssen bezahlt werden; ich muß wo anders unterzukommen suchen. Sehr natürlich! —

DER WIRTH. Wo anders? Sie wollen ausziehen, gnädiger Herr? Ich unglücklicher Mann! ich geschlagner Mann! Nein, nimmermehr! Eher muß die Dame das Quartier wieder räumen. Der Herr Major kann ihr, will ihr sein Zimmer nicht lassen; das Zimmer ist sein; sie muß fort; ich kann ihr nicht helfen. - Ich gehe, gnädiger Herr —

v. TELLHEIM. Freund, nicht zwey dumme Streiche für einen! Die Dame muß in dem Besitze des Zimmers bleiben. —

DER WIRTH. Und Ihro Gnaden sollten glauben, daß ich aus Mißtrauen, aus Sorge für meine Bezahlung? — Als wenn ich nicht wüßte, daß mich Ihro Gnaden bezahlen können, so bald Sie nur wollen. — Das versiegelte Beutelchen, —fünfhundert Thaler Louisdo, stehet darauf, — welches Ihro Gnaden in dem Schreibepulte stehen gehabt; — ist in guter Verwahrung. —

v. TELLHEIM. Das will ich hoffen; so wie meine übrigen Sachen. — Just soll sie in Empfang nehmen, wenn er Ihnen die Rechnung bezahlt hat. —

DER WIRTH. Wahrhaftig, ich erschrack recht, als ich das Beutelchen fand. — Ich habe immer Ihro Gnaden für einen ordentlichen und vorsichtigen Mann gehalten, der sich niemals ganz ausgiebt.

— Aber dennoch, — wenn ich baar Geld in dem Schreibepulte vermuthet hätte —

v. TELLHEIM. Würden Sie höflicher mit mir verfahren seyn. Ich verstehe Sie. — Gehen Sie nur, mein Herr; lassen Sie mich; ich habe mit meinem Bedienten zu sprechen.

(*LM*, II, 177.6-178.5)

Especially compared to the effusiveness of the Innkeeper, Tellheim's style here is spare to the point of being elliptical; "Freund, nicht zwey dumme Streiche für einen!". In contrast to the long periods of the Innkeeper, which constantly generate subordinate clauses, Tellheim speaks in terse sentences communicating the same inexorable pessimistic logic which has made him renounce Minna. Here Tellheim uses barely any adjectives, restricting his utterances to almost skeletal subject-verb-object constructions, or at most, to brief periphrases. The resulting tone is politely cold, and, taking into consideration the "Freund" with which Tellheim addresses the Innkeeper, not a little condescending, for, when he is speaking sincerely to the widow of his former adjutant, Tellheim says, "Ihr Gemahl war mein Freund; ... ich war immer karg mit diesem Titel."

When he is alone with Just, Tellheim's tone is easier and more relaxed, partly because he addresses his servant with the familiar "du". Beyond this, however, there are other elements which contribute to a tone of greater familiarity. Tellheim is more accessible to Just than to the Innkeeper, making possible Just's touching persuasion of Tellheim to keep him on as his servant in Act I, Scene 8. It is only with Just and Werner that he has this familiar, almost jocular tone, expressing himself freely, calling Just "Bestie" and confessing to him "Ich habe keinen Heller baares Geld mehr...", whereas in the following scene, he is to depict his plight so much more decorously.

Quite a different modulation of Tellheim's tone occurs when Frau Marloff, the widow of his former "Rittmeister" comes to pay her husband's debt to him. His initial reaction upon seeing her is: "Um des Himmels willen, gnädige Frau!

welche Veränderung!", an exclamation which gives a hint
of the change in his style which is to follow in the next scene.
After being seen as the self-controlled officer, coldly re-
proving the tactless Innkeeper, or jocularly upbraiding a
surly servant, Tellheim becomes most spontaneous and human
in his actions, even if only momentarily. A hint escapes here
of the ardent Tellheim we are to encounter in Act V:

v. TELLHEIM. Reden Sie frey, gnädige Frau! Vor mir dürfen Sie
Sich Ihres Unglücks nicht schämen. Kann ich Ihnen worinn
dienen?
DIE DAME. Mein Herr Major —
v. TELLHEIM. Ich beklage Sie, gnädige Frau! Worinn kann ich
Ihnen dienen? Sie wissen, Ihr Gemahl war mein Freund, mein
Freund, sage ich; ich war immer karg mit diesem Titel.
DIE DAME. Wer weiß es besser, als ich, wie werth Sie seiner
Freundschaft waren, wie werth er der Ihrigen war? Sie würden
sein letzter Gedanke, Ihr Name der letzte Ton seiner sterbenden
Lippen gewesen seyn, hätte nicht die stärkere Natur dieses traurige
Vorrecht für seinen unglücklichen Sohn, für seine unglückliche
Gattinn gefordert —
v. TELLHEIM. Hören Sie auf, Madame! Weinen wollte ich mit
Ihnen gern; aber ich habe heute keine Thränen. Verschonen Sie
mich! Sie finden mich in einer Stunde, wo ich leicht zu verleiten
wäre, wider die Vorsicht zu murren. — O mein rechtschaffner Marloff! Geschwind, gnädige Frau, was haben Sie zu befehlen? Wenn
ich Ihnen zu dienen im Stande bin, wenn ich es bin —
DIE DAME. Ich darf nicht abreisen, ohne seinen letzten Willen
zu vollziehen. Er erinnerte sich kurz vor seinem Ende, daß er als
Ihr Schuldner sterbe, und beschwor mich, diese Schuld mit der
ersten Baarschaft zu tilgen. Ich habe seine Equipage verkauft, und
komme seine Handschrift einzulösen. —
v. TELLHEIM. Wie, gnädige Frau? darum kommen Sie?
DIE DAME. Darum. Erlauben Sie, daß ich das Geld aufzähle.
v. TELLHEIM. Nicht doch, Madame! Marloff mir schuldig?
Das kann schwerlich seyn. Lassen Sie doch sehen. (er ziehet sein
Taschenbuch heraus, und sucht) Ich finde nichts.

(*LM*, II, 180.8-34)

Tellheim's tone is more emotional, less impersonal in the passage above than in his dialogue with the Innkeeper. Lessing

achieves this by loosening the terseness of Tellheim's speech to a degree.

Repetition is one way in which this looseing is effected. Tellheim repeats his offer of aid to Frau Marloff three times within this passage, and emphatically repeats the words "mein Freund". His emotion is also expressed by his increased use of exclamations. Tellheim's penchant for under-statement is clearly evident here. Unlike Just, the Innkeeper, and Frau Marloff, all of whom rather unrestrainedly give vent to their feelings, Tellheim, even in a situation which so touches him, retains his composure, even if under strong self-constraint.

The tension between his feeling and his composure is particularly clear in the speech on lines 14-19, above. Frau Marloff has just finished depicting the death of her husband, her speech made doubly affecting and emphatic through the relatively highly concentrated use of attributives: "Ihr Name [würde] der letzte Ton seiner sterbenden Lippen gewesen seyn, hätte nicht die stärkere Natur dieses traurige Vorrecht für seinen unglücklichen Sohn, für seine unglück-liche Gattinn gefordert." For the sake of his composure, which, however, he regains quickly, Tellheim implores her to stop. His speech, "Sie finden mich in einer Stunde, wo ich leicht zu verleiten wäre, wider die Vorsicht zu murren", hides his truly difficult circumstances behind a mask of peri-phrasis and understatement, emphasized by his use of the subjunctive. Instead of mentioning what troubles really beset him, he names only abstract destiny, "die Vorsicht"; instead of using a stronger verb, such as "klagen" or "schreien", Tellheim uses the moderate, almost ironical "murren". In the widow's presence, Tellheim permits himself only one more word in memory of his dead "Rittmeister"; "O mein recht-schaffner Marloff!", typically praising an ethical quality, rather than saying "guter" or "armer" Marloff. This is another instance of the studied understatement with which Tellheim achieves his controlled and yet, in this scene, very human tone. In the first act, then, through careful mani-

pulation of stylistic features as well as a conscious choice of
the characters who confront Tellheim, Lessing has shown us
essential qualities of the Major, building up, layer upon carefully created layer, his dignity, his goodness, his generosity,
and, on the other hand, his initial pessimism, his firmly maintained deduction that the world, even in the guise of an Innkeeper, is against him. He has also shown the varied range of
tone of which Tellheim is capable, the coldly polite and military with the Innkeeper, the more familiar and jocular tone
with Just, and finally, that of the man of feeling, sympathetic
and yet controlled, which is also to characterize him in his
initial scenes with Minna. Yet all of these qualities and tones
are plausibly compatible with each other within the same
character.

In a symmetrical relationship to the exposition of Tellheim's
character and tone in Act I is the way in which Minna's
character and the range of her emotional nuances are shown
in Act II. In the analyses of the styles of the Innkeeper and
Franciska, we have already had glimpses of Minna's style.
Like Tellheim, Minna is reserved and cool with the Innkeeper.
She speaks few words with him, but clearly makes her point
when necessary. Just as Tellheim does not lower his language
to the level which Just uses in talking to the Innkeeper, so
Minna does not take on the tone which Franciska uses with
him. (Cf. p. 204.)

There is symmetry, too, between the tones in which both
Minna and Tellheim speak to their servants. As we have noted
before, Franciska is indeed Minna's "liebste Gespielinn", but
Minna, in speaking to her, only rarely loses sight of the fact
that she is her servant. In the same degree in which Tellheim's
tone is more intimate when he is talking to Just, Minna is
more communicative when she is speaking with Franciska
than with the Innkeeper. In the first scene of the second
act, it is her playful side which first comes to light, the
feature which is to be most significant for her further action
within the play, just as Tellheim's apparent inflexibility and
pessimism are most conspicuous in his first appearance. Thus,

when Franciska says, "Wir werden, vor langer Weile, uns putzen müssen, und das Kleid versuchen, in welchem wir den ersten Sturm geben wollen.", Minna plays with the concept of storming a fortress and, giving an intriguing hint of the coming exposition, says, "Was redest du von stürmen, da ich bloß herkomme, die Haltung der Kapitulation zu fordern?" (Cf. quotation on p. 211, lines 13-19.) Minna speaks to Franciska of that which is most characteristic and important for her, "das Herz", an essential concept for her vocabulary. In speaking with Franciska, she alternates between the earnestness of this mood, in which she contemplates the hoped-for reunion with Tellheim, and the bantering tone of the maid, as in her laughing response to Franciska's remark about keeping the mouth under lock and key to restrain the heart. (Cf. quotation on p. 211, lines 29-35.) Laughter indicated in the dialogue is also successfully used here, as elsewhere, to emphasize Minna's gay character. In showing Minna successively with Franciska and the Innkeeper, and, later in the play, with Riccaut, and in varying the tone in which she speaks with each, Lessing has shown her to be a young woman not only of wit, heart, and grace, but also of dignity and tact.

As a final preparatory demonstration of Minna's character to the audience, Lessing shows the full exuberance of optimism of her soul in her joy on hearing that Tellheim is in Berlin. In her language in the following scene, the confusing mixture of feelings of reverent gratitude and almost wanton joy which she describes at the end of the passage is most accurately caught. Franciska has momentarily left the room, leaving Minna alone with her exultation:

DAS FRÄULEIN. Ich habe ihn wieder! — Bin ich allein? — Ich will nicht umsonst allein seyn. (sie faltet die Hände) Auch bin ich nicht allein! (und blickt aufwärts) Ein einziger dankbarer Gedanke gen Himmel ist das vollkommenste Gebet! — Ich hab ihn, ich hab ihn! (mit ausgebreiteten Armen) Ich bin glücklich! und frölich! Was kann der Schöpfer lieber sehen, als ein fröliches Geschöpf! — (Franciska kömmt) Bist du wieder da, Franciska? — Er jammert dich? Mich jammert er nicht. Unglück ist auch gut. Vielleicht, daß ihm der Himmel alles nahm, um ihm in mir alles wieder zu geben!

FRANCISKA. Er kann den Augenblick hier seyn — Sie sind noch in Ihrem Negligee, gnädiges Fräulein. Wie, wenn Sie Sich geschwind ankleideten?

DAS FRÄULEIN. Geh! ich bitte dich. Er wird mich von nun an öfterer so, als geputzt sehen.

FRANCISKA. O, Sie kennen Sich, mein Fräulein.

DAS FRÄULEIN. (nach einem kurzen Nachdenken) Wahrhaftig, Mädchen, du hast es wiederum getroffen.

FRANCISKA. Wenn wir schön sind, sind wir ungeputzt am schönsten.

DAS FRÄULEIN. Müssen wir denn schön seyn? — Aber, daß wir uns schön glauben, war vielleicht nothwendig. — Nein, wenn ich ihm, ihm nur schön bin! — Franciska, wenn alle Mädchens so sind, wie ich mich ietzt fühle, so sind wir — sonderbare Dinger. — Zärtlich und stolz, tugendhaft und eitel, wollüstig und fromm — Du wirst mich nicht verstehen. Ich verstehe mich wohl selbst nicht. — Die Freude macht drehend, wirblicht. — (*LM*, II, 201.14-202.6)

We see Minna here at the height of her exuberance. Her mood alternates between reverent, albeit somewhat overly theatrical gratitude and unfettered joy and relief. This is particularly expressed by the repetition of "Ich hab ihn!", with which Minna has interspersed her speech ever since recognizing Tellheim's ring. The final adjectives "drehend, wirblicht", unusually expressive adjectives for Lessing, further contribute to the lightness of the tone, bordering almost upon giddiness. Especially, however, the antithetical adjectives, "Zärtlich und stolz, tugendhaft und eitel, wollüstig und fromm" convey her state of mind, concentrating all that has gone before; prayer and her being in her negligee are in harmony in her joy, which lets her speak in paradox, even to the point at which she can say, "Unglück ist auch gut." Minna's joy is paradoxical to her, and this is expressed not only in her actions, her rapid alternation of attitudes, but also, most strikingly, in her language.

At the end of the second act, after they have been shown in a variety of situations, the first, almost catastrophic encounter of Minna and Tellheim takes place. In this and subsequent encounters, the tonal varieties which have been indicated in minor expositions come to full expression, more intensely, and with a wider dimension of significance. This may be seen in the final scene of Act II. Both Minna and Tellheim are still acting and speaking from their original emotional and intellectual positions. Minna is radiantly confident as to the outcome of her trip, Tellheim still firm in his renunciation of Minna because of his wounded pride and because he is now "der Unglückliche". Minna has just wrung from Tellheim his declaration that he still loves her, and is trying to fend off the qualification implied by his "Ja, ja! – Allein –":

Das Fräulein. Geduld! — Sie lieben mich noch: genug für mich. — In was für einen Ton bin ich mit Ihnen gefallen! Ein widriger, melancholischer, ansteckender Ton. — Ich nehme den meinigen wieder an. — Nun, mein lieber Unglücklicher, Sie lieben mich noch, und haben Ihre Minna noch, und sind unglücklich? Hören Sie doch, was Ihre Minna für ein eingebildetes, albernes Ding war, — ist. Sie ließ, sie läßt sich träumen, Ihr ganzes Glück sey sie. — Geschwind kramen Sie Ihr Unglück aus. Sie mag versuchen, wie viel sie dessen aufwiegt. — Nun?

v. Tellheim. Mein Fräulein, ich bin nicht gewohnt zu klagen.

Das Fräulein. Sehr wohl. Ich wüßte auch nicht, was mir an einem Soldaten, nach dem Prahlen, weniger gefiele, als das Klagen. Aber es giebt eine gewisse kalte, nachläßige Art, von seiner Tapferkeit und von seinem Unglücke zu sprechen. —

v. Tellheim. Die im Grunde doch auch geprahlt und geklagt ist.

Das Fräulein. O, mein Rechthaber, so hätten Sie Sich auch gar nicht unglücklich nennen sollen. — Ganz geschwiegen, oder ganz mit der Sprache heraus. — Eine Vernunft, eine Nothwendigkeit, die ihnen mich zu vergessen befiehlt? — Ich bin eine große Liebhaberinn von Vernunft, ich habe sehr viel Ehrerbietung für die Nothwendigkeit. — Aber lassen Sie doch hören, wie vernünftig diese Vernunft, wie nothwendig diese Nothwendigkeit ist.

v. Tellheim. Wohl denn; so hören Sie, mein Fräulein. — Sie nennen mich Tellheim; der Name trift ein. — Aber Sie meynen, ich sey der Tellheim, den Sie in Ihrem Vaterlande gekannt haben; der blühende Mann, voller Ansprüche, voller Ruhmbegierde; der seines ganzen Körpers, seiner ganzen Seele mächtig war; vor dem die Schranken der Ehre und des Glückes eröffnet standen; der Ihres Herzens und Ihrer Hand, wann er schon ihrer noch nicht würdig war, täglich würdiger zu werden hoffen durfte. — Dieser Tellheim bin ich eben so wenig, — als ich mein Vater bin. Beide sind gewesen. - Ich bin Tellheim, der verabschiedete, der an seiner Ehre gekränkte, der Krüppel, der Bettler. — Jenem, mein Fräulein, versprachen Sie Sich; wollen Sie diesem Wort halten ?—

DAS FRÄULEIN. Das klingt sehr tragisch! — Doch, mein Herr, bis ich jenen wieder finde, — in die Tellheims bin ich nun einmal vernarret, — dieser wird mir schon aus der Noth helfen müssen. — Deine Hand, lieber Bettler! (indem sie ihn bey der Hand ergreift)

V. TELLHEIM. (der die andere Hand mit dem Hute vor das Gesicht schlägt, und sich von ihr abwendet) Das ist zu viel! — Wo bin ich? — Lassen Sie mich, Fräulein! — Ihre Güte foltert mich! — Lassen Sie mich.

DAS FRÄULEIN. Was ist Ihnen? wo wollen Sie hin?

V. TELLHEIM. Von Ihnen! —

DAS FRÄULEIN. Von mir? (indem sie seine Hand an ihre Brust zieht) Träumer!

V. TELLHEIM. Die Verzweiflung wird mich tod zu Ihren Füßen werfen.

DAS FRÄULEIN. Von mir?

V. TELLHEIM. Von Ihnen. — Sie nie, nie wieder zu sehen. — Oder doch so entschlossen, so fest entschlossen, — keine Niederträchtigkeit zu begehen, — Sie keine Unbesonnenheit begehen zu lassen — Lassen Sie mich, Minna! (reißt sich los, und ab)

DAS FRÄULEIN. (ihm nach) Minna Sie lassen? Tellheim! Tellheim! (*LM*, II, 204.21-206.3)

The epithets which Minna uses to describe Tellheim in the passage above, and those which he uses to describe himself are significant elements in determining the tone of each of them. Tellheim sees himself in a tragic light as "Der Unglückliche" and "der verabschiedete, der an seiner Ehre gekränkte, der Krüppel, der Bettler", and is able to speak of himself positively only in the past tense. Minna can admit that this *sounds* tragic, but is never convinced that it is so potentially. With a teasing use of adjectives of endearment, she blunts the barbs which Tellheim turns against himself with loving irony; "der Unglückliche" becomes "mein lieber Unglücklicher"; "der Bettler" becomes "lieber Bettler". Tellheim tries to rush off

the stage in the deepest perplexity and confusion of feeling at
Minna's demand, "Deine Hand, lieber Bettler!", the ironic
epithet coupled with the possessive in the intimate second
person singular form breaking the formal decorum of their
relationship. Minna, in her optimism and innocence, cannot
sense his problem and calls him, again rebukingly, "Träumer!"
These are not the only instances of Minna's almost playful
use of words in this passage, especially of Tellheim's words.
When he had first entered, Tellheim had said: "Seitdem mir
Vernunft und Nothwendigkeit befehlen, Minna von Barnhelm
zu vergessen: was für Mühe habe ich angewendet!" (*LM*,
II, 203.29-30). In lines 19-23, above, Minna questions this
statement with a mock seriousness, playing on "Vernunft" and
"Nothwendigkeit" and the adjectives associated with them;
"Ich bin eine grosse Liebhaberinn von Vernunft, ich habe
sehr viel Ehrerbietung für die Nothwendigkeit, aber lassen
Sie doch hören, wie vernünftig diese Vernunft, wie nothwendig diese Nothwendigkeit ist." Despite the earnestness of
the encounter, and despite Minna's own essential seriousness
towards Tellheim, the analytical playfulness of Minna's tone,
in such contrast to the controlled resignation of the officer, is
further enhanced by other of her vocabulary items in this
passage. Thus, such a verb as "auskramen" seems oddly un-
fitted in tone to its object "Unglück" and is, indeed, an
intentional solecism, meant, once again, to convey her naive
confidence that Tellheim need only, quite literally, unpack
his troubles before Minna, and everything will be made
right again. It is in the spirit of the same kind of girlish
straightforwardness that Minna says, "In die Tellheims bin
ich nun einmal vernarret", the adjective here carrying a
colloquial overtone which is in teasing contrast to Tellheim's
mortified earnestness, and to the mention of love early in
the passage. Minna's description of herself as "ein eingebildetes, albernes Ding" also contributes to this effect. Her
impulsiveness is also underlined by the two consequent verb
shifts, "... was Ihre Minna für ein eingebildetes, albernes
Ding war – ist. Sie ließ, sie läßt sich träumen, ... " Each of

these stylistic touches, laid on by Lessing with a most conscious hand and more painstakingly than ever before, help to create for Minna a style which is at once playful and pithy, at once ironically light and essentially sincere in its tone.

In this passage, Tellheim's tone is the exact opposite of Minna's. In greater amplitude in this passage, and even more in the next passage to be examined, we see emerge again the qualities of his language already shown in Act I. His terseness, even dryness of tone under ordinary circumstances covers a deeply feeling nature which, when aroused, expresses itself with considerable force. There are vivid flashes of this expressiveness apparent in the present passage. Highly significant in this respect is the speech on lines 23-35, above, in which Tellheim begins to tell Minna why he cannot claim her hand. The structure of the speech is very logical, even rhetorical, distinguishing between the Tellheim who was and the one who is, culminating appositively in the question to Minna, "Jenem, mein Fräulein, versprachen Sie Sich; wollen Sie diesem Wort halten?" (lines 34-35, above). Yet, despite the rigorousness of the logic, how much pathos, usually suppressed by Tellheim, there is in this speech! The adjective "blühende" is unusually graphic, and the emotional and rhetorical quality is further heightened by the emphatic repetition of the predicative adjectives and their complementary nouns, "voller Ansprüche, voller Ruhmbegierde", and the mutually complementary genitive objects in the next clause, "der seines ganzen Körpers, seiner ganzen Seele mächtig war"; finally, the image, conventional as it may be, of the gates of honor and fortune, and the comparison of himself with his dead father further increase the pathos of Tellheim's speech, justly occasioning Minna's gently ironic remark that all of this sounds very tragic. The formal logical structure of the passage and its relatively strong emotional content are, and in the writer's opinion intentionally so, antithetical, giving a sort of emblematic image for Tellheim's character; the exterior logically consistent, the interior laden with barely contained emotion. Goaded by Minna's over-

whelming goodness and her apparent misunderstanding of
his situation, the despair and confusion which Tellheim feels
finally do break out in his speech (lines 41 ff., above), the
logical connection of his syntax breaking down into a series of
exclamations ending in the emphatic, "Ihre Güte foltert
mich!", the verb here again a particularly strong one for
the normally moderate Tellheim. As Meyer-Benfey says,
at this point, all communication between Minna and Tellheim must break down into inarticulateness,[9] and a period of
respite for both must interpose before contact is taken up
again.

When Tellheim and Minna next confront each other, in
Act IV, Scene 6, the situation has changed barely at all. Both
have some hint that the external circumstances, the problem
of Tellheim's exoneration, might be moving towards a
solution, but nothing is definite concerning this point as yet.
Tellheim has sent Minna a letter explaining his situation to
her, which, though she claims not to have done so, she has
read, but not entirely understood. She still believes, and tells
Tellheim:

Was haben Sie denn gegen das Lachen? Kann man denn auch
nicht lachend sehr ernsthaft seyn? Lieber Major, das Lachen erhält uns vernünftiger, als der Verdruß. Der Beweis liegt vor uns.
Ihre lachende Freundinn beurtheilet Ihre Umstände weit richtiger
als Sie selbst.   (*LM*, II, 238.28-32)

Consistently with this argument, she pursues the same course
which she took in Act II, Scene 9, to attempt to raise the
major from the melancholy contemplation of his misfortune
through a teasing minimization of his troubles, by reminding
him of what he does have in order to turn his mind away from
the spectre of his supposedly lost honor. Thus, goaded once
again, Tellheim explains to Minna and, for the first time, to
the audience, in what the question of his lost honor centers:

v. TELLHEIM. Sie erinnern Sich, gnädiges Fräulein, daß ich Ordre
hatte, in den Aemtern Ihrer Gegend die Kontribution mit der

---

[9]   Meyer-Benfey, *op. cit.*, p. 51.

äussersten Strenge baar beyzutreiben. Ich wollte mir diese Strenge ersparen, und schoß die fehlende Summe selbst vor. —

Das Fräulein. Ja wohl erinnere ich mich. — Ich liebte Sie um dieser That willen, ohne Sie noch gesehen zu haben.

v. Tellheim. Die Stände gaben mir ihren Wechsel, und diesen wollte ich, bey Zeichnung des Friedens, unter die zu ratihabirende Schulden eintragen lassen. Der Wechsel ward für gültig erkannt, aber mir ward das Eigentum desselben streitig gemacht. Man zog spöttisch das Maul, als ich versicherte, die Valute baar hergegeben zu haben. Man erklärte ihn für eine Bestechung, für das Gratial der Stände, weil ich sobald mit ihnen auf die niedrigste Summe einig geworden war, mit der ich mich nur im äussersten Nothfall zu begnügen, Vollmacht hatte. So kam der Wechsel aus meinen Händen, und wenn er bezahlt wird, wird er sicherlich nicht an mich bezahlt. — Hierdurch, mein Fräulein, halte ich meine Ehre für gekränkt; nicht durch den Abschied, den ich gefordert haben würde, wenn ich ihn nicht bekommen hätte. - Sie sind ernsthaft, mein Fräulein? Warum lachen Sie nicht? Ha, ha, ha! Ich lache ja.

Das Fräulein. O, ersticken Sie dieses Lachen, Tellheim! Ich beschwöre Sie! Es ist das schreckliche Lachen des Menschenhasses! Nein, Sie sind der Mann nicht, den eine gute That reuen kann, weil sie üble Folgen für ihn hat. Nein, unmöglich können diese üble Folgen dauren! Die Wahrheit muß an den Tag kommen. Das Zeugnis meines Oheims, aller unsrer Stände —

v. Tellheim. Ihres Oheims! Ihrer Stände! Ha, ha, ha!

Das Fräulein. Ihr Lachen tödtet mich, Tellheim! Wenn Sie an Tugend und Vorsicht glauben, Tellheim, so lachen Sie so nicht! Ich habe nie fürchterlicher fluchen hören, als Sie lachen. — Und lassen Sie uns das Schlimmste setzen! Wenn man Sie hier durchaus verkennen will: so kann man Sie bey uns nicht verkennen. Nein, wir können, wir werden Sie nicht verkennen, Tellheim. Und wenn unsere Stände die geringste Empfindung von Ehre haben, so weiß ich was sie thun müssen. Doch ich bin nicht klug: was wäre das nöthig? Bilden Sie Sich ein, Tellheim, Sie hätten die zweytausend Pistolen an einem wilden Abende verloren. Der König war eine unglückliche Karte für Sie: die Dame (auf sich weisend) wird Ihnen desto günstiger seyn. — Die Vorsicht, glauben Sie mir, hält den ehrlichen Mann immer schadlos; und öfters schon im voraus. Die That, die Sie einmal um zweytausend Pistolen bringen sollte, erwarb mich Ihnen. Ohne diese That, würde ich nie begierig gewesen seyn, Sie kennen zu lernen. Sie wissen, ich kam uneingeladen in die erste Gesellschaft, wo ich Sie zu finden glaubte. Ich kam blos Ihrentwegen. Ich kam in dem festen Vorsatze, Sie zu lieben, - ich liebte Sie schon! — in dem

festen Vorsatze, Sie zu besitzen, wenn ich Sie auch so schwarz und
häßlich finden sollte, als den Mohr von Venedig. Sie sind so
schwarz und häßlich nicht; auch so eifersüchtig werden Sie nicht
seyn. Aber Tellheim, Tellheim, Sie haben doch noch viel ähn-
liches mit ihm! O, über die wilden, unbiegsamen Männer, die nur
immer ihr stieres Auge auf das Gespenst der Ehre heften! für alles
andere Gefühl sich verhärten! — Hierher Ihr Auge! auf mich,
Tellheim! (der indeß vertieft, und unbeweglich, mit starren Augen
immer auf eine Stelle gesehen) Woran denken Sie? Sie hören mich
nicht?   (*LM*, II, 239.19-240.35)

Tellheim's "Lachen des Menschenhasses" is a sharply ironic
reproach to Minna's light-hearted view of his situation, to her
insistence on being "Ihre lachende Freundinn". The way in
which Lessing introduces Tellheim's sarcastic laughter, however, is as important to the effect of this device as the laughter
itself. For not only is the laughter itself ironic in the extreme:
so is Tellheim's general style in the passage. In telling Minna
of how his honor came to be questioned, Tellheim speaks as
though he were giving a military report. This effect is achieved
through the choice of vocabulary and through a sentence
structure more involved and cumbrous than that which
Tellheim customarily uses. Such military, financial, and legal
technical terms as "Ordre", "Kontribution", "die zu
ratihabirende Schulden", "Valute", and "Gratial", coming
from specifically technical realms, do much to set the precise,
even pedantic quality of Tellheim's narration. Then too, the
use of long dependent infinitive phrases, such as "daß ich
Ordre hatte ... die Kontribution mit der äussersten Strenge
baar beyzutreiben", or "... weil ich sobald mit ihnen auf die
niedrigste Summe einig geworden war, mit der ich mich nur
im äussersten Nothfall zu begnügen, Vollmacht hatte", contrast strongly with the normally terse and straightforward
style of Tellheim, substituting for it a more formal, carefully
modifying, clause-studded sentence structure. The total effect
of the use of these devices is to sharpen the irony of Tellheim's
discourse, to bring the bitter laughter, which climaxes the
parody of military and legal language, into even bolder relief.
In this passage, Minna retains very much her style of the

second act. Her speech is straightforward, her sentences terse
and uncluttered. The insistent, emphatic, driving quality of
her speech here is established by a concentration of carefully
combined features. One of these is emphatic adverb placement; "Sie sind der Mann nicht, ...", "... unmöglich können
diese üble Folgen dauren"., "... lachen Sie so nicht!", "Sie
sind so schwarz und häßlich nicht";. In addition to the
emphatic placement, either initial or final, of these adverbs,
we again find emphatic verb repetition and reinforcement;
"Wir können, wir werden Sie nicht verkennen, ...", "Ich kam
uneingeladen..., ich kam blos Ihrentwegen, ... Ich kam mit
dem festen Vorsatze, Sie zu lieben, ..." The relatively vivid
adjectives which Minna uses in this passage serve to reinforce
this emphatic effect; "... die wilden, unbiegsamen Männer,
die nur immer ihr stieres Auge auf das Gespenst der Ehre
heften!" Thus, in the first phase of the play's main action,
from Act II, Scene 9 to Act IV, Scene 6, the phase in which
Minna is directly attempting to turn Tellheim's mind from
his wounded pride and to her, Minna's tone is light, exclamatory, spontaneous, and generally gay, whereas Tell-
hiem's tone is characterized by a contained terseness which,
on occasion, can give way to an outburst of despair, as at the
end of the second act, or to a bitter parodistic irony which
expresses the depth of his momentary misanthropy.

In the last scenes of Act IV and through most of Act V,
the situation as set forth in the first four acts of the play is
suddenly reversed through Minna's pretense of having been
disinherited by her uncle because of her refusal to marry the
man he had chosen for her. This ruse has the desired effect on
Tellheim. His sense of honor and justice is suddenly aroused,
and he wishes to rush to Minna's defense, to marry her and
leave Berlin with her immediately. But now, Minna seemingly
refuses to let Tellheim make the same sacrifice which he had
refused to let her make, throwing back at him his argument
that equality between the partners is the sole basis for a happy
marriage. Just as Tellheim has argued that he was no longer
the same man who had won Minna's love, Minna claims that

she is no longer a worthy wife for Tellheim, and is merely
"ein Sächsisches verlaufenes Fräulein". Not only are the
attitudes of the characters suddenly and dramatically exchanged. One of the unique stylistic features of *Minna von
Barnhelm* is the fact that their very styles of speaking, their
tones, are exchanged, as the following passage reveals:

v. TELLHEIM. ... Ich ward Soldat, aus Partheylichkeit, ich weiß
selbst nicht für welche politische Grundsätze, und aus der Grille,
daß es für jeden ehrlichen Mann gut sey, sich in diesem Stande
eine Zeitlang zu versuchen, um sich mit allem, was Gefahr heißt,
vertraulich zu machen, und Kälte und Entschlossenheit zu lernen.
Nur die äusserste Noth hätte mich zwingen können, aus diesem
Versuche eine Bestimmung, aus dieser gelegentlichen Beschäfti-
gung ein Handwerk zu machen. Aber nun, da mich nichts mehr
zwingt, nun ist mein ganzer Ehrgeiz wiederum einzig und allein,
ein ruhiger und zufriedener Mensch zu seyn. Der werde ich mit
Ihnen, liebste Minna, unfehlbar werden; der werde ich in Ihrer
Gesellschaft unveränderlich bleiben. — Morgen verbinde uns das
heiligste Band; und sodann wollen wir um uns sehen, und wollen
in der ganzen weiten bewohnten Welt den stillsten, heitersten,
lachendsten Winkel suchen, dem zum Paradiese nichts fehlt, als
ein glückliches Paar. Da wollen wir wohnen; da soll jeder unsrer
Tage — Was ist Ihnen, mein Fräulein? (die sich unruhig hin
und herwendet, und ihre Rührung zu verbergen sucht)
   DAS FRÄULEIN. (sich fassend) Sie sind sehr grausam, Tellheim,
mir ein Glück so reizend darzustellen, dem ich entsagen muß.
Mein Verlust —
   v. TELLHEIM. Ihr Verlust? — Was nennen Sie Ihren Verlust?
Alles, was Minna verlieren konnte, ist nicht Minna. Sie sind noch
das süsseste, lieblichste, holdseligste, beste Geschöpf unter der
Sonne; ganz Güte und Großmuth, ganz Unschuld und Freude! —
Dann und wann ein kleiner Muthwille; hier und da ein wenig
Eigensinn — Desto besser! desto besser! Minna wäre sonst ein
Engel, den ich mit Schaudern verehren müßte, den ich nicht
lieben könnte. (ergreift ihre Hand, sie zu küssen)
   DAS FRÄULEIN. (die ihre Hand zurück zieht) Nicht so, mein
Herr! — Wie auf einmal so verändert? — Ist dieser schmeichelnde,
stürmische Liebhaber der kalte Tellheim? — Konnte nur sein
wiederkehrendes Glück ihn in dieses Feuer setzen? — Er erlaube
mir, daß ich, bey seiner fliegenden Hitze, für uns beide Ueber-
legung behalte. — Als er selbst überlegen konnte, hörte ich ihn
sagen: es sey eine nichtswürdige Liebe, die kein Bedenken trage,

ihren Gegenstand der Verachtung auszusetzen. — Recht; aber
ich bestrebe mich einer eben so reinen und edeln Liebe, als er. —
Jetzt, da ihn die Ehre ruft, da sich ein großer Monarch um ihn
bewirbt, sollte ich zugeben, daß er sich verliebten Träumereyen
mit mir überließe? daß der ruhmvolle Krieger in einen tändelnden
Schäfer ausarte? — Nein, Herr Major, folgen Sie dem Wink Ihres
bessern Schicksals —

v. TELLHEIM. Nun wohl! Wenn Ihnen die große Welt reizender
ist, Minna, — wohl! so behalte uns die große Welt! — Wie klein,
wie armselig ist diese große Welt! — Sie kennen sie nur erst von
ihrer Flitterseite. Aber gewiß, Minna, Sie werden — Es sey! Bis
dahin, wohl! Es soll Ihren Vollkommenheiten nicht an Bewun-
derern fehlen, und meinem Glücke wird es nicht an Neidern ge-
brechen.

DAS FRÄULEIN. Nein, Tellheim, so ist es nicht gemeynt! Ich weise
Sie in die große Welt, auf die Bahn der Ehre zurück, ohne Ihnen
dahin folgen zu wollen. — Dort braucht Tellheim eine unbe-
scholtene Gattinn!   (*LM*, II, 254.17-255.28)

At Minna's assumption of her pose of having been disinherited,
Tellheim's actions and view of the situation have radically
changed. As he himself puts it, "Meine ganze Seele hat neue
Triebfedern bekommen" (*LM*, II, ?46.27-28). This fact
undeniably expresses itself in Tellheim's language in the
passage above. He now has all of Minna's former exuberance
of style. All of the long pent-up passion flows freely from him.
Lessing achieves this effect in the same way as in defining Minna's style; through a lavish use of adjectives and exclamatory
phrases, in strong contrast to the contained and generally
rather bloodless speech of Tellheim in the first four acts. In
Tellheim's flights of passionate fancy, the adjectives accu-
mulate ever more densely. Between lines 1 and 12, above,
Tellheim contents himself with single attributives; thereafter,
in his enthusiasm, no less than three will do; "... und wollen
in der ganzen weiten bewohnten Welt den stillsten, heitersten,
lachendsten Winkel suchen, ..." His delight in superlatives
carries on into his next speech and the adjectival accumulation
continues: "Sie sind noch das süsseste, lieblichste, holdseligste,
beste Geschöpf unter der Sonne." Tellheim's exuberance is
is also expressed in a sudden indulgence in repetitions, such as,

"Desto besser! desto besser!" and "nun wohl! ... wohl!" His syntax is considerably less organized, as we see from his use of adverbial phrases; "ganz Güte und Großmuth, ganz Unschuld und Freude! – Dann und wann ein kleiner Muthwille; hier und da ein wenig Eigensinn." At times he becomes incomprehensibly anacoluthic, as when he says, "Aber gewiß, Minna, Sie werden – Es sey! Bis dahin, wohl!", presumably referring to a point of time in the future. As occurs only rarely among Lessing's characters in the comedies, Tellheim is here animated by a thought which he cannot communicate. In short, for all intents and purposes, Tellheim has taken on the tonal scale previously identified with Minna, strengthened by even more passion and richness of expression.

Minna, on the other hand, has, clearly with parodistic intent, taken on the tone in which Tellheim was wont to speak earlier. On lines 30-43, above, the resemblance between Minna's present tone and Tellheim's former one is especially apparent. Notably, she speaks of Tellheim in the third person singular, although not as a form of second person address. Her tone, in echoing his words from the previous act, is as cold as Tellheim's is warm, as stiff as Tellheim's had been earlier, an effect accomplished by the same devices which had been used then; more involved sentence-structure, featuring suspension through adverbial clauses. An element of sarcasm is added to Minna's tone through her choice of words, for example, her opposition of "der ruhmvolle Krieger" with the "tändelnde Schäfer", the second element of which puts the first in a pejorative light.

To see how meticulously Lessing matches the tone of each character to the situation in which he finds himself, we need only look at the scene between Tellheim and Werner which takes place just after the Major has been informed by Just that Minna has redeemed the ring which had been pawned to the Innkeeper. Tellheim thinks that all of this has been a ruse to break their engagement. Werner arrives with the money which Tellheim had asked him to get, only to find that his commander has changed his mind once more:

WERNER. Hier bin ich schon, Herr Major! —

v. TELLHEIM. (ohne ihn anzusehen) Wer verlangt dich? —

WERNER. Hier ist Geld! tausend Pistolen!

v. TELLHEIM. Ich will sie nicht!

WERNER. Morgen können Sie, Herr Major, über noch einmal so viel befehlen.

v. TELLHEIM. Behalte dein Geld!

WERNER. Es ist ja Ihr Geld, Herr Major. — Ich glaube, Sie sehen nicht, mit wem Sie sprechen?

v. TELLHEIM. Weg damit! sag ich.

WERNER. Was fehlt Ihnen! — Ich bin Werner.

v. TELLHEIM. Alle Güte ist Verstellung; alle Dienstfertigkeit Betrug.

WERNER. Gilt das mir?

v. TELLHEIM. Wie du willst!

WERNER. Ich habe ja nur Ihren Befehl vollzogen. —

v. TELLHEIM. So vollziehe auch den, und packe dich!

WERNER. Herr Major! (ärgerlich) ich bin ein Mensch —

v. TELLHEIM. Da bist du was rechts!

WERNER. Der auch Galle hat —

v. TELLHEIM. Gut! Galle ist noch das beste, was wir haben.

WERNER. Ich bitte Sie, Herr Major, —

v. TELLHEIM. Wie vielmal soll ich dir es sagen? Ich brauche dein Geld nicht! (*LM*, II, 258.26-259.14)

In his acute disappointment over Minna's apparent perfidy, Tellheim takes on a tone more radically misanthropic, sharper and terser than ever before. From the "stürmischer, schmeichelnder Liebhaber" of the previous scene, he is once again "der kalte Tellheim", belaboring poor Werner with a sarcasm bordering on brutality.

The sharpness of the tone is caused by an extreme shortening of the sentences, by a complete stripping away from Tellheim's speech of all polite circumlocutions. Essential to the effect of the passage and to the shock which it imparts not only to Werner, but also to the audience, is the way in which the links between the speeches are established. Tellheim rapidly turns each of Werner's statements into a barb which he hurls back upon his unwitting friend. Thus he picks up Werner's appeal: "Ich habe ja nur Ihren Befehl vollzogen", turning the verb "vollziehen" back against Werner: "So vollziehe auch den, und packe dich!" Werner's objections to being treated in such a way are cut short brutally by Tellheim's acerbic comments. Although Tellheim once again resumes his normal tone and the play progresses to its harmonious end, this abrupt final twist in its mood is a retarding element of great ingenuity, in whose effectiveness the style, in setting the tone of the dialogue, plays a significant role.

Minna von Barnhelm, as the last major "Lustspiel" which Lessing created, shows a full utilization of the stylistic devices of characterization whose development has been traced in the preceding chapters of this study. Each of the characters has been provided with his particular pattern and range of speech, with all of the characters, however, remaining on the colloquial level of style. The new dimension which has been added in *Minna von Barnhelm* is that of tonal nuance, changing as the dynamics of the dramatic situation dictate, but almost exclusively in the case of Minna and Tellheim. Since they are the dynamic characters in the comedy, the other characters being more or less static in their functions, this is only natural. To the many factors which have been adduced to explain the perennial popularity of *Minna von Barnhelm*, at least on the German stage, such as its patriotic quality, its particularly felicitous blending of specifically timely elements with universally valid human ones in its plot, there must be added the flexible and realistic quality of its language, which Lessing has manipulated with uncanny accuracy to impart to each character a distinctive voice and to Minna and Tellheim an expressive tonal range unprecedented in the German comedy up to that time and only rarely equalled since.

The significant difference between *Minna von Barnhelm* and its predecessors lies in the treatment of the main characters, Minna and Tellheim. They are in strong contrast to the woodenly rhetorical or sentimentally declamatory stage lovers of Lessing's earlier comedies, who were definitely in a subordinate position in relation to the main, the comic characters, at least in their function as lovers. By making Minna and Tellheim the central characters of the play, Lessing has given them an individual status unique among the lovers of his comedies. Adrast and Juliane in *Der Freygeist* are still general characters, a Freethinker and a religious young lady who might appear in any number of plays of the same kind, despite the slight individualizing touches which Lessing used in their representation. But Minna and Tellheim, through their carefully drawn idiosyncrasies of temperament and action expressed by carefully utilized stylistic means, cannot be identified or exhausted as character types. they are individuals lovingly created for this play and no other, viable in its reality and in no other.

VI. CONCLUSION

The foregoing study, tracing the practical development of Lessing's use of language in the comedies from his earliest complete play, *Der junge Gelehrte*, to his comic masterpiece, *Minna von Barnhelm*, shows no revolutionary changes, no significant turning point, as would, for example, a similar study of his tragedies. Rather, we see a gradual, organic development of improved stylistic techniques almost from one play to the next. We saw that, in *Der junge Gelehrte*, Lessing had developed quite early an ability to bring to life upon the stage the standard types of the French-oriented Saxon comedy, who spoke an artistic approximation of socially appropriate levels of colloquial prose. This ability made Lessing the equal of his older contemporaries as a manipulator of the language of comedy. In the plays written between 1748 and 1750, Lessing, retaining the same general features of language, eliminated one after the other the failings which were still to be found in *Der junge Gelehrte*. The two functions of language in comedy, characterization and communication, still performed by two distinct stylistic modes in the early plays, were combined in ever more subtle ways. *Der Misogyne* is the first play in which these two functions have fully merged. In *Die Juden* and *Der Freygeist*, it was seen how Lessing began to penetrate beyond the simple depiction of types in his comedies and, in the language of these plays, began to make the characters speak in a somewhat more individualized way than in the earlier plays. As characters, however, as the theory of comedy required, they were still considerably generalized. Passing through the fragments which Lessing produced before 1763, and which, for all for their experimental nature and ranging through various literary epochs for their sources, display little novelty or improvement in Lessing's conception of comic language, we come to *Minna von Barnhelm*, the climax of Lessing's practice in comedy. It was demonstrated that, for the characters besides Minna and Tellheim, the stylistic characterizations were essentially analogous to those found in the plays written before 1750. Lessing has made specific individuals of Tellheim and Minna, partly through expository devices, but most significantly through the individual ways in which they are made to speak. Their tone responds in the most delicate nuance to the particular circumstances of their confrontation at each moment. It is this unique combination of the universally typical moment of feeling with completely individual characterization, a combination which Lessing achieved only this one time in his career as a comic playwright, which has made *Minna von Barnhelm* ever popular upon the German stage. It is the individual personality rather than the general type which endears itself to the beholder and moves him.

Certainly Lessing's achievement of creative manhood since his last comedy before *Minna*, the events of the Seven Years' War, and the intricate web of biographical circumstances which are said to play a part in *Minna von Barnhelm* contributed to its indefatigable appeal as a comedy. But just as certainly, Lessing's mastery of the language of comedy, his full use of the techniques acquired during his literary apprenticeship in Leipzig, and his penetration beyond these to a new conception of the expression of character in comedy must also be considered factors vital to its charm. The highly charged and individual language of the widow in *Die Matrone von Ephesus* gives us a hint that Lessing might have further pursued the trend begun in *Minna von Barnhelm*, creating a firmer foundation for the future of German comedy, had not his numerous other interests drawn him forever from the comic genre.

For Lessing the function of comedy was normative; to heal vice through laughter at its folly and, failing that, to preserve freedom from vice through laughter. To these ends, he showed his audiences artistic representations of persons much like themselves in character, manner, and speech, with whose situations they might compare their own. In this study, we have attempted to describe Lessing's perfecting of a language suitable to this aim, one which was colloquial and yet artful, pithy and yet witty, for the characters who populate the lively world of his comedies.

SOURCES CONSULTED

PRIMARY SOURCES

Gellert, Christian Fürchtegott, "Das Loos in der Lotterie", in *Neue Bey-träge zum Vergnügen des Verstandes und Witzes*, 4 vols. (Bremen-Leipzig, 1744-57), III, pts. 5 and 6.

Goldoni, Carlo, *Tutte le Opere*, ed. Giuseppe Ortolani, 14 vols. (Milan, 1935-56).

Gottsched, Johann Christoph, *Versuch einer Critischen Dichtkunst*, 4th edn. (Leipzig, 1751).

Gottschedin, Luise Adelgunde Viktorie, "Die Pietisterey im Fischbein-Rocke", in *Deutsche Literatur; Reihe Aufklärung*, III, ed. F. Brügge-mann (Leipzig, 1935).

Houdar de la Motte, Antoine, *Œuvres...*, 10 vols. (Paris, 1754).

La Fontaine, Jean de, *Œuvres*, 12 vols. (Paris, 1890).

Lessing, Gotthold Ephraim, *Sämtliche Schriften*, Hrsg. von Karl Lachmann, dritte ... Auflage besorgt durch Franz Muncker, 23 vols. (Stuttgart, Berlin & Leipzig, 1886-1924).

——, *Lessings Werke*, ed. Julius Petersen and Waldemar von Olshausen, 25 vols. with 3 vols. of notes, and 2 vols. of indexes (Berlin-Leipzig-Vienna-Stuttgart, n.d.).

Petronius, *The Satyricon*, trans. William Arrowsmith (New York, 1960).

Plautus, *Plautus: with an English Translation* by Paul Nixon, 5 vols. (London and Cambridge, Mass., 1928).

——, *The Comedies of Plautus*, trans. Henry Thomas Riley, 2 vols. (London, 1889).

Weiße, Christian Felix, *Beytrag zum deutschen Theater*, 5 vols., (Leipzig, 1768).

——, *Lustspiele*, 3 vols. (Leipzig, 1783).

SECONDARY SOURCES, DICTIONARIES, AND GRAMMARS

Adelung, Johann Christoph, *Versuch eines vollständigen grammatisch-kritischen Wörterbuches der Hochdeutschen Mundart...*, 5 vols. (Leipzig, 1774-86).

Aikin-Sneath, Betsy, *Comedy in Germany in the First Half of the Eighteenth Century* (Oxford, 1936).

Albrecht, Paul, *Leszings Plagiate*, 6 vols. (Hamburg and Leipzig, 1891).

Arnold, Robert F., *Das deutsche Drama* (München, 1925).

Beare, Mary, *Die Theorie der Komödie von Gottsched bis Jean Paul* (Bonn, 1927).

Behschnitt, Kurt, *Lessings Ansichten von der deutschen Sprache* (Breslau, 1915).

Belouin, G., *De Gottsched à Lessing* (Paris, 1909).

Bergethon, Kaare Roald, *Lessing's Theory of Translation*, Diss. Cornell Univ., Ithaca, N.Y. (1940).

Bergson, Henri, "Laughter", in *Comedy*, ed. Wylie Sypher (Garden City, 1956).

Biedermann, Flodoard von, *Lessings Gespräche* (Berlin, 1924).

Biedermann, Karl, *Deutschland im 18. Jahrhundert*, 4 vols. (Leipzig, 1854-80).

Blackall, Eric A., *The Emergence of German as a Literary Language* (Cambridge, 1959).

Böckmann, Paul, *Formgeschichte der deutschen Dichtung*, vol. I (Hamburg, 1949).

Borden, Charles Ernest, *The Original Model for Lessing's 'Der junge Gelehrte'* (= *University of California Publications in Modern Philology*, vol. 36, no. 3) (Berkeley, 1952).

Braun, Julius W., *Lessing im Urtheile seiner Zeitgenossen*, 3 vols. (Berlin, 1884-97).

Brewer, Edward V., "Lessing and the Corrective Virtue in Comedy", *JEGP*, XXVI (1927), pp. 1-23.

Brown, F. Andrew., "The Conversion of Lessing's Freigeist", *JEGP*, LVI (1957), pp. 186-202.

Brüggemann, Fritz, "Der Kampf um die bürgerliche Welt-und Lebensanschauung in der deutschen Literatur des 18. Jahrhunderts", *DVjS*, 3. III (1925), pp. 94-127.

——, "Lessings Bürgerdramen und der Subjektivismus als Problem. Psychogenetische Untersuchung", *Jahrbuch des Freien Deutschen Hochstifts*, 1926, pp. 69-110.

Carrington, Herbert, *Die Figur des Juden in der dramatischen Litteratur des XVIII. Jahrhunderts* (Heidelberg, 1897).

Cohn, Hilde D., "Die beiden Schwierigen im deutschen Lustspiel: Lessing, *Minna von Barnhelm* — Hofmannsthal, *Der Schwierige*", *Monatshefte*, XLIV (1952), pp. 256-69.

Coym, Johannes, *Gellerts Lustspiele, Palaestra*, II (Berlin, 1899).

Creizenach, Wilhelm, *Zur Entstehungsgeschichte des neueren deutschen Lustspiels* (Halle, 1879).

Curme, George Oliver, *A Grammar of the German Language*, 2nd rev. edn. (New York, 1952).

Drews, Wolfgang, *Gotthold Ephraim Lessing in Selbstzeugnissen und Bilddokumenten* (= *Rowohlts Monographien*, 75) (Hamburg, 1962).

Dunkle, Harvey I., "Lessing's 'Die Juden': an Original Experiment", *Monatshefte*, XLIX (1957), pp. 323-29.

Düsel, Friedrich, *Der dramatische Monolog in der Poetik des 17. und 18. Jahrhunderts und in den Dramen Lessings* (= *Theatergeschichtliche Forschungen*, XIV) (Hamburg-Leipzig, 1897).

Emigholz, Erich, *Lessings sprachliche Form im Drama: Untersuchungen zum Problem Vers-Prosa in Lessings Dramen unter gleichzeitiger Abgrenzung vom Drama der Klassik*, Diss. Münster (1955).

Fischer, Kuno, *G. E. Lessing als Reformator der deutschen Literatur* (Stuttgart-Berlin, 1904).

Fischer, Wilhelm, "Lessing über das 'weinerliche' und das 'rührende' Lustspiel", *Mozart-Jahrbuch*, 1954, pp. 7-13.

Fricke, Gerhard, *Studien und Interpretationen* (Frankfurt, 1956).

——, "Bemerkungen zu Lessings 'Freigeist' und 'Miss Sara Sampson'", in *Studien zur deutschen Sprache und Literatur*, 3 (Istanbul, 1956), pp. 30-66.

Funke, Erich, "Stil- und Sprachausdruck in Lessings Faustfragment", *Monatshefte*, XXVI (1934), pp. 4-10.

Garland, H. B., *Lessing: The Founder of Modern German Literature*, 2nd edn. (London, 1962).

Grimm, Jakob und Wilhelm, *Deutsches Wörterbuch* (Leipzig, 1854ff).

Grisebach, Eduard, *Die Wanderung der Novelle von der treulosen Wittwe durch die Weltlitteratur*, 5th edn. (Berlin, 1886).

Guthke, Karl S., "Lessingforschung 1932 bis 1962", *DVjs*, XXXVIII, (1964) Sonderheft, pp. 68-169.

Haynel, Woldemar, *Gellerts Lustspiele* (Emden-Borkum, 1896).

Heitner, Robert R., "Lessing's Manipulation of a Single Comic Theme", *MLQ*, 18 (1957), pp. 183-98.

Hettner, Hermann, *Geschichte der deutschen Literatur im 18. Jahrhundert* (Leipzig, 1928).

Holl, Karl, *Geschichte des deutschen Lustspiels* (Leipzig, 1923).

——, *Zur Geschichte der Lustspieltheorie* (= *Literarhistorische Forschungen*, 44) (Berlin, 1911).

Kettner, Gustav, *Lessings Dramen im Lichte ihrer und unserer Zeit* (Berlin, 1904).

Kies, Paul P., "The Sources of Lessing's 'Die Juden'", *Philological Quarterly*, VI (1927), pp. 406-10.

——, "Lessing's Early Study of English Drama", *JEGP*, XXVIII (1929), pp. 16-34.

——, "Lessing's Relation to Early English Sentimental Comedy", *PMLA*, XLVII (1932), pp. 807-26.

Langen, August, "Deutsche Sprachgeschichte vom Barock bis zur Gegenwart", *Deutsche Philologie im Aufriß*, ed. Wolfgang Stammler, 3 vols. (Berlin, 1952), I, 1078ff.

Lehmann, August, *Forschungen über Lessings Sprache* (Braunschweig, 1875).

Mann, Otto, "Grundlagen und Gestaltung des Lessingschen Humors", *Zeitschrift für Ästhetik*, 31 (1937), pp. 1-31.

——, *Lessing, Sein und Leistung*, 2nd, edn. (Hamburg, 1961).

Markwardt, Bruno, "Studien über den Stil G. E. Lessings im Verhältnis zur Aufklärungsprosa", *Wissenschaftliche Zeitschrift der Universität Greifswald: Gesellschafts- und sprachwissenschaftliche Reihe*, 3 (1953-4), pp. 151-80; 4 (1954-5), pp. 1-34, 177-208; 5 (1955-6), pp. 297-338.

Mertens, F., "Zu Lessings jungem Gelehrten", *Zeitschrift für den Deutschen Unterricht*, 10 (1896), pp. 512-13.

Metzger, Willi, *Die Entwicklung von Lessings Briefstil* (= *Giessener Beiträge zur deutschen Philologie*, XIX) (Giessen, 1927).

Meyer, Richard M., "Zwei Dramen Lessings", in: Meyer, Richard M.. *Aufsätze literarhistorischen und biographischen Inhalts*, I (Berlin, 1911), pp. 146-63.

Meyer-Benfey, Heinrich, *Lessings Minna von Barnhelm* (Göttingen, 1915).

Minor, Jakob, *Christian Felix Weiße und seine Beziehungen zur deutschen Literatur des 18. Jahrhunderts*, (Innsbruck, 1880).

Mohri, Wilhelm, *Die Technik des Dialoges in Lessings Dramen* (Elbersfeld, 1929).

Müller-Fraureuth, Karl, *Wörterbuch der obersächsischen und erzgebirgischen Mundarten*, 2 vols. (Dresden, 1911).

Nolte, Fred O., "Lessing and the Bourgeois Drama", *JEGP*, XXXI (1932), pp. 66-83.

Oehlke, Waldemar, *Lessing und seine Zeit*, 2 vols. (Munich, 1919).

Paul, Hermann, *Deutsche Grammatik*, 5 vols. (Halle a.S., 1919).

Peisel, Herbert Horst Johannes, *Die Lebensform Lessings als Strukturprinzip in seinen Dramen* (Philadelphia, 1941).

——, "Damon und Leander; Eine kleine Studie zur weiteren Förderung der Einfühlung in die Geistes- und Gemütswelt Lessings," *German Quarterly*, XXXIV (1961), pp. 385-408.

Petsch, Robert, "Lessings Dramen", *Neue Jahrbücher für das klassische Altertum, Geschichte und deutsche Literatur und für Pädagogik*, 17 (1906), pp. 206-28.

——, "Die Kunst und Charakteristik in Lessings Minna von Barnhelm", *Zeitschrift für den deutschen Unterricht*, 26 (1912), pp. 285-305.

——, "Die Matrone von Ephesus: Ein dramatisches Bruchstück von Lessing", *Dichtung und Volkstum*, (*Euphorion*), 41 (1941), pp. 87-95.

Price, Lawrence M., *The Reception of English Literature in Germany* (Berkeley, 1932).

Reinhardstoettner, Kurt von, *Plautus: spätere Bearbeitungen plautinischer Lustspiele* (Leipzig, 1886).

Rempel, Hans, *Tragödie und Komödie im dramatischen Schaffen Lessings* (= *Neue Forschung*, 26) (Berlin, 1935).

Ricklefs, Jürgen, "Lessings Theorie vom Lachen und Weinen", in *Dankesgabe für Albert Leitzmann*, ed. Fritz Braun and Kurt Stegmann von Pritzwald (Jena, 1927), pp. 7-66.

Rindskopf, Siegmund, "Der sprachliche Ausdruck der Affekte in Lessings dramatischen Werken", *Zeitschrift für den deutschen Unterricht*, XV (1901), pp. 545-84.

Robertson, John George, *Lessing's Dramatic Theory* (Cambridge, 1938).

Schlenther, Paul, *Frau Gottsched und die bürgerliche Komödie* (Berlin, 1886).

Schmid, Christian Heinrich, *Chronologie des deutschen Theaters* (n.p., 1775), ed. Paul Legband, in *Schriften der Gesellschaft für Theatergeschichte*, I (Berlin, 1902).

Schmidt, Erich, *Lessing: Geschichte seines Lebens und seiner Schriften*, 4th edn., 2 vols. (Berlin, 1923).

Schreiber, S(arah) Etta, *The German Woman in the Age of Enlightenment: A*

Study in the Drama from Gottsched to Lessing (= *Columbia University Germanic Studies*, 19) (New York, 1948).

Schuchmann, Hans, *Studien zum Dialog im Drama Lessings und Schillers* (Giessen, 1927).

Spieß, Otto, *Die dramatische Handlung in Lessings 'Emilia Galotti' und 'Minna von Barnhelm'*, in *Bausteine zur neueren deutschen Literatur*, II (Halle a.S., 1911).

Staiger, Emil, *Die Kunst der Interpretation*, 2nd edn. (Zürich, 1957).

Steffen, Hans, *Sprachkritik und Sprachhaltung bei Molière und Lessing*, in *Worte und Werte: Bruno Markwardt zum 60. Geburtstag*, ed. Gustav Erdmann and Alfons Eichstaedt (Berlin, 1961), pp. 383-97.

Stockum, Th. C. van, "Lessings Dramenentwurf 'Die Matrone von Ephesus'", *Neophilologus*, XLVI (1962), pp. 125-33.

Tyrol, Fritz, *Lessings sprachliche Revision seiner Jugenddramen* (Berlin, 1893).

Ulmer, Bernhard, "The Leitmotiv and Musical Structure in Lessing's Dramas", *Germanic Review*, 22 (1947), pp. 13-31.

Ure, Peter, "The Widow of Ephesus: Some Reflections on an International Theme", *The Durham University Journal*, New Series, Vol. XVIII, No. 1 (December 1956), pp. 1-9.

Vail, Curtis C. D., *Lessing's Relation to the English Language and Literature* (New York, 1936).

Zwierzina, Konrad, "'Der Schlaftrunk' von Lessing", *Euphorion*, 16, Supplement (1916), pp. 63-72.

INDEX

STUDIES IN GERMAN LITERATURE

ANGLICA GERMANICA

MOUTON & CO · PUBLISHERS · THE HAGUE